SOCIAL JUSTICE AND DEUTERONOMY

SOCIETY OF BIBLICAL LITERATURE

DISSERTATION SERIES

David L. Petersen, Old Testament Editor
Pheme Perkins, New Testament Editor

Number 136

SOCIAL JUSTICE AND DEUTERONOMY
The Case of Deuteronomy 15

by
Jeffries M. Hamilton

Jeffries M. Hamilton

SOCIAL JUSTICE AND DEUTERONOMY
The Case of Deuteronomy 15

Scholars Press
Atlanta, Georgia

SOCIAL JUSTICE AND DEUTERONOMY
The Case of Deuteronomy 15

Jeffries M. Hamilton

Ph.D., 1990
Princeton Theological Seminary

Advisor:
Patrick D. Miller, Jr.

Library of Congress Cataloging in Publication Data

Hamilton, Jeffries M.
Social justice and Deuteronomy : the case of Deuteronomy 15 / Jeffries M. Hamilton.
p. cm. — (Dissertation series / Society of Biblical Literature ; no. 136)
Includes bibliographical references.
ISBN 1-55540-747-1 (alk. paper). — ISBN 1-55540-748-X (pbk. : alk. paper)
1. Bible. O.T. Deuteronomy XV—Criticism, interpretation, etc.
2. Social justice—Biblical teaching. I. Title. II. Series:
Dissertation series (Society of Biblical Literature) ; no. 136.
BS1275.2.H445 1992
222'.1506—dc20

92-25380
CIP

Printed in the United States of America
on acid-free paper

Contents

Acknowledgements

I would like to acknowledge two types of support, both of which were necessary for this dissertation to see completion.

The first and most fundamental support came from my parents, Harold and Jane, who instilled in me a knowledge of the Bible and a love of learning, from other spiritual parents, who caused that knowledge and love to grow, and from my wife, Sarah, who suffered my frequent and long trips to "Deuteronomy-land" and who provided as well a listening ear whose judgment could be trusted and whose advice was sound without fail.

The second support came from teachers along the way, especially the faculty at Union Theological Seminary in Virginia, Dr. James L. Mays and Dr. W. Sibley Towner, and the faculty at Princeton Theological Seminary during my time there, Dr. J. J. M. Roberts, Dr. Katharine D. Sakenfeld, Dr. Dennis T. Olson, Dr C. Leong Seow, and Dr. Judith E. Sanderson. In addition, particular mention should be made of my classmates at Princeton, Jeffrey S. Rogers and Wesley Toews. We got each other through.

A special sort of gratitude goes to Dr. Patrick D. Miller, Jr. and to Mary Ann Miller who have been both intellectual and emotional parents beginning with my first postgraduate course in the Old Testament and continuing to the present.

Abbreviations

AfO	Archiv für Orientforschung
AJSL	*American Journal of Semitic Languages and Literatures*
AnBib	Analecta Biblica
ANET3	*Ancient Near Eastern Texts Relating to the Old Testament, Third Edition*
AOS	American Oriental Series
AS	*Assyriological Studies*
ASOR	American Schools of Oriental Research
BA	*Biblical Archeology*
BASOR	*Bulletin of the American Schools of Oriental Research*
BDB	Brown, Driver, and Briggs, *Hebrew and English Lexicon of the Old Testament*
BERes	The Babylonian Expedition of the University of Pennsylvania. Series D: Researches and Treatises.
BHS	Biblia Hebraica Stuttgartensia
Bib	*Biblica*
BJS	Brown Judaic Studies
BZ	*Biblische Zeitschrift*
CAD	*The Assyrian Dictionary of the Oriental Institute of the University of Chicago*
CBQ	*Catholic Biblical Quarterly*
CE	Codex Eshnunna
CH	Codex Hammurabi
EcuBibSt	Ecumenical Biblica Studies
EvQ	*Evangelical Quarterly*

FRLANT	Forschungen zur Religion und Literatur des Alten und Neuen Testaments
HTR	*Harvard Theological Review*
HUCA	*Hebrew Union College Annual*
IDBSup	Supplementary Volume to *Interpreter's Dictionary of the Bible* (G. A. Buttrick, Ed.)
ICC	International Critical Commentary
Int	*Interpretation*
JAOS	*Journal of the American Oriental Society*
JBL	*Journal of Biblical Literature*
JCS	*Journal of Cuneiform Studies*
JANESCU	*Journal of the Ancient Near Eastern Society of Columbia University*
JNES	*Journal of Near Eastern Studies*
JNSL	*Journal of Northwest Semitic Languages*
JPS	Jewish Publication Society
JSOT	*Journal for the Study of the Old Testament*
JSOTSup	Journal for the Study of the Old Testament—Supplement Series
LXX	Septuagint
MAL	Middle Assyrian Laws
NCB	New Century Bible Commentary
NICC	New International Critical Commentary
NTS	*New Testament Studies*
OBT	Overtures to Biblical Theology
Or	*Orientalia*
OTL	Old Testament Library
OTS	*Oudtestamentische Studiën*
PBI	Pontifical Biblical Institute
PersRelSt	*Perspectives on Religious Studies*
RA	*Revue d'assyriologie et d'archéologie orientale*
RB	*Revue biblique*
RIDA	*Revue Internationale des Droits de l'Antiquité*
RSV	Revised Standard Version
SBLDS	Society of Biblical Literature Dissertation Series
SBT	Studies in Biblical Theology
SCM	Student Christian Movement
SDIOP	Studia et Documenta ad Iura Orientis Pertinentis
SP	Samaritan Pentateuch
Symbolae David	*Symbolae Iuridicae et Historicae Martino David Dedicatae*
TCL	Textes cuneiformes, Musée de Louvre

TDOT	G. J. Botterweck and H. Ringgren (Eds.), *Theological Dictionary of the Old Testament*
THAT	E. Jenni and C. Westermann (Eds.) *Theologisches Handwörterbuch zum Alten Testament*
VAB	Vorderasiastische Bibliothek
VS	Verbum Salutis
VT	*Vetus Testamentum*
VTSup	Vetus Testamentum Supplements
ZA	*Zeitschrift für Assyriologie*
ZAW	*Zeitschrift für die alttestamentliche Wissenschaft*

Introduction

The many problems which proceed from the existence of poverty in our society have been brought to the fore in recent years by discussions both national and international. Homelessness, hunger, single-parent households, child care, enabling the poor to obtain adequate mental and physical health care—these are some of the social and political issues which have their bases at least in part in the larger issue of systemic and deep-rooted poverty. Some observers have even begun to describe the shape of a permanent underclass, dependent on the largess of government and the generosity of individuals to supplement what they can obtain for themselves through their own limited means and impoverished imaginations in order to eke out their survival.[1]

The facts, even the broad outlines, of these problems are more or less agreed upon. What finds little agreement, however, is the way in which society is to respond to these problems. What role is government to play in the care of the poor and dependent? Even more basically, what attitude is society as a whole and the persons who make up that society

[1] One notes as an indication of the existence of this underclass, for instance, a recent report by the Census Bureau which details how government payments—Social Security, Medicare, food stamps, and the like—reduce the number of people who would otherwise be below the poverty line from 50.6 million to 36.5 million. See Robert Pear, "U. S. Pensions Found to Lift Many of Poor," *New York Times*, 28 December 1988, Sec. A, pp. 1, 20.

to have toward those who have a special need for care because of their position or capabilities? Or again, what are the societal values which lie behind the ways we choose to respond to these people in special need of care?

Each of these questions has many possible responses, each response representing an often well-defined, even well-meaning, political position. What is more important for those who are possessed of faith convictions, however, is the manner in which their own attitudes and values can be shaped by the attitudes and values present in Scripture. The first step toward allowing Scripture to shape our attitudes and values and from there the way we respond to those in our society in special need of care is to find texts in the Old and New Testament whose content has some resonance with contemporary problems.

This dissertation proposes to undertake an examination of the attitudes and values toward social justice found in the book of Deuteronomy. It will use as its primary text Dt 15. This chapter contains two pieces of legislation pertinent to the task at hand: the law contained and commented on in Dt 15:1-11, which deals with the release of loans by creditors at seven-year intervals, and the law contained and commented on in Dt 15:12-18, which deals with the release of slaves in the seventh year of their servitude. Together, these two release-laws exhibit many of the attitudes which the book of Deuteronomy has toward the disadvantaged, the religious and moral values which lie behind those attitudes, and the legislation which proceeds from them.[2]

The book of Deuteronomy is an especially fruitful text for this kind of study for two reasons. First, as commentators have noted for many years,[3] Deuteronomy displays a particular concern for those who have none of the built-in supports which Israelite society normally provided—specifically those supports provided by one's tribe and family. This concern is expressed through the oft-repeated refrain which points to the

---

[2] P. Miller delineates three areas of concern addressed by the laws of Deuteronomy. They are the worship of God, the care of those who are needy and weak, and the system of leadership which will govern the nation. He calls Dt 15 "the definitive chapter for discerning the centrality of Deuteronomy's concern that access to the blessing of God be available to all members of the community, including those who, out of need and position, are least likely to enjoy that blessing." See "The Way of Torah," *Princeton Seminary Bulletin* 8/3 (1987), 17-27, esp. 25.

[3] Among them are S. R. Driver, *A Critical and Exegetical Commentary on Deuteronomy* (ICC; New York: Charles Scribner's Sons, 1895), esp. xxivf; M. Weinfeld, *Deuteronomy and the Deuteronomic School* (Oxford: Clarendon, 1972), 282-297; and A. D. H. Mayes, *Deuteronomy* (NCB; Grand Rapids: Eerdmans, 1979), 72.

widow, the orphan, and the sojourner as objects of particular concern.[4] This humanitarian tendency is present in Dt 15 as well, which, though it holds out the ideal of a land without poverty (Dt 15:4), recognizes that it is the ongoing existence of the poor which causes the law to be given (Dt 15:7, 11).

Second, the book of Deuteronomy is especially important in attempting to allow our response to social justice issues to be informed and shaped by Scripture because it has cast a shadow of influence throughout the Old Testament and into the New.[5] The most visible evidence of this shadow of influence is the set of books running from Joshua through 2 Kings which scholars have called the "Deuteronomic History" because it has been written in the style and with the theological perspective of Deuteronomy. Indeed, the chapters of Deuteronomy itself which frame the corpus of laws (that is, chs. 1-3 and 31-34) are said to be part of this History. They create a book which self-consciously places the portrait of the ideal society imparted in the legal corpus in a specific historical moment: the gathering of the people of YHWH on the plains of Moab, just on the brink of the promised land. This literary artifice serves to place the Torah before the people at a moment of decision. Deuteronomy asks what will be the appearance of the nation of God's people which is about to come into being. The History which follows tells the story of what happens after God's people have their land.

Yet this shadow of influence is felt in less direct ways as well. Many of the prophetic books bear the imprint of the theological perspective of Deuteronomy. Isaiah 36:1-39:8 is virtually identical to 2 Kings 18:13-20:19. Much of Jeremiah shares vocabulary and style with the Deuteronomic books. An example of this phenomenon in Jeremiah has a direct bearing on Dt 15. In the course of the episode of the freeing of slaves and their re-enslavement under King Zedekiah (Jer 34), Jeremiah receives a Word of YHWH which quotes directly from Dt 15 (cf. Jer 34:8 and Dt 15:1, 12). The issues which find legal expression in Dt 15 are exhibited in Isa

---

4 On the particularly vulnerable position occupied by these three classes, see D. Gowan, "Wealth and Poverty in the Old Testament: The Case of the Widow, the Orphan, and the Sojourner," *Int* 41 (1987), 343-344.

5 N. Lohfink, for example, refers to a "Deuteronomic phenomenon" in the Bible, by which he means the influence which the Deuteronomic school has had throughout the Bible (N. Lohfink, "The Cult Reform of Josiah of Judah: 2 Kgs. 22-23 as a Source for the History of Israelite Religion," in *Ancient Israelite Religion*, ed. P. D. Miller, P. D. Hanson, and S. D. McBride [Philadelphia: Fortress, 1987], 459).

58:6 and 61:1-2 as well.[6] This pair of texts is received into the New Testament as the text on which Jesus preaches his inaugural sermon (Luke 4:16-21).[7]

Thus the concern for social justice exhibited in a special way by the book of Deuteronomy in general and by Dt 15 in particular has made itself felt in an ambit far beyond its own narrow bounds. This makes it a text especially deserving of attention by those who would seek to allow their response to social justice issues in the present to be informed and shaped by Scripture.

The dissertation will begin with an examination of the structure, logic, and imagery of the passage. It will then seek further illumination on the attitudes and values of the passage by comparison and contrast with those attitudes and values found in laws and edicts analogous to the release-laws from the ancient Near East and in its parallels in Exodus and Leviticus. The dissertation will then try to place this text in the context of Deuteronomy.

The first chapter explores the rhetorical dimensions of Dt 15. It does this primarily in two ways. First, the structure of the text is explored as a way of determining how the logical sequence of presentation and argument employed by the text serves to ensure assent and compliance in its hearers. Second, the chapter focuses on the phrasing and imagery employed by the text to anchor the text's argument with emotional moorings.

The second chapter deals with the ancient Near Eastern analogies to the release-laws of Dt 15. In particular those texts which have some bearing on the issues of manumission of slaves and release of loans (the two components of Dt 15) are studied. Such material includes the *mīšarum* and *andurārum* edicts (periodic royal acts which released taxes, loans, and slaves), pertinent sections of the cuneiform Law Codes, and personal contracts and bills of sale. While these texts are placed in their historical contexts and attention is paid to their philological difficulties,

---

6 Note that Isa 61:1 uses the technical vocabulary of manumission found in Jer 34. This term, *dĕrôr,* is philologically related to the Akkadian term *andurārum,* which will be spoken of below.

7 Another example not as directly related to the topic at hand is that of the Temptation, where the temptations of the devil are responded to by Jesus' quoting certain texts from Deuteronomy (cf. Matt 4:1-11, Luke 4:1-1; the quoted texts are Dt 8:3, 6:16, and 6:13 though their order varies between Matt and Luke). Note also that the first half of the pair of texts Jesus is said to have identified as the Great Commandment is the *Shema* from Deuteronomy (Dt 6:4f; cf. Matt 22:34-40, Mark 12:28-34, and Luke 10:25-28).

the primary focus of this chapter is on the system of care for those in special need. Thus these ancient Near Eastern texts serve both to illuminate certain obscure features of the release-laws in Deuteronomy and to sketch out another possible set of attitudes and values toward issues of social justice.

The third chapter deals with the legal parallels to Dt 15 found in Exodus and Leviticus, more specifically those groups of legal material referred to as the Covenant Code (Exod 20:22-23:33) and the Holiness Code (Lev 19-26). As with the ancient Near Eastern texts, the biblical legal parallels in Exodus and Leviticus are examined with two purposes in mind. The first purpose is served through an examination of the manumission and debt-release components of these groups of laws as a way of further defining what is going on in Dt 15. In keeping with the second purpose, this chapter treats the texts from these two legal codes isolated as having immediate bearing on the just ordering of society as self-contained systems of social justice. This is done, as with the ancient Near Eastern material, in order to compare the attitudes and values they exhibit in this regard with the Deuteronomic system of social justice and its outworking in Dt 15.

The fourth chapter draws on the findings of the first three as it seeks to explore in a more integrated fashion the attitudes and values toward issues of social justice which prevail in the whole of the laws of Deuteronomy. The chapter looks first at the position Dt 15 occupies in the sequence of laws in Deuteronomy in order to determine its relative import. Then the chapter draws comparisons with the other laws in Deuteronomy dealing with attendant issues in order to see how they correspond or fail to correspond in attitude with Dt 15. At this point, an attempt will be made to define the basic premises of a deuteronomic system of social justice and the way that system of social justice is like or unlike other systems as evidenced by the Near Eastern analogies and biblical parallels.

A concluding chapter then takes this definition and suggests ways in which it may be applied to the contemporary situation of the believing community. These suggestions are offered in light of certain hermeneutical difficulties which arise when one tries to move from a biblical text to the present. In addition, these suggestions are presented in such a way as to bear similarity to the basic premises of a deuteronomic system of social justice offered in chapter four.

It is hoped that in such a manner, sensitive attention can be paid both to the integrity of the text from which the contemporary reader hears resonance with contemporary problems and to the need to locate and define the terms of that resonance in such a way as to be helpful to that reader. Thus the dissertation seeks to thread its way between the twin dangers of obscurity, an over attention to issues of antiquarian import, and of glibness, a too-easy move from ancient text to present-day context.

I

The Rhetoric of Deuteronomy 15

Several dimensions of the text before us have relevance to an attempt to determine its place within and affinities to the system of social justice which prevails in the book of Deuteronomy as a whole. The study begins in this chapter with an examination of the text itself, specifically its *structure* and its *language*. Together, these two dimensions of the text can be thought of as the *rhetoric* of the text.[1]

---

[1] Structure is being included under this rubric because organization is clearly a component of rhetorical effectiveness. I am aware of the difficulty in using the terms "rhetoric" and "rhetorical." In biblical studies, the examination of texts under these rubrics has found many adherents in recent years, particularly after the Presidential Address of J. Muilenberg to the Society of Biblical Literature (published as "Form Criticism and Beyond," *JBL* 88 [1969] 1-18). Muilenberg appears to define rhetorical criticism as having two concerns: the careful delineation of the limits of the text so that one is dealing with a discrete literary unit, and the observation within that unit of what I would term stylistic features—e.g., parallel structures, literary devices such as chiasm, and strophes or stanzas. While this kind of analysis certainly has a great part to play in determining the way in which a text engages in "the art of using words effectively" (Webster's), it strikes me as a form of literary criticism more akin to that of the New Critics than "rhetorical criticism" proper. My own understanding of the term "rhetorical criticism" is closer to that of T. Eagleton (*Literary Theory: An Introduction* [Minneapolis: University of Minnesota, 1983] 205-206) who in calling for a return to rhetorical criticism in literary studies defines it as that mode of examining texts which pays particular attention to the way those texts are constructed and the

The Structure of Deuteronomy 15

Taking up the first of the two areas under the larger rubric of the rhetorical dimension of the text, then, the structure of Dt 15:1-18 can be expressed in very broad terms at the outset. The two halves (1-11, the *šĕmiṭṭāh* law, and 12-18, the manumission law) bear similarities in structure: the law proper, or what will be referred to as the "heading-law" (vv 1 and 12), and several succeeding sections which deal with matters of interpretation, explanation, exhortation, or example (vv 2-11 and 13-18).

One sees immediately that the law itself, while setting the agenda for discussion, is structurally a very small part of the text. The structure of the text, seen even in these broad terms, points us in the direction of a concern to do more than simply rehearse pertinent laws. The concern is less with observance than with the significance of observance. Like the Near Eastern Law Codes, the promulgation of the release-laws in this fashion is not primarily a presenting of the minimal requirements of social stability. In the case of the Law Codes, as we shall see,[2] the primary concern is to establish some correspondence between social reality and the order which underlies that reality. In the case of the deuteronomic text before us, the primary concern is to set forth how society ought to operate. Stated another way, the primary concern is of what values society should have when it approaches problems which at first glance can be taken as merely a matter of legality or illegality.

This characterization must be borne out by subsequent analysis, but one should note that this characterization is not new. Indeed, M. Weinfeld makes an observation very close to ours concerning this very passage.[3] This characterization is also in part a restating on the basis of structure of what has been termed the homiletical, hortatory, or paranetic style of Deuteronomy. S. R. Driver observed that this style was developed with the intention of moving and influencing its readers by bearing the reader "into long and rolling periods," thereby holding them enthralled.[4] Most influentially, G. von Rad characterized the Deuteronomic style as "out and out paranetic, a wooing and imploring form of

---

culturally pregnant language they use (the two parts to be examined under this rubric in the present chapter) in order to achieve certain effects, such as persuasion, exhortation, etc.

[2] Below, pp 56-62.

[3] *Deuteronomy and the Deuteronomic School*, 3.

[4] *Deuteronomy*, lxxxvi-lxxxvii.

address."[5] N. Lohfink has tried to bring some focus to this characterization with respect to Dt. 5-11 by maintaining the priority of the attitude out of which paranesis arises and which gives a discernable form to its literary remains, which attitude and form might produce a crystallization of various sub-genres into a literary text.[6] More recently, S. D. McBride characterizes the purpose of Dt. as "constitutional".[7]

It must be noted that our tentative statement of the underlying concern of the text, seen from the perspective of an observation of its structure as making manifest its rhetorical intent, goes beyond simply labelling the work or any one part of it homiletical, hortatory, or paranetic. Deuteronomy certainly partakes of all of these styles. In trying to lay out the rhetorical dimensions of Dt 15, we can not be content with only characterization but must also concern ourselves with the nature of the attitude which motivates the production of this kind of text, with the shape of that which it is intended to evoke (that is, the shape of the ideal society), and with the rhetorical strings it pulls in order to manipulate the reader into assent to that aim. In other words, what we are after is an anatomy of evocation and exhortation,[8] a limning of the way in which this text (any text) communicates its vision of how life in the land should be and why it thinks this vision is important, worth investing with persuasive rhetoric.

The way in which structure fits into an anatomy of evocation is by uncovering the relative weight given to the various sections of a text to make plain the sequence of associations which leads the reader through the text. In each of these cases, it is apparent that a concentration on the structure of this or any text is a process of abstraction.[9]

But even within this concentration on structure there are levels of abstraction. At the highest level of abstraction, the two release-laws of Dt 15:1-18 can each be spoken of as law and consequence, or human act of obedience and divine recompense. In this respect, the two laws share

---

[5] G. von Rad, *Old Testament Theology*, vol. 1 (Trans. D. M. G. Stalker; New York: Harper and Bros., 1962), 220. See also his *Deuteronomy: A Commentary* (Trans. D. Barton; OTL; Philadelphia: Westminster, 1966), 19.

[6] N. Lohfink, *Das Hauptgebot* (AnBib 20; Rome: PBI, 1963), 271-272.

[7] S. D. McBride, "Polity of the Covenant People: The Book of Deuteronomy," *Int* 41 (1987), *passim*, but esp. 235-236, and note his qualification of von Rad's characterization of Dt. on 232 n9.

[8] "Anatomy" here in the archaic sense of the division of a phenomenon into its component parts in order to make a detailed study.

[9] This in contrast to a concentration on phrasing, vocabulary, and syntax, which particularizes the text.

form with the immediately preceding law concerning the triennial tithe for the maintenance of the Levite (14:28//15:1//15:12; 14:29b//15:10b//15:18b).[10] Examples of this basic structure can be multiplied: Dt 16:15 ("Seven days you shall hold festival for YHWH your God . . . for YHWH your God will bless you in all your crops and in all your activity and you will have nothing but joy") or Dt 5:16 ("Honor your father and your mother . . . in order that your days be long and good come to you upon the land which YHWH your God is giving you")[11] and others.

On this level of abstraction, then, the release laws share with other laws of a similar basic formulation the concern to connect statement of law (or desired behavior) and consequence (in this case, reward for behaving in that manner). M. Weinfeld discusses this connection of law and reward, what he calls the "core of deuteronomic literature", as part and parcel with the presence of wisdom elements in deuteronomic material.[12]

The natural connection between wisdom and legal texts (their common connection through the court) has been noted in several

[10] On the paralleling of 14:28f and 15:1-11, see S. A. Kaufman, "The Structure of Deuteronomic Law," *Maarav* 1/2 (1978-79), 129. The additional parallel with 15:12-18 has been inferred here.

[11] R. Sonsino cites these as examples of laws with motive clauses introduced by simple (that is, single as opposed to composite) conjunctions (*Motive Clauses in Hebrew Law* [SBLDS 45; Chico: Scholars, 1980], 70-71). That this is not an adequate category for our purposes is made evident by the fact that Dt. 15:10b is not introduced by a simple conjunction (rather, by the phrase *kî biglal haddābār hazzeh*) and yet is recognizably of the same structure at this level of abstraction. See also Dt 18:9, 12b for a negative example of this same construction. More helpful is the scheme provided by P. Buis (*Le Deutéronome* [Paris: Beauchesne, 1969], 459-462; Buis acknowledges his dependence on Lohfink's work in *Das Hauptgebot*, though Buis is more accessible at this point). Buis' category "Schema bref" is the most like our observed structure; indeed, he cites Dt. 5:16 as an example. That both Dt 15:1-11 and 12-18 are anything but brief and yet can be said to be patterned on this scheme is due to the high level of abstraction we are at present working on. A theological categorization like that of J. Levenson ("The Theologies of Commandment in Biblical Israel," *HTR* 73 [1980], 17-33) places this kind of movement from law to consequence with those laws whose explanation is of a rational, explanatory nature (27-28); similarly, M. Weinfeld (*Deuteronomy and the Deuteronomic School*, 307) calls this "the doctrine of reward" or "material motivation" (356, see esp. his category 2a). Obviously both the fact that so much transpires between proclamation of the law proper and proclamation of divine reward and the theological or ideological implications of the nature of that reward are issues which will be returned to. For the present we must be content with observation.

[12] *Deuteronomy and the Deuteronomic School*, 307-319, esp. 312 where he cites all of 14:29, 15:10, and 15:18.

places.[13] At this juncture, the connection between wisdom and law enables us to make the observation about our text's rhetoric that the sequence "law-consequence" is a customary one for instruction and exhortation. The idea of reward following on correct behavior, for instance, is found in Prov 28:27 ("The one who gives to the poor will lack nothing, while the one who shuts his eyes is full of curses").[14] Phrased in this manner, it evokes compliance on the basis of reason, or what might be called "enlightened self-interest." What follows now is a tracing out of this sequence of "law-consequence" in the structure of first Dt 15:1-11 (the *semittah* law) and then 15:12-18 (the manumission law).

The Structure of the Šĕmiṭṭāh Law

The structure of the *šĕmiṭṭāh* law (vv 1-11) is complex and bears careful examination. More highly articulated in its structure than the manumission law which follows, the *šĕmiṭṭāh* law works on its hearers by means of carefully reasoned argument. To take a particular instance of the complexity of this unit, we might cite the relationship between the two pieces we have called "law" and "consequence."

---

13 See J. Levenson, "The Theologies of Commandment," 27; D. J. McCarthy, *Treaty and Covenant* (AnBib 21A; Rome: PBI, 1978), 163n12; B. Gemser, "The Importance of the Motive Clause in Old Testament Law," *Congress Volume, 1953* (VTSup 1; Leiden: E. J. Brill, 1953) 64-66; and M. Weinfeld *Deuteronomy and the Deuteronomic School*, 53-58 (Weinfeld is here arguing against von Rad's theory of a Levitical origin of Deuteronomy on the basis of its wisdom content which Weinfeld understands as excluding a sacerdotal setting. This analysis must be tempered by the comments of Levenson and McCarthy that wisdom cannot be confined to the scribal class nor priestly circles excluded from political/ courtly/learned spheres). While we are not dealing here with apodictic law, E. Gerstenberger's seminal work on the relation of the law to the transmission of "tribal ethos" should be mentioned. See his *Wesen und Herkunft der ʿapodiktischen Rechts'* (Neukirchen-Vluyn: Neukirchener Verlag, 1965). While Gerstenberger's grammatical analysis is open to question (see e.g. the trenchant comments of J. Bright in "The Apodictic Prohibition: Some Observations," *JBL* 92 [1973], 185-204), still, his drawing a connection between this type of law and wisdom has proven fruitful for such observations of a more general nature. Bright's tentative endorsement of the covenant-treaty form as the most likely point of origin for apodictic law ("The Apodictic Prohibition," 203) does not gainsay this connection for the reason cited by Levenson and McCarthy, viz., the common court setting of the social strata engaged in both wisdom and politics (i.e., those involved in covenant-treaty making). This subject will re-emerge as we discuss the Mesopotamian Law Codes in the next chapter (pp 58-59 and *passim*).

14 The citation is from Weinfeld's discussion of "blessing" as part of the "doctrine of reward" in wisdom and deuteronomic literature. (*Deuteronomy and the Deuteronomic School*, 312-313.)

Within the *šĕmiṭṭāh* law, the blessing itself which is the consequence of observing the law (that is, 15:10b) is, of course, not directly affixed to the law of release (that is, 15:1) but more properly ought to be seen as part of that section which might be called "further instruction with regard to act and attitude." As such, its structural connection to v 1 should be seen as an indirect indication of what attends upon compliance with the law in the particular case of reluctance to lend as the seventh year approaches (the immediate subject of this unit). Its instructional relationship to v 1 is, if anything, heightened by this qualification since in this case it provides the positive aspect of possible consequences, of which v 9b is the negative aspect in the case of disobedience. In order to see this connection more clearly and its counterpart in the manumission law of 15:12-18, we must descend to a more particular level of abstraction, the end result of the analysis of which will be a working out of the structure of the passage in some detail.

In the most general sense, of course, this now tripartite scheme (law-negative consequence-positive consequence) is found elsewhere in Deuteronomy. It reflects the pattern found in Dt 28, which enumerates the blessings and curses attendant upon obeying or not obeying.[15] A similar sequence is found in the law concerning honest measurement (Dt 25:13-15, where the sequence is "law-positive consequence-negative consequence").

In the particular area of instruction denoted in 15:7-11 (that section which contains both the negative and positive consequence of the *šĕmiṭṭāh* law), the boundaries of behavior and their consequences are set forth. Indeed, they are set out in relation to the heading-law (that is, the law found in 15:1) as a means of showing those for whom the law is meant to provide: the poor and needy.

The relationship of heading-law and enumerated consequence illustrating the boundaries of behavior and those for whom the law is intended is present in the case of the dual consequences found in vv 9b and 10b. This relationship between heading-law and enumerated consequence is made evident when one examines in detail the verses we will call "Further Instruction with Reference to Act and Attitude" (i.e., vv 7-11).

Because we are holding up this connection between law and consequence, our analysis of the structure of the whole of the *šĕmiṭṭāh* law (i.e.,

---

15 This does not suppose an editorial connection between these two portions of Dt, merely a structural parallel which carries with it similar rhetorical, evocative weight.

15:1-11) will proceed in reverse order, and we will begin with that unit which contains the consequences of the legislation: vv 7-11.

Further Instruction With Reference to Act and Attitude (vv 7-11)

Our analysis starts with the observation that the unit is bounded by two references to the one on whose behalf the law is given—the poor one (vv 7 and 11). While both of these references to the poor one begin with the particle *kî*, their syntax is quite different. The first reference in v 7 presents us with a hypothesis ("*if* there is among you a poor one . . .") which stands in contrast to the ideal vision spoken of in v 4 ("There shall be no poor among you"). The second reference is not hypothetical but rather tells the hearer the situation to which the behavior here enjoined is to be a response ("For the poor will not cease in the midst of the land").

Within the boundaries set by these two references to the poor one we notice a high prevalence of commands of various sorts:

1a. *do not* harden your heart (*lōʾ* + imperfect) and
1b. *do not* close your hand (*lōʾ*+ imperfect);
2a. *surely* open your hand (infinitive + imperfect) and
2b. *surely* lend (infinitive + imperfect);
3. *be careful lest* you harbor a base thought and your eye begrudge and you do not give (imperative + dependent clause);
4. *surely* give (infinitive + imperfect);
5. *do not* let your heart begrudge (*lōʾ*+ imperfect).

Indeed, the density of commands which use infinitives is without parallel elsewhere in Deuteronomy. Deuteronomy 15 contains eight such verb forms. Only one other chapter contains as many as four (chapter 7) and only two others contain as many as three (chapters 13 and 27); all other chapters contain fewer than three of these verb forms. Already we begin to gain an impression of the great weight which is being placed on Dt 15. This relative weight is the subject of the fourth chapter of this study, but for now suffice it to say that the high prevalence of commands in general and of the construction "infinitive + imperfect" shows the care which is being taken to dictate the way in which this text affects its audience.

There is apparent in these commands an alternation between negative and positive commands leading away from the hypothetical statement of the situation ("if there be any poor among you") to the declarative restatement of the situation ("there will never cease to be poor ones in the land"). The restatement of the situation then leads in turn to a ringing conclusion which in effect restates the heading-law, only this time in the emotive, practical terms in which the preceding discussion on attitude has taken place (v 11b: "therefore I am commanding you that you should surely open your hand to your needy and poor kin in your land"). The intent of the law is at this point made explicit: that the release of loans is for the benefit of the poor.

This unit thus alternately pushes and pulls the hearer through negative and positive commands to this practical and emotive restatement of the heading-law. Throughout this process, both act and attitude are present. Indeed, as we shall see shortly in discussing the language used (on pp. 47-52), the very terms employed ensure that both act and attitude are at once present since heart, hand, eye, and the verbs which describe what they do straddle both arenas. It comes as no surprise, therefore, when the motivational element of the section, v 10b ("for in return for this thing, YHWH your God will bless you in all your deeds and in all your undertakings") carries this same duality of act and attitude: God's favorable attitude toward the compliant hearer of the legislation issues in the favorable outcome of that one's concerns.[16]

The structure of the section thus consists of the statement of a hypothetical situation to which the legislation at hand is a response (v 7a). That the *šĕmiṭṭāh*-law is a proper response becomes apparent as the hearer is led through a series of alternating negative and positive commands dealing with the actions and attitudes which the hearer is to have in light of this situation (vv 7b-10a). To clinch the matter, the attitude and action of God in response is given as a motivating factor (v 10b). The situation is then restated as fact, indeed a fact which will not go away (v 11a), and the summary of the law, now with its attendant attitudes made manifest, is given (v 11b).

That the whole of this unit is to be taken as tightly bound to the heading-law (the *šĕmiṭṭāh*-year legislation) is made explicit by the reappearance of the technical term for this law, *šĕmiṭṭāh*, in v 9. What we are given in vv 7-11, then, is not just negative and positive consequence, but

[16] C. Mitchell (*The Meaning of BRK "to Bless" in the Old Testament* [SBLDS 95; Atlanta: Scholars, 1987] esp. 165-167) comes to this conclusion in his examination of the term "to bless": "The factor that makes a blessing a blessing is the relationship between God and the person blessed. God blesses because of his favorable attitude toward a person or group of people. A blessing is any benefit or utterance which God freely bestows in order to make known to the recipient and to others that he is favorably disposed toward the recipient." Clearly both attitude and act are components of divine blessing.

a skillfully devised portrait-in-miniature of the law and the impact which this law will have: curse or blessing and the need to guard one's thoughts and actions.

Clearly this is exhortation addressed to those who have the capacity to affect the shape of society. They are shown to have not only the capacity to affect the shape of social reality but also the capacity to bring upon the whole of society either curse or blessing, depending on how they act toward those for whom the heading-law seeks to provide.

The Portrait of the Obedient People (vv 4-6)

That it is the poor on whose behalf the law is given is apparent in the unit we have already characterized in passing as an ideal portrait (i.e., vv 4-6) as well, but this characterization cannot be allowed to stand without qualification.

Many commentators take these verses to be secondary.[17] Others feel that the contrast between vv 4-6 and those which follow is intentional, that of the ideal which follows from obedience and the real which accompanies disobedience[18] or of future possibility as opposed to present reality.[19]

These questions are of lesser importance to the task at hand than the effect which the presence of this unit has on the way the law affects its audience, that is, what having this section here *does* to the hearer which renders the presentation of the law more effective than it would otherwise be. As with the previous unit so too with this one we will understand the task at hand to be concerned with discerning the structure of the text as a rhetorical entity rather than trying to recreate the legislation at an earlier stage.

With these two goals in mind (that is, the resolution of its place in the line of argument in the *šĕmiṭṭāh* law and its structure as a rhetorical

---

17 E.g., A. D. H. Mayes (*Deuteronomy*, 248) points to similarities with texts outside the Code itself (7:12f with its portrait of the ideal should observance be the norm and 4:21 with its similar use of the word "inheritance" as here in 15:4-6) as proving them to be closely analogous to these verses and therefore showing them to be part of a later stage of editing than the law itself. The point about the secondary nature of these verses is made as well in Buis, *Le Deutéronome* 257; von Rad, *Deuteronomy* 106; and Seitz, *Redaktionsgeschichtliche Studien zum Deuteronomium* (Stuttgart: W. Kohlhammer, 1971), 169.

18 J. Rennes, *Le Deutéronome* (Geneve: Editions Labor et Fides, 1967) 80.

19 D. Schneider, *Das fünfte Buch Mose* (Wuppertal: R. Brockhaus, 1982) 155. P. Craigie (*The Book of Deuteronomy* [NICC; Grand Rapids: Eerdmans, 1976] 237) appeals to both of these in combination.

entity), the unit we have labeled "The Portrait of an Obedient People" has a certain linearity to it: there will be no poor because YHWH will bless but only if you obey with the result that[20] YHWH blesses you, and so your relationship to other nations will be as lender, not borrower.

As one can see from this brief paraphrase, there are actually two portraits given in this section, or perhaps two dimensions of the one portrait of the obedient people. The hearer is told that there will be no poor because God will bless the land. The hearer is also told that the relationship which will obtain between the nation and other nations will be that of lender, not borrower; ruler, not ruled.

Additionally, two elements of this portrait are emphasized through the use of emphatic constructions: that YHWH will indeed bless (infinitive + imperfect, v 4b) and that the people should indeed obey (infinitive + imperfect, v 5a) with the result that YHWH will bless. The two dimensions of the ideal portrait thus sandwich the conditions upon which that portrait depends: God's blessing and the people's obedience.

It is this pair of conditions (divine blessing and human obedience) which carry over into the next section, the unit we have called "Further Instruction with Reference to Act and Attitude" (i.e., vv 7-11) and have just discussed. Stated in terms of the sequence we observed at the highest level of abstraction, we begin to see that the sequence "law-consequence" permeates the law both in the sweep of the whole law and within its component parts. In the case of vv 7-11 there are present both the negative and positive consequences following upon disobedience or obedience and a vigorous restatement of the law in emotive terms. In the case of the present section, "The Portrait of the Obedient People" (i.e., vv 4-6), both elements are present in the portrait of the society with neither poverty within the nation nor borrowing from those without the nation, an ideal which the portrait tells us arises from God's blessing, a blessing that in turn depends on careful observance.

The effect is then an inescapable confronting of the reader with both the expectations of the legislation and the consequences which follow so that assent becomes logical (the hearer is given not just one but several statements of what is at stake) and compliance necessary.

Explanation of the Law (vv 2-3)

The final unit appended to the heading-law to be discussed with respect to the *šĕmiṭṭāh* law we shall label "Explanation of the Law" (vv 2-

---

[20] On the use of *kî* as a resultative, see R. Williams, *Hebrew Syntax: An Outline*[2] (Toronto: Univ. of Toronto, 1984) pars. 450 and 527.

3). As S. Kaufman observes, it is self-evident from the fact that this explanation was deemed necessary that Deuteronomy has borrowed the term *šĕmiṭṭāh* and is using it in a new way.[21] However one understands the relationship of this text to the fallow year for the land in Exod 23:10f which also employs the verb *šmṭ*, it is plain that the text does not assume that we know the content of the law (this is evident in v 2a: "Now this is the manner of the *šĕmiṭṭāh* . . . ").

Unlike the other two units appended to the heading-law whose lines of argument were structured logically rather than formally, the unit labelled "interpretation of the law" is structured as an in-and-out argument, a chiasm:[22]

1. every holder of a pledge/loan under his control shall *release*
  2. *what he has received* (by pledge/loan) from his neighbor[23];
    3. he shall not *exact* (the loan)
      4. of *his neighbor, his kin,*
        5. for the "Release" of YHWH has been proclaimed;
      4.' of the *foreigner*
    3.' you may *exact* (the loan),
  2.' but *that which is yours* from your kin
1.' you shall *release* from your control.

21 "Social Welfare Systems of Israel," 282.

22 Cf. *Redaktionsgeschichtliche Studien*, 168. Seitz is here arguing that this structure indicates the grafting of v 3 onto an original interpretation present in v 2, in part on the basis of the prevalence of *rē(a)ᶜ* in v 2 and *ʾāḥ* in v 3, the switch from 3rd to 2nd person subject, and the contrast provided in v 3 between exacting a loan from the kinsperson and yet allowing exaction of loans to the foreigner. Mayes (*Deuteronomy*, 247) agrees with this analysis. Again, our concern is with the rhetoric of the text as a whole, in its final form. More will be said especially about the presence of both "neighbor" and "kin" later.

23 The translation given here of this difficult verse follows that of R. North, in "*Yâd* in the Shemitta-Law," *VT* 4 (1954) 196-198. The difficulty lies in who is doing what to whom. Drawing upon a study by Koschaker detailing the action of guaranteeing a loan by handing over a pledge, North concludes that the guarantor is symbolically delivered over into the power of the creditor. The pronominal suffix ("his") attached to "hand" refers to the creditor, however, and not the one who borrows, since that is the manner in which the transaction is spoken of in the examples cited by Koschaker. The verb *nšh* in the relative clause which follows therefore involves receiving a pledge as a condition of making a loan. Construing the action this way accords well with the related laws at Dt 24:6 and 10-13 which tell what the creditor may and may not do with pledges. North's translation of this phrase is "every holder of a pledge at his disposition shall release what he has received-by-pledge-loan-contract with his neighbor."

The in-and-out argument in this case works to highlight the behavior required (release of loans by the creditor) and the warrant for requiring that behavior (by appeal to the authority of YHWH). In fact, this appeal to the authority of YHWH as the grounds by which the law is given authority is the central point on which the structure of the section turns.

In this section the sequence "law-consequence" does not underlie the argument as it does in the following two sections (that is, vv 4-6 and 7-11). Rather, the text is here interpreting the heading-law and so is weighted toward the content of that law and its justification.

Summary and Observations

The structure of the first of our two release-laws (the release of loans) proves itself to be highly articulated and calculated to produce the desired effect in its audience (that is, observance). This *šĕmiṭṭāh* law consists of the bald statement of the law (15:1) and the outworking of that law in three units, explanation (2-3), portrait of the ideal (4-6), and further instruction (7-11). Each of these three appended units is structured in such a way as to lead the audience both within the immediate argument of each section and in consort with one another to an inescapable confrontation with the issues at stake here.

This close scrutiny of the structure of argument in Dt 15:1-11 has led to many insights into the reasoning which lies behind its arrangement. The chief of these is the prevalence of the sequence "law-consequence" as a pattern which seeks to evoke observance. This sequence appeals primarily to the reason of the audience by pointing out that which the audience stands to gain or lose. In the case of the section labelled "The Portrait of the Obedient People," a positive face is put on this sequence: observance of the *šĕmiṭṭāh* law leads by way of divine blessing to the twin ideals of no poor in the land and no indebtedness to other nations. In the case of the section labelled "Further Instruction with Reference to Act and Attitude," the case contrary to the "absence of poverty" ideal is put and a negative face is drawn in the sequence: lack of response to the poor when the *šĕmiṭṭāh* year looms leads to iniquity and the cry to God to redress wrong.[24] But there is a positive side as well: giving without guile leads to blessing.

---

24 R. Boyce (*The Cry to God in the Old Testament* [SBLDS 103; Atlanta: Scholars, 1988], 41-42) observes in connection with this occurrence of the cry to God that it represents an expansion of the paradigm of cry narratives in the area of the identity of the participants: God rather than king, the poor rather than the absolutely marginalized (widow, orphan).

Another motif which this close scrutiny has uncovered is the grounding of the substance of the law in the authority of YHWH. In this particular case, the Deuteronomic justification for the law differs from that displayed in similar parts of the Covenant Code which, as we shall see,[25] appeal to the *character* of the deity as one who hears the outcry of the wronged (cf. Exod 22:21-23, 24-26; 23:6-8). The motif of the outcry of the wronged is of course, present in the "Further Instruction" section (i.e., the passage just discussed, Dt 15:9b). In the case of the interpretation of the *šĕmiṭṭāh*-year law in 15:2-3, however, the appeal is not to the *character* of the deity so much as to the *authority* of the deity, and it is this authority which underlies the whole of the argument. This is social justice mandated by divine warrant.

The Structure of the Manumission Law

In contrast to the highly articulated structure of the law contained in 15:1-11, in the case of 15:12-18 (the manumission law), the structure of the passage is not as highly articulated. And yet it too shows evidence of a great deal of care taken in the structuring of its argument. As with the *šĕmiṭṭāh* law, the motif of "law-consequence" is applied to the subject of manumission and done so in a way that care is taken to show the situation which the law addresses and the situations which create difficulties for observance.

Having made these general comments, however,we must admit at the outset that there are features of the manumission law which are difficult to explain as logical components of the structure of the law, that is, of its line of argument.

What the Law Intends (vv 16-18)

The structural difficulties hinge on 15:16-17, which poses problems for any structural scheme.[26] The closing of the passage as a whole in v 18

---

[25] Below, pp 88-89 and 90-91.

[26] Some commentators view these verses as a secondary intrusion into the flow of 12-18. Seitz (*Redaktionsgeschichtliche Studien*, 172) sees 16f as secondary on the grounds that v 18 deals with manumission as does the rest of the passage while 16f does not. Seitz sees this type of interjection as similar to that of 15:4-6, which breaks up the flow from 15:2-3 to 7-11, though he acknowledges that the law with 16f included corresponds to its Covenant Code parallel (Exod 21:5f), which also takes up the subject of the slave who wishes to remain in service even though manumission is offered. Mayes (*Deuteronomy*, 252) notes the parallel with the Covenant Code legislation and also notes that v 18 does not fit after v 15 either, since v 15 concludes the preceding section. He sees v 18 as the conclusion to the whole slave law which has

with a caution about one's attitude toward manumission challenges us to try to understand the passage as a rhetorical entity with a single subject: manumission.[27] There is a sense in which Mayes' division of the law into two subsections (13-15, 16-18) is correct,[28] with certain nuances: v 18 must be divided into two parts. Dt 15:18b serves as the conclusion to the law as a whole and so displays in bookend fashion with v 12 the hortatory sequence "law-consequence." In this it is similar to 15:10b (the statement of blessing) with which it is similar in phrasing and vocabulary. Dt 15:18a, however, can be said to serve as the conclusion to the section we will call "What the Law Intends"—16-18a. Again, however, 18a departs from 16-17 in insisting on the primacy of manumission as the subject of the text. It underscores the fact that 15:12 is still the heading-law and that the scenario introduced in v 16 ("it may happen that . . . ") does not represent a case over against that heading law but an appendix to it.

In a sense, vv 16-18 within the manumission law serve a function similar to vv 7-11 in the *šĕmiṭṭāh*-law. Both units introduce a situation contrary to that which the audience has been led to expect by the section which precedes: the poor who are among you despite the ideal painted in vv 4-6 (in v 7a), the slave who refuses to go out from servitude despite the parallel drawn to Israel's own remembrance of harsh servitude in

---

two subsections (12-15, 16-18) each with a similar structure: a casuistic law followed by general exhortation. Dt 15:18 then serves as an overall conclusion to the manumission law and as the exhortation which concludes the second subsection (vv 16-18). Mayes admits the difficulty with this view that v 18 deals with manumission and not permanent bondage and so is awkward as a hortatory conclusion to 16f. P. Buis (*Le Deutéronome*, 259) characterizes 16f as an exception which is included here as elsewhere in ancient law. It is thus included on the basis of a desire to exhaust the subject at hand before moving on. Buis does not comment on the difficulties posed by the abrupt return to manumission when the passage is brought to a close in v 18. F. Horst (*Das Privilegrecht Jahwes* [FRLANT 45; Göttingen: Vandenhoeck & Ruprecht, 1930], 75-78) solves the structural difficulties posed by this passage by positing a development of the text at the hands of three editors. Again, the Covenant Code parallel makes this position difficult to hold without qualification. In addition, while it is likely that any text in Deuteronomy bears the imprint of several hands, the problem we are posing to ourselves is the way in which the final form of the release-laws operates rhetorically, that is, the way they seek to evoke assent and compliance. Obviously, knowing that this final form is the result of some editing helps us only slightly in trying to puzzle out the effect which that final form is intended to have on its audience.

[27] To make this observation is to render problematic Seitz's chiastic structure for vv 13-18, since his argument relies on the omission of 16f from the structure.

[28] *Deuteronomy*, 252.

Egypt from which YHWH ransomed them (in v 16).[29] Putting the contrary case opens the way to discuss the attitude of those who have the power to comply or not comply with the heading-law. In the case of 15:7-11, those with the power to comply are enjoined to do so even in the face of the *šĕmiṭṭāh* year—the good or ill condition of society as a whole rests on their ungrudging compliance. It is important to notice that the behavior in view in 15:7-11 is not, strictly speaking, related to the heading-law as it is spelled out in the interpretation (vv 2-3): it is not the release of loans which is in view but the continued willingness to lend to the poor despite release. By analogy, it is not manumission which is in view in 15:16-18a but the restricted conditions under which manumission can be forfeited and the way in which that restriction affects the attitude of the owner.

It is the awareness that 16f is a restriction to a single case of the exceptions to the heading-law which is our clue for understanding how v 18a relates to 16f. When we see 16f as an exception to the behavior required by the heading-law, then the thrust of that law (that all slaves should go out of service in the seventh year) is never lost. Vv 16f spell out the *only* circumstance in which the intention of the heading-law can be abrogated, and v 18a spells out the attitude which should prevail in those who have the power to see to the fulfillment of that intention. In the face of temptation to force perpetual servitude or to coerce from the enslaved a willingness to perpetuate their position of absolute dependence, v 18a counsels a willingness to comply with the behavior required by the heading-law *and* its underlying intent (that *all* should go out).

Thus while it is the attitude of the enslaved which is directly available to us in vv 16f, v 18a shows us that what is also being addressed is the attitude of the master. The law intends for all to go out. Only the desire of the slave can negate this intention. Therefore those who can effect release should not consider release a hardship nor try to coerce the dependent into renouncing manumission.

In this sense the attitude of those who have the capacity to see that the behavior required by the heading-law is carried out is in view just as

[29] Note too the syntactical parallel between 15:7 and 16 which, though not exact, is suggestive: the verb of narration (*hyh*) introduces a qualifying statement. In both cases, the verb is preceded by a disjunctive particle (*kî* in 7; the conjunction *wāw* which when used with *hyh* often denotes a turning point in speech in 16—on the use of *whyh ky* to signal the beginning of a subsidiary concern [*unterfall*], see I. Cardellini, *Die biblischen "Sklaven"-Gesetze*, [BBB 55; Bonn: Peter Hanstein, 1981], 274 text and 274 n27).

in 15:7-11 with respect to the *šĕmiṭṭāh* year. The heading-law in 15:1 and its interpretation in vv 2-3 create the conditions under which behavior not directly covered by the law (lending to the poor) might seem onerous. Yet that onerous act should still be done since blessing or curse rides on it.

Similarly, the heading-law in 15:12 and its interpretation in vv 13-14 create the conditions in which behavior not directly covered by the law (not coercing renunciation) might seem onerous.[30] Yet that onerous act should still be done since the service of the servant has been a boon to the master, and blessing will follow a manumission which is not given grudgingly.

This interpretation, which subsumes the exception to the heading-law under the intent underlying that heading-law (that all should go out from servitude), is borne out by comparison with the parallel legislation in Exod 21:2-6. In the Covenant Code legislation, the exceptions to the heading-law (which otherwise bears such great similarity to that in Dt 15) are spelled out in detailed and exhaustive fashion. The goal is clearly to restrict the circumstances in which confusion can arise.

This is not the case in Dt 15:16f. Here, no attempt is made to spell out the circumstances which lie behind or create the desire for renouncing manumission. Only the attitude of the slave is spoken of, not the circumstances of that slave (married or not, childless or having children).

In the case of the Covenant Code law, the section spelling out the exceptions to release serves to restrict those who may go out (the wife whom the slave has married before entering service may go out, but not the one whom the slave is given after entering service). The deuteronomic legislation, in contrast, places restrictions on those who may *not* go out (*only* those who love their present circumstances). Thus, in contrast to its Covenant Code parallel, this passage is not concerned with describing in detail those who may or may not go out from slavery but with describing the circumstances under which going out may be refused. Such a contrast between these two texts reinforces our point that 15:16f should be read under the general intention that all should go out.

The sudden switch back to the attitude of the owner then, as we have said, seems not so jarring since it too limits the barriers which can be placed between the slave and that slave's manumission. Indeed, the implied intention that all should go out becomes in effect a second consequence of the heading-law.

---

30 Doubly so, since it is not only the slave who departs but with him or her a provision from the stocks of the former master.

In this manner, vv 16-18 can be given the label "What the Law Intends." As we have said, in this respect it holds a place in the argument similar to that which vv 7-11 holds in the *šĕmiṭṭāh*-year law. And just as vv 7-11 spell out the twin consequences of one's behavior with respect to the law, so too does the unit in vv 16-18 close with a similar dual enumeration of consequence, in this case the two positive consequences of divine blessing and manumission to all after a limited term of service. Already the rhetorical sequence "law-consequence" is clearly prominent.

But as with vv 7-11 in the *šĕmiṭṭāh*-year law, so here the section labelled "What the Law Intends" also spells out the nature of the behavior deemed appropriate in light of the heading-law: the right to renounce manumission is restricted (thereby implying the intention that all should go out) and the right of the owner to begrudge the slave her or his going out is prohibited.[31]

Internal History (v 15)

There is yet another conceptual parallel between the place of vv 16-18 in the rhetorical structure of the manumission law and that of vv 7-11 in the *šĕmiṭṭāh*-year law. This additional parallel has already been alluded to but should be discussed now in greater detail. This parallel has to do with the relationship which these two sections have to the sections which precede them—the section we have labelled "The Portrait of the Obedient People" in the case of the *šĕmiṭṭāh* law and the present one which we shall call "Internal History."

In the case of vv 7-11 there is on the surface a great deal of tension between that unit and the one preceding in vv 4-6. One says that there will be no poor; the other says that there will always be poor. Vv 4-6, as we have seen, stress two themes: the ideal portrait and the importance of observance. It is the second of these, the importance of observance, which carries over into vv 7-11 in which observance in the specific situation with which the unit is concerned (lending to the poor as the *šĕmiṭṭāh* year approaches) is rewarded by divine blessing.

---

31 Note the presence of the "*lōʾ*-prohibitive" at 18a: *lōʾ yiqšeh bĕʿêneka* etc. On this form of prohibition, see most conveniently J. Bright, "The Apodictic Prohibition," 186-189.

Similarly, v 15, while not as highly articulated in structure as are vv 4-6, nonetheless serves to elicit obedience from the audience and so appeals to the historical memory of the nation.[32]

In the *šĕmiṭṭāh* law, vv 4-6 appeal to the relationship between the ideal of absence of poverty and obedience and so make no further appeal other than an implied one to the authority of YHWH whose voice has given the law.[33]

In the manumission law, however, the appeal made in v 15 is more complex. It establishes an emotional parallel between the situation of the whole people of God as slaves in Egypt to the Hebrew slave in the land. In this way it enjoins the owner of the slave to follow the example of YHWH in obtaining release for that one. In this calling to mind of slavery in Egypt, the possibility that some will not wish to be free seems remote.

This unit on the surface stands in some tension with the following verses. V 16 begins the unit labelled "What the Law Intends" with an apparently contradictory situation: that of the slave who does not wish to go out. And yet as we have seen, the theme of obedience to the intention of the law carries over into vv 16-18 as they spell out not merely exceptions to the heading-law but severe restrictions to any temptation to inhibit the carrying out of the intention of the heading-law.

It is in this similar pattern of surface contrast and sub-surface continuity that the respective units of 15:1-11 and 12-18, labelled "The Portrait of the Obedient People"//"Internal History" and "Further Instruction with Reference to Act and Attitude"//"What the Law Intends" (that is, vv 4-6//15 and 7-11//16-18), show a structural parallel. In both cases the effect is to reinforce the sequence "law-consequence" by inserting a note on the importance of observance or obedience. And in both cases the theme of observance being rewarded with divine blessing is present. Indeed, the wording of reward is almost identical.[34]

Explanation of the Law (vv 13-14)

Like the *šĕmiṭṭāh* law, the manumission law follows the initial statement of the heading-law (in this case, v 12) with an explanation. In the

---

32 The *internal history* of the people of YHWH—see the comments to follow in Chapter Three, pp 89-91, on the use of internal history to safeguard the inclusion of those who stand in danger of being excluded from the protection of the law.

33 Cf v 5a: "If only you are sure to heed the voice of YHWH your God."

34 Cf. 15:10b: "because for this YHWH your God will bless you in all your work (*maʿaśekā*) and in all you undertake."

18b: "So YHWH your God will bless you in all that you do (*taʿăśeh*)."

case of the *šĕmiṭṭāh*-year law, the persuasive sequence "law-consequence" is reinforced at this point by stressing the divine warrant for the law. This is the case with the explanation of the law given in the manumission law, though in a less direct fashion. That the theme of divine warrant is present in the explanation of the manumission law given in vv 13-14 requires some elucidation.

We have noted above how the structure of the interpretation of the *šĕmiṭṭāh* law serves to highlight the behavior required by the law (release of loans by the creditor) and the warrant for requiring that behavior (by appeal to the authority of YHWH).

These same two themes are struck in vv 13-14, the explanation of the manumission law, though again the unit is not as highly articulated in structure. This unit divides itself into two sections along the lines of the two themes just outlined: the behavior required by the heading-law (that is, the slave will be provided for out of the bounty of the owner's property—vv13-14a) and the warrant for requiring that behavior (that is, the owner provides for the slave out of the bounty which comes from YHWH's blessing of the land—v 14b[35]). It is of course the latter of these two themes where divine warrant is present. Stated in a more straightforward fashion, the meaning here is that just as God has blessed you, you shall provide for the slave who goes free. This is warrant by example.

Summary and Observations

Thus the various subsections in the manumission law fulfill a structural function similar to the corresponding subsections in the *šĕmiṭṭāh*-

35 The rendering of the text at this point in both the LXX and SP makes the relationship between divine blessing and provisioning the slave even clearer. The LXX reads "*katha eulogēsen se kurios ho theos sou, doseis auto* (according to the manner in which the Lord your God has blessed you, you shall give to him)," and the SP reads "*kʾšr brkk yhwh ʾlhyk ttn lw* (just as YHWH your God has blessed you, you shall give to him)." That the Masoretes also understand the relationship between the clauses of v 14 this way is apparent in the placement of the *ʾatnaḥ* beneath *miyyiqbekā*, thereby creating a break in the flow of the sentence. This means that the blessing of YHWH is understood not as being conferred *upon* the owner's property (in which case the verse would read "you shall liberally provide for that one from your flock and threshing-floor and vineyard with which YHWH your God has blessed you"—no break) but that the blessing of YHWH is understood to belong to the latter part of the verse in a manner similar to LXX and SP (thus: "you shall liberally provide for that one from your flock and threshing-floor and vineyard; just as YHWH your God has blessed you, so you shall give to that one"—break between 14a and 14b).

year law section. With respect to the overall argument of the manumission law, then, they likewise stress the warrant for the law (in this case, providing for the slave since or as YHWH has provided for them), a call for observance of the law, and a description of the consequences of observance in a particular situation. Like the *šĕmiṭṭāh* law, and despite tensions within the text and a less highly articulated structural pattern, the manumission law also follows the sequence "law-warrant-call to obedience-positive consequence."

Or to make the point graphically:

15:1	heading-law	15:12
15:2-3	warrant	15:13-14
15:4-6	call to obedience	15:15
15:7-11	consequence in specific situation	15:16-18

Remarkably, this sequence not only follows in a general way observable patterns in wisdom literature, as noted above, but corresponds to the description of what goes on in arguing a case articulated by a modern dissector of arguments, Stephen Toulmin.[36] We shall next examine this similarity and in so doing will analyze the two release-laws on a level of abstraction mid-way between the highest level (the sequence "law-consequence") and the detailed level of abstraction we have just finished examining.

The Structure of the Release Laws and Effective Argumentation

Saying that traditional descriptions of the shape and uses of arguments are too bound to the model of mathematical proofs[37] and are consequently not up to the task of explaining what really goes on in arguments, Toulmin turns instead to the realm of jurisprudence for his model.

According to this way of describing the line an argument takes, when one wishes to establish the viability of a *claim* or assertion, one has recourse to several courts of appeal, or rather several types of statements by which the claim is supported. Each of these types of statement can be seen as a response to or an anticipation of a challenge made to the claim by an imagined skeptical interlocutor.

---

[36] *The Uses of Argument* (London: Cambridge, 1958). The model which follows is taken from pp 97-107.

[37] That is, the "All A's are B; C is an A; therefore C is a B" model.

One such question made or anticipated is "What have you got to go on?" The claimant responds to such a challenge by making appeal to certain facts or *data* which establish the necessity or possibility of her claim.

Having produced her data, the claimant may find herself faced with a further challenge which asks her to produce the step by which she moved from data to claim. Toulmin phrases this challenge colloquially "How did you get there?" and calls the type of statements by which this challenge is answered *warrants* (rules, principles, or inference-licenses)—statements which act as bridges between the claimant's data and her conclusion. They are statements *in terms of which* one moves from facts to conclusion. They are often referred to implicitly and not explicitly. Some warrants allow the claimant to state her claim with a great deal of force; others allow only a tentative assertion.

In either case, the claim is made on the basis of modal *qualifiers* (such as "necessarily" or "presumably") and is made acknowledging certain conditions of exception or *rebuttal* which indicate circumstances in which the authority of the warrant no longer holds.

Warrants for making a claim are not only qualified and set out in light of certain "unlesses" (exceptions or rebuttals); they also need to stand up to the question "Why do you think that?"—they need support from *backing statements* which allow one to presume or to trust the validity of arguing from data to claim on the basis of one's justifying warrants.

Toulmin displays this model for an argument like this:[38]

D (data) ————————→ So, Q (qualifier), C (claim)
↓ ↓
Since W (warrant) Unless R (rebuttal)
↓
On account of B (backing)

Or in terms of a sample argument:[39]

Harry was born in Bermuda ————————→ So, presumably, Harry is a British subject
↓ ↓
Since Unless
↓ ↓
A man born in Bermuda will Both his parent were aliens/ he has become a

38 *Ibid.*, 104.

39 *Ibid.*, 105.

generally be a British subject   naturalized American/ . . .
↓
On account of
↓
The following statutes
and other legal provisions:

It should be apparent that there is a great deal of correspondence between the structure of an argument according to Toulmin's model and the structure of the presentation of the release-laws of Dt 15. Both as a way of illustrating this correspondence and as a way of sharpening our understanding of the way in which the structure of the release-laws had been composed with an eye towards greatest effect in evoking assent and compliance in its audience, we would do well to diagram the structure of the release-laws (based on the analysis of their structure which has preceded) along the lines of Toulmin's model.

The *šĕmiṭṭāh* law, according to the categories of Toulmin's model, has this structure (notice that I am reversing the order of terms Rebuttal and Qualifier for the sake of clarity):

Data (1, 2abc, 3) ⟶ So, Qualifier (7-8, 11), Claim (10b)
↓   ↓
Since   Unless
Warrant (2d)   Rebuttal (9-10a)
↓
On account of
Backing (4-6)

Where

Data = the law (v 1) and its interpretation (2abc, 3)

Since

Warrant = the law is of YHWH (2d)

On account of

Backing = heeding the voice of YHWH, from which follows a society with neither internal nor external poverty (4-6)

So, unless

Rebuttal/Exception = the refusal to accept the authority of the divine origin of the law (the Warrant) leads to ill will and lack of generosity (9-10a)

Presumably

Qualifier = the poverty which provides the occasion for observance will continue

And

Claim = observance/obedience will be rewarded by the blessing of YHWH

Similarly, the manumission law, according to the categories of Toulmin's model and the preceding analysis, has this structure:

Data (12,13,14abd) ⟶ So, Qualifier ([18a]), Claim ([16-18a],18b)
↓ Since ↓ Warrant (14c) ↓ On account of Backing (15)
↓ Unless ↓ Rebuttal (16-18a)

Where

Data = the law (12) and its interpretation (13-14abd)

Since

Warrant = YHWH's blessing of the land has created the conditions for well-being and hence the warrant for provisioning the slave (14c)

On account of

Backing = the empathy due the slave because of the sense of commonality evoked by the recollection of servitude in Egypt (15a) and the obedience due YHWH because of YHWH's redemptive act (15b)

So, unless

Rebuttal/Exception = the slave renounces his or her right to manumission or the owner begrudges the slave that right (16-18a)

Presumably

Qualifier = there will continue to be those who serve their terms (18a, by implication)

And

Claim = all shall go out (implied by the restriction of the exceptions in 16-18a) and obedience/observance will be rewarded by the blessing of YHWH (18b)

The structure delineated through employing Toulmin's model places us on a level of abstraction midway between the highest level (the sequence "law-consequence" or its nuanced form "law-warrant-call to obedience-consequence") and the more detailed comments which grew out of an examination of the interrelationships present among the various units which make up the release-laws.

On this level of abstraction, at least three observations come into focus which were not apparent at the other two levels of abstraction.

First of all, this model serves to highlight the evocative effect of the presentation of the two release-laws. It is clear from diagramming the line of argument of the two release-laws this way that the argument carries us skillfully and inexorably from the datum of the law to the claim that obedience will elicit divine blessing. This is simply another, more precise way of saying what has been said before, that here as elsewhere in Deuteronomy the purpose of the rhetoric with which the laws are presented is persuasion, exhortation, and evocation.

Second and more importantly, diagramming the release-laws in this manner brings to the surface a structural interconnection between the two release-laws. One notices that what appears in the *semittah* law in the place of the argument's claim (that obeying this law will be rewarded with blessing) becomes in the manumission law a warrant justifying the move from Data to Claim (that because YHWH has blessed the property of the owner, then some of the bounty of that property should go to the slave at the end of his or her servitude).

It is certainly the case in the Deuteronomic laws that divine blessing appears simply as a motive clause, the punch line to exhortation. It is also the case with respect to these two release laws that there is a certain amount of narrative linearity to YHWH's blessing. The blessing promised in the one becomes the grounds for a new demand in the other when the two are viewed as persuasive arguments toward the claim that obedience is met with a positive consequence. YHWH's blessing serves to interlock the two release-laws.

Third, another pair of argument features which interconnect the two release-laws is that which appears as a Qualifier in the *šĕmiṭṭāh* law, namely that poverty will continue to provide the occasion for obedience. As will be apparent in our analysis of the ancient Near Eastern documents, poverty and the indebtedness which is its companion are among the chief reasons for slavery in these cultures.[40] Stated in terms of Toulmin's model, the Qualifier in the *šĕmiṭṭāh* law has become an implied datum in the manumission law (that is, it is the fact that many sell themselves into slavery because of their indebtedness which makes the manumission law necessary). Again, there is a certain narrative connection between the two laws.[41] It is as if having made one argument, the compiler of the Deuteronomic laws must then make the other.

Persuasive argument, legal or otherwise, depends upon more than structure to retain the interest of its audience, however. Artistry in language and phrasing also contributes to a compelling and evocative

---

[40] I. Mendelsohn, "Slavery in the Ancient Near East", *BA* 9 (1946), 78-80. The biblical texts Mendelsohn cites as confirmation of this observation are Lev 25:39-54, 2 Kgs 4:1-2, Am 2:6, Is 50:1, Neh 5:1, Exod 21:2-3, and our text.

[41] This is another way of saying that these two laws display with respect to one another the kind of thematic association typical of the Mesopotamian and biblical law codes. On the presence of this phenomenon, see S. Kaufmann, "The Structure of Deuteronomic Law," *passim*.

argument. It is to the manner in which these release-laws strive to evoke assent and compliance on the level of the words they use rather than the argument structure they employ[42] that we now address ourselves.

THE LANGUAGE OF THE CHAPTER

Put another way, a discussion of the language of the text has to do with the particular vocabulary which its framer has chosen. This is language which has been chosen carefully to complement the argument of the text (that is, its structure). This complementarity serves to engage the audience on the level of both reason and emotion, since the particular vocabulary chosen here is highly evocative. We will allow our presentation of this level of the text to be directed by the various evocative words which make up the text.[43] Under this guiding feature, two subdivisions will be treated, namely those words having somatic fields of meaning,[44] and those words having relational connotations.

Somatic Vocabulary

The three primary somatic or body terms used in this passage to arrest the attention of the audience are *yād* (hand), *lēbāb* (heart, soul, etc.),

---

42 I am making a distinction between the "structure" of the release-laws and their "story" level in much the same way in which narratologists distinguish between the *fabula* of a narrative and the *story* related in the narrative. The fabula of a narrative is the series of logically or chronologically related events caused or experienced by the actors in the narrative (that is, the structure of the argument). The story of the narrative consists of the *particular* way the narrative is related. The fairy tale "Puss in Boots," for instance, can be told in many different ways, even change radically in terms of its particulars, and still be recognized as the same narrative. In the case of the release-laws, the two laws of Dt 15 have a recognizably similar structure of argument, and they therefore can be said to be relating the same narrative ("There is a law and it should be observed in order to receive blessing") while differing on the level of story, one telling the narrative in such a way that the law of the *šěmiṭṭāh* year is related, while the other telling the narrative in such a way that manumission law is related. On this distinction, see M. Bal, *Narratology: Introduction to the Theory of Narrative* (Toronto: Univ. Press, 1985).

43 I am at this point apparently collapsing two of Bal's narrative categories, *story* (see previous note) and *text* (that is, the actual "words-on-a-page" which may differ from one "edition" of the story to the next). This apparent collapsing of these two categories is both apparent and real. It is real to the extent that my analysis rests heavily on a single "text," the MT, but only apparent to the extent that other texts will also receive attention (e.g., the LXX, the SP).

44 On the "prominent use of body language" in this passage, see Miller, "The Way of Torah," 26.

and *ʿáyin* (eye). Each has connotations both within itself and in consort with the others.

As R. North has shown,[45] *yād* is here to be understood as referring to the power which the creditor has over the debtor. The debtor (or, more specifically, the guarantor) is delivered into the custody of the creditor—either through the pledge of self, a dependent, or some possession.[46] Therefore, the debtor is said to be "under the power of" or "in the hand of" the creditor who holds the pledge. This is the sense of the word in Dt 15:2 and 3. It is similar to the more general use of the term to denote possession (cf. Dt 13:18 of spoil, and 1 Sam 14:34 of an ox or 1 Sam 16:2 of a heifer) and the use of the term as meaning "in the power of" or "in the custody of" found elsewhere (cf. Dt 23:32 of having no power and Gen 41:35 of the authority of the ruler).[47] This usage of the term accords with the observation made above that the law is addressed to those who have the capacity to shape society—in this case, the holder of the loan.

The observation about the one to whom the law is addressed was made with reference to vv 7-11, the unit of the *šĕmiṭṭāh* law labelled "Further Instruction with Reference to Act and Attitude". *Yād* is used with respect to those who have the capacity to shape society. Here, the one addressed is the creditor who is tempted not to lend as the year of release approaches. That one is said to be contemplating shutting (*qpṣ*) their hand from the poor kin (v 7). Instead, the text enjoins the one who has the power to shape society to "open (*ptḥ*) your hand to your poor and needy kin," to lend to the poor one sufficient to meet need (vv 8 and 11—in each case the verb appears with its infinitive accompanying in the emphatic position).

Thus the word "hand" is used to cover all the actions of the one to whom the *šĕmiṭṭāh*-year law is addressed. Those who have such capacity are to release (v 2), not close (v 7), open (v 11). As such, "hand" also ties the ends of the law together and makes it clear that the whole text is given from a single perspective with a single goal in mind, that is, the amelioration of the situation of the poor who are the object of the action "handed" to the powerful in each case.

---

45 "*Yād* in the Shemittah Law," 196-199.

46 On the last, cf. Dt 24:10-13, 17f where the noun "pledge" (*ʿăbôṭ*) occurs as in 15:6b in its cognate verbal form. See also Hab 2:6f where the piling on of pledges (i.e. indebtedness) is named as punishment for those who despoil others, using an intensified noun from the same root as in Dt 24 and 15 (*ʿabṭîṭ*).

47 These examples are taken from P. Ackroyd, "*Yād*", *TDOT* V 407 and 419.

In the case of the action described by that which the hand of the powerful is to do in vv 7-11, there is an accompanying attention given to the attitude of the one who acts. This pairing of attitude and action is most apparent in v 7, where the audience (the powerful) is given a two fold prohibition: *not* to harden your heart and *not* to close your hand. The use of the verb *ʾmṣ* (to harden) with *lēbāb* is particularly noteworthy, as it appears also in the incident concerning King Sihon of Og in Dt 2, the first and prototypical conquest of the new generation,[48] where YHWH is said to have hardened (*ʾmṣ*) the heart of the king of Bashan. Thus for the powerful to harden their hearts against the poor is for them to find themselves in the same camp with Sihon, who was given over for conquest. As with *yād*, there is a collocation of attitude and act—the needs of the poor are resisted (as Sihon resisted Israel's claim to passage), but those who so resist put themselves at risk (a risk, in the case of the *šěmiṭṭāh* law, whose character is withheld from the audience until v 9b).

The heart is paired with another organ in its other two appearances—it appears with "eye" (*ʿáyin*) in v 9 and by implication in v 10 as well, since "heart" here takes on the verb which had denoted the action of the eye previously ("to [seem] evil"—*rʿh*). This skillful conjoining of "heart" and "eye" through the use of them in parallel in v 9 (the heart "having a base thought," the eye "[seeming] evil" [*rʿh*]), and the use of "heart" in v 10 along with the verb previously used with "eye" (*rʿh*) compresses the attitude to be avoided in its second appearance. The two phrases need not be repeated; they are both present in the use of the subject of one phrase ("heart") and the verb of the other ("[seem] evil").

This has the effect of placing greater emphasis on that which the audience is to do. On the negative side of the picture (v 9), the bad attitude of the potential creditor is emphasized by the length of the clauses dealing with that attitude, eighteen words in all, not counting the reaction of the spurned one. That action which is left undone receives but three words. As the argument proceeds (in v 10) from the curse, the action which is to be done receives emphasis through the use of the emphatic infinitive, while the bad attitude is compressed.[49]

In these core verses of the argument of vv 7-11, bad attitude leads almost incidentally to bad action; good action *avoids* almost incidentally bad attitude. This is the point of the unit as a whole: generosity, open-

---

48 Mayes, *Deuteronomy* 134-135; von Rad, *Deuteronomy* 43-44.

49 Though still numerically smaller (three words to five), the location of the positive action (*before* the sentence about attitude) and its verbal emphasis gives it greater weight.

handed giving to the poor, is an action without guile or rationalization, while a closed fist is preceded by a hard heart and eyes that see evil.

Those eyes that view with evil in v 9 appear at two points in Dt 15. The first we have just discussed in its relation to "heart." The second occurrence is in v 18, in that section we called "What the Law Intends" in the manumission law. In our discussion of this section above, we noted that this section serves a similar function in the argument of the manumission law as that served by the section of the *šĕmiṭṭāh* law we called "Further Instruction with Reference to Act and Attitude." One should not make too much of this correspondence, or be tempted to say that the appearance of "eye" in both laws forges a link between them. *ʿÁyin* frequently appears in sentences showing attitude and is used in this manner in Deuteronomy at several points.[50]

The use of "eye" at these two points, therefore, is not unusual. The two uses do signal us, however, to a common concern with attitude—the same commonality which led us to associate these two units structurally. The usage of "eye" confirms on the level of the passage's language what we had supposed in analyzing its structure—that the law takes care to take notice of the attitudes of its audience and to delineate the attitudes which are inappropriate.[51]

Relational Vocabulary

The words to be discussed here consist of those words and phrases which affect the audience by speaking of the relational qualities shared by the persons involved. This category affects the audience in that so naming the principals in the two release-laws tends to create within the law itself a personal relationship, a kinship or non-kinship, among those groups. It also works to create this personal relationship between the categories of persons used in the law and the audience to whom the law is given.

---

50 See for example Dt 7:6 (not have mercy); 12:8, 25; 13:19 (doing what seems pleasing to oneself); 17:2 (doing what is evil in the eyes of YHWH); and 28:54, 56 (to seem bad to one).

51 The other anatomical word employed by the passage is *ʾōzen*, "ear," which is used simply to refer to the part of the slave which was to be pierced as a sign of perpetual servitude. I. Mendelsohn (*Slavery in the Ancient Near East* [New York: Columbia University, 1949], 49) says that the ear was presumably pierced in order to attach a tag of some sort, as a hole alone would heal over. Mayes (*Deuteronomy*, 252) supposes that the one so tagged would have preferential status as one whose debt has been discharged. The text does not provide enough information to decide this one way or another.

The chief of these relational terms is *ʾāḥ*, "kin". The other terms will be discussed as they are related to this one.

As has been noted in myriad places,[52] *ʾāḥ* often carries the broader connotation of "compatriot," "fellow-citizen," or, to stick to a relational term, "kin" rather than the more narrow connotation of "brother" which it holds in other places. That this is often the case in its appearances in Deuteronomy has also been noted often.[53] Indeed, a textual discrepancy occurs at the first point at which *āḥ* appears; and it seems to have arisen precisely as a result of the connotations carried by this relational term.

The SP at 15:2c does not have the conjunction between "his [the creditor's] neighbor" (*rēʿēhû*) and "his kin" (*ʾāḥîw*), apparently understanding the syntactical relationship between the two terms as explicative (and so one would translate "he shall not oppress his neighbor, his kin") rather than as referring to two different groups, a reading which is possible with the inclusion of the conjunction as in the MT (and so one might translate "he shall not oppress his neighbor or his kin").[54] G. Seitz supposes that the presence of both terms within the *šĕmiṭṭāh* law reflects an editorial expansion of the pre-deuteronomic form of the law.[55] That pre-deuteronomic form is found in vv 1-2, with the presence of *ʾāḥ* in v 2 being a gloss. The use of "neighbor" (*rē[a]ʿ*) in these two verses confirms its pre-deuteronomic provenance.[56] This is probably the case. Since we are in this study trying to work out an anatomy of the means by which the text before us evokes assent and compliance in its audience, however, more must be said.

First, the composer of the text as we have it has made a deliberate choice in retaining "neighbor" from the law as it existed previously and adding to it the more normal deuteronomic term for kin or compatriot—

---

52 E.g., BDB 26 (reference here); H. Ringgren, "*āch*", *TDOT* I 190; E. Jenni, "*āḥ*", *THAT I*, 99-100; etc.

53 E.g., Driver, *Deuteronomy*, 175; Mayes, *Deuteronomy*, 124; Weinfeld, *Deuteronomy and the Deuteronomic School*, 229; Kaufman, "Deuteronomy 15 and the Recent Dating of P," in *Das Deuteronomium* (ed. N. Lohfink; Leuven: University Press, 1985), 275; and Miller, "The Way of Torah," 26.

54 The translational contrast made apparent by these two texts is precisely that found between the RSV and *Tanakh*, respectively, at this point.

55 *Redaktionsgeschichtliche Studien*, 168.

56 This does not exhaust Seitz' arguments in favor of a predeuteronomic origin for vv 1-2. Seitz also sees the impersonal form of the law with an unspecified subject and the lack of the normal deuteronomic appositive ("your God") following YHWH in v 2b as further indications of its pre-deuteronomic origins. *Redaktionsgeschichtliche Studien*, 168 n234 notes the lack of the conjunction *wāw* before "kin" in the SP of v 2b as evidence for its being taken as a gloss.

that is, *'ah*. That this conjoining of two nearly synonymous terms (in the way they are being used here) is deliberate can be demonstrated by the fact that in many instances Deuteronomy chooses to employ *ʾāḥ* when *rē(a)ᶜ* would be adequate or is even more customary elsewhere. Deuteronomy frequently makes use of *ʾāḥ* in the broader sense of "kin" or "compatriot" rather than simply a blood relative (cf. Dt 15:2, 3, 7, 9, 11, 12; 17:15; 19:18f; 22:1-5; 23:20f; and 25:3). This usage of *ʾāḥ* occurs in the Holiness Code, which postdates the Deuteronomic Code (cf. Lev 19:17; 25:25, 35, 36, 39, 47), but it does not occur in the Covenant Code, which predates the Deuteronomic Code. In some cases Deuteronomy so employs *ʾāḥ* in reshaping legal custom to suit its own agenda when a different relationship obtains elsewhere (cf. Dt 22:1-5 and Exod 23:4f).

In other cases Deuteronomy prefers to use *ʾāḥ* to define the relationship between the principals when *rē(a)ᶜ* could as easily serve. An example is the expanded form of the law concerning the judge's role in a case of false witness in Dt 19:15-21. The Decalogue's prohibition against false witness in both Exod 20:16 and Dt 5:20 uses the term "neighbor" (*rē[a]ᶜ*) to refer to the one against whom the false witness is made. In accordance with more typical deuteronomic practice, the one against whom the false witness is made is spoken of as "kin" (*ʾāḥ*) in Dt 19:18f.

A clearer example is not a direct parallel but demonstrates the point we are making. In the respective sections of laws in Exod and Dt dealing with men who quarrel, the description of the quarrel is quite similar syntactically. Though the legal points made in Exod 21:18f (injury incurred by one of the parties at the hand of the other) and Dt 25:11f (injury to the sexual organ of one at the hand of the wife of the other) are different, each begins with a similar grammatical construction. In both cases the description of the quarrel includes an action which one does to the other (Exod) or each to each (Dt); that is, the construction *ʾîš wĕ* . . . occurs where the second noun is meant to stand for "the other." In Exod, *rē(a)ᶜ* is used for this purpose while in Dt *ʾāḥ* serves. Both of these constructions carry the same sense, that is, "the other,"[57] yet even in this, Deuteronomy's preference for *ʾāḥ* in defining relationships within the nation is apparent.

On the other hand, of the fourteen occurrences of *rē(a)ᶜ* in the legal corpus of Deuteronomy, there is only one other instance outside of 15:2

57 BDB, 26 (meaning 4) and 946 (meaning 3). Indeed, in Isa 19:2, *both* are used in this sense in parallel clauses.

in which *rē(a)ᶜ* appears alongside *ʾāḥ*.[58] This instance is that of Dt 13:7 (Eng 13:6), which introduces the law about resisting the enticements of another to follow other gods. In this case, both *ʾāḥ* and *rē(a)ᶜ* occur in a list of likely enticers, a list which is intended to exhaust those who are close enough to the audience to be dangerous in this regard. It occurs in the sequence of laws on this subject which comes progressively closer to the hearer (1. 12:30-13:1[Eng 12:29-31], the dispossessed in the land; 2. 13:2-6 [Eng 1-5], prophets and diviners; 3. 13:7-12 [Eng 6-11], close relations). Here *rē(a)ᶜ* is translated "friend" on the strength of the attached relative clause "who is as your spirit" (*ʾăšer kĕnapšĕkā*) rather than the broader sense of "neighbor" or "fellow-citizen" as elsewhere. It refers to one (the friend) who is distinct from the blood relation (the "kin" [*ʾāḥ*]).

Thus only in the occurrence of *rē(a)ᶜ* in Dt 15 is it paired with *ʾāḥ* to refer to the same person or group of persons—namely the compatriot to whom the creditor owes release. The pairing cannot simply be dismissed on the grounds that it merely reflects an editorial seam in the text. It is in rhetorical effect a turning of both barrels on the audience so that the identity of those to whom the obligation to release the loan holds true is given the widest possible compass. In this case, as opposed to some of the *andurārum* edicts from Mesopotamia (to be discussed in the next chapter, pp 53-56), for example, there is no doubt that this law is intending to address all the financial relationships within the land. This intention could conceivably be blurred had only one of these terms appeared, since both *rē(a)ᶜ* and *ʾāḥ* appear elsewhere in Deuteronomy in their more narrow connotations of "friend" (Dt 13:7) or "neighbor" (23:25f), and "brother" (13:7, or 25:5-10 concerning levirate obligation), respectively.

The contrast between the release owed the neighbor or kin—that is, all who dwell within the land as members of the "family of YHWH"[59]—is

58 The others are the laws concerning the cities of refuge (Dt 19:1-13, four occurrences) which reflect a pre-deuteronomic custom; the prohibition of the removal of the neighbor's landmark (Dt 19:14) which has its reflex in the curses of Dt 27 (cf. 27:17); the laws concerning cases of rape (Dt 22:23-27, two occurrences) which perhaps employ *rē(a)ᶜ* under the influence of the Decalogic prohibition against adultery (the sequence is begun with the subject of adultery in 22:22); the law limiting taking of the neighbor's produce (Dt 23:25 and 26 [Eng 24 and 25]) which employs "neighbor" in its spatial sense; and the law concerning the garment taken in pledge from the neighbor (Dt 24:10) which has its parallel in Exod 22:26f. These account for eleven occurrences. The other three are Dt 13:7 and 15:2 (two occurrences), both to be discussed.

59 N. Lohfink ("The People of God" in *Great Themes in the Old Testament* [Edinburgh: T & T Clark, 1982] 117-133) demonstrates the familial connotations of

underlined by the contrasting lack of such an obligation with respect to the foreigner (*nokrî,* see 15:3) and the surrounding nations (*gôyîm,* see 15:6). Unlike those persons outside the community, those within the community are to be understood as "kin," "friend" and "neighbor," words which define a relationship in which compassion and care are to be the norm.[60]

Therefore when *ʾāḥ* is used in apposition with "a poor one" (*ʾebyôn*) in 15:7(a and b) and in 15:9, it is already clear that the widest possible relational associations are meant. Similarly, to close one's fist against such the poor one (15:7), to look with displeasure upon one's obligation to give to a poor kin (15:9) is something one has done when such is done to *any* in the community.

It is similar with the single occurrence of *ʾāḥ* in the manumission law. We have noted the way in which the lines of argument of the *šĕmiṭṭāh* law and the manumission law interconnect such that the point of qualification in the first (that the poverty which is the occasion for observance will continue) then serves as an implied datum in the manumission law (in the sense that this same state of poverty will result in many selling themselves into slavery).

On the level of the text's language this same interconnection appears. On this level the interconnection is created by the repetition of *ʾāḥ*. The *ʾāḥ* is identified specifically as the poor one in the part of the *šĕmiṭṭāh* law which deals with attitude (i.e. vv 7-11). Therefore when this *ʾāḥ* sells self to the "you" (the audience) of the law, it is understood that this is the same *ʾāḥ* who is said to be "the poor one" in the preceding law.

As with the pairing of *ʾāḥ* and *rē(a)ʿ* in the *šĕmiṭṭāh*-year law, *ʾāḥ* is paired with another term in the manumission law. This second term spells out the identity of the one who sells self into slavery. It underscores the emotional tie to the audience which that term is meant to evoke. In the manumission law, the term with which *ʾāḥ* is paired is *ʿibrî/ʿibrîyyâ*. In both these particulars, the deuteronomic version of the manumission law departs from that of the Covenant Code. In Exod 21:1-6 the enslaved is not referred to as "kin," nor is the feminine form given. Thus Deuteronomy takes care, on the one hand, to identify the relational status of the slave (he or she is part of the "family" of which the nation is comprised) and, on the other hand, to give the widest possible compass to those covered by the manumission law.

---

such phrases as *ʿam* YHWH or *ʿammî* spoken by YHWH and therefore with *ʿam* generally with reference to the community of Israelites.

60 Miller, "The Way of Torah," 26.

As will be discussed in chapter 3 (pp 83-85), the term *ᶜibrî* (and, here, *ᶜibrîyyâ*) is meant to be evocative of more than just social status. *ᶜIbrî* connotes in its occurrences in these two laws the experience of slavery in Egypt when the Israelites were *ᶜibrîm*. The one, the *ʾāḥ*, who sells self into slavery is to be thought of still as "one of you," specifically as one of you as you were when you were in Egypt.

Thus, as in the use of *ʾāḥ* in the *šĕmiṭṭāh* law, so here too the audience is being treated to a two-pronged rhetorical device. In this case, the intention is to ensure that the one who becomes enslaved retains that one's identity as kin. But not only this. The one who is to be thought of as kin though now enslaved is also to be thought of as in a state with ties to one of the most evocative traditions in the nation's "internal history": that of slavery in Egypt when the whole of the national family was *ᶜibrîm*.

Naturally, v 15 makes this point as well. The law rehearses in miniature the episode of slavery in Egypt and redemption by YHWH in order to reinforce the association of the kin who sells self into slavery with the period of Egyptian servitude in order to evoke the closest possible emotional relationship between the subject of the law (the female or male slave) and those for whom the law is intended to dictate behavior.

Additionally, because the blessing by YHWH of the audience's enterprises within the land (15:14b and 18b) is dependent upon that act of redemption, this relationship between slave and audience colors the whole of the law, indeed, the whole of Israel's experience in the land. It is because of this coloration that certain other images receive heightened emphasis: the one who sends the slave out is to provide from that one's property a "rich necklace" (*haᶜănêq taᶜănîq*)[61] for the kindred now released from enslavement. The owner of the slave owes to the slave, because that one is kin, a generous portion of the bounty which the land, given by YHWH who redeems from slavery, provides. Both slave and owner share the experience of having been *ᶜibrî* and so the produce of the land which is YHWH's gift to the redeemed Egyptian *ᶜibrîm* belongs to both.[62] In other words, the act of releasing the Hebrew slave is in effect a

---

[61] P. Miller, Jr. "The Human Sabbath: A Study in Deuteronomic Theology," *Princeton Seminary Bulletin* 6 (1985), 94 n15.

[62] One must note in qualification, and yet in confirmation of this tie into the "internal history" of the Egyptian experience, the lingering subordinate status of the one who goes out "free" (*ḥopšî*). I. Mendelsohn ("New Light on the *Ḫupšu*", *BASOR* 139, 9-11) termed those of this class in Alalakh "free-born people" who stood in social rank between the land-owning aristocracy and the slave class. E. Lipiński ("L'Esclave Hebreu", *VT* 26 [1976], 123) cites 1 Sam 17:25 (he translates "and his father's house he will make mighty in Israel" [*et sa maison paternelle, il la rendra puissante en Israel*]) as

recreation in miniature of the divine act of redemption from Egyptian servitude, right down to the provision of resources to the newly free.[63]

Thus in both the *šĕmiṭṭāh* law and the manumission law, the relational term *ʾāḥ* plays a crucial role in establishing the emotional tone of the passage. In both cases, however, the word is not allowed any ambiguity in compass but is pushed to the widest possible association by pairing it with another, equally evocative term—namely, *rē(a)ʿ* and *ʿibrî/ʿibrîyyâ*.

Summary and Conclusion

While it is beyond the scope of a concluding section to rehearse the many exegetical points uncovered in the preceding analyses of the structure and phrasing of the release-laws of Dt 15, some observations can be made which will bring together these analyses in a broad fashion.

---

evidence in favor of what might be called an "absolute" understanding of the term. However, as N. Lohfink notes ("*Ḥopšî*," *TDOT* V 115-116), I Sam 17:25 is very likely a late text, and the usage here can indicate merely the general application of what was once a term with a narrower meaning. It appears likely that the term refers to "emancipated slave," about which, however, modern conceptions of freedom cannot be applied (Lohfink, 117). N. Lemche ("*ḤPŠY* in 1 Sam xvii 25," *VT* 24 [1974] 373f and "The Hebrew Slave: Comments on the Slave Law Ex. xxi 2-11," *VT* 25 [1975], esp. 139-142) details the arguments in favor of understanding *ḥopšî* as referring to some sort of private clientage to the former master or collective dependency on the state. As Lemche notes, however, it is clear from the rich dowry given the slave upon release (Dt 15:14, the passage under discussion) that the status here cannot be taken to mean continued dependence. Additionally, the contrast with the "perpetual slave" (*ʿébed ʿôlām*) in Dt 15:17 makes it difficult to see continued dependence being meant, perhaps reflecting further development in usage toward an absolute sense of freedom. The ambiguity inherent in the term remains, however, and is in fact another parallel between the manumission law and the act of redemption from Egypt: just as those freed from Egyptian bondage are now bound to YHWH (Dt 6:20-25), so too manumission for the "Hebrew slave" does not gain for that one absolute freedom but membership in the community which is bound to God (Lohfink, 118).

63 A less direct, perhaps even unintentional, evocation of Egyptian servitude in the other (that is, the *šĕmiṭṭāh*) law can be traced out through the observation that the term used for exaction of a loan, which appears in vv 2 and 3 as a finite verb (*yiggōś* and *tiggōś*, respectively), is of the same root (*ngś*) as the noun in the form of a participle (*nōgēś*) which refers in Exodus 3 and 5 to the Egyptian taskmasters. This root in both of these forms appears in a variety of contexts, however, many of them having no obvious relation to the period of Egyptian servitude, and so the connection must be allowed to remain a tantalizing possibility. In any case, the use of this term places us in the realm of oppressor and oppressed rather than simply that of amelioration of a business burden.

As befits such a rhetorically pregnant text, much of our exegesis has focused on the audience *to* whom the law is directed and the social group *for* whom the law is given. What has become apparent in both the analysis of the structure of the text and the analysis of its language is that great care has been taken to identify these two groups.

From this perspective, the text might be said to be functioning with respect to these two groups (which are characters in any legal text, though other legal texts may have additional characters as well) in a fashion similar to that which is at work in the Holiness Code—namely, the law serves in part to define the relationships which exist among the principals of society (the native, the kin, the resident alien, the foreigner, etc.). This similarity will become more apparent when we turn to that body of law in chapter 3.[64]

Yet this observation cannot be made without a great deal of qualification. As we observed in the functioning of relational terms in this passage, those terms are pushed by their association with other terms to embrace the widest possible compass. This is a type of definition of relationship which serves the aim of inclusion rather than restriction. Thus the audience is made to be aware of itself as all of those who have the capacity to shape society within the scenario set out by these two laws, and that awareness is given the widest possible scope by the consequences attached to observation of or obedience to the law.

Similarly, the groups cared for by the provisions of the law are defined in the widest possible terms—they are any within the family of YHWH who stand in special need of this kind of care. No attempt is made to restrict the identity of those toward whom the audience is obliged to give the care prescribed in the law.

To anticipate discussion to follow, this is a kind of definition which has affinities with the tendency toward inclusion that can be observed in the Covenant Code.[65]

Thus Deuteronomy 15, within the narrow confines of its own sphere of action, displays a rhetorical process which takes care both to define its principals and to launch that definition toward inclusion. Deuteronomy 15 seeks to make assent and compliance unavoidable in two ways: The persuasive manner in which its argument is structured (a manner which at several points highlights the obligation of the audience and the identity of the ones being cared for) and the particular vocabulary employed (a vocabulary which highlights the connections between

---

64 See below, esp. pp 94-96.

65 See below, pp 94.

attitude and act and which evokes a relationship between the audience and those in need of care which is of a most intimate nature)—in short, by the rhetorical skill exhibited in its structure and language.

Related to this point is the tendency exhibited in both biblical and cuneiform law to attempt to be exhaustive in dealing with any particular legal subject. Because of the rhetorical qualities of this text, however, this exhaustiveness can be seen to exist in narrative fashion and with some sense of anticipation rather than simply rehearsal. In this our text is similar to the extraordinary edicts providing release from debt (the *mīšarum* edicts, discussed below on pp 48-53) which both outline the practice desired and anticipate abuse. In the release laws of Deuteronomy 15, this quality is displayed where the attitude of the audience is anticipated and instruction given as to the correct attitude one should have when faced with particular situations in which this law has some bearing.

Allied with this is the attempt to make regular what was formerly extraordinary. In the Mesopotamian material, as we shall see,[66] the release of slaves in the third year of their service rather than only at the intervals set by the decrees of release bears this out. The periodization of release in Deuteronomy 15 is clear and has not been commented on in this chapter, though it will play a part in placing the passage in the larger structure of deuteronomic law.[67]

Behind and in the midst of all of this, of course, is the presence of YHWH who both gives warrant to the law (thereby evoking assent) and who matches compliance with blessing. In this, of course, YHWH differs from the gods of the ancient Near East, who, though they served these functions relative to the law, could not be said to be the *source* of the law, and so the law was dependent on the discernment of those responsible for its promulgation.

The contrast thus made apparent between YHWH as warrant, rewarder, and source of the law underlines what is made explicit elsewhere in Deuteronomy: that YHWH is the only deity to be reckoned with and that because YHWH has given them the law, Israel will be seen as a wise nation. Just as the Mesopotamian Law Codes are transformed by being placed in the context of royal apology and so being made to function in some instances in more than one manner,[68] so too the context in which the release-laws have been placed (the monotheistic character of deuteronomic theology) makes them serve a purpose beyond the strictly

66 Below, pp 69-70.
67 See below, pp 107, 110, and 114.
68 See the discussion below, pp 60-62.

legal—they are now a part of a body of law which is constitutional of the wise and just nation and witness to the wisdom and justice of the deity who in the past redeemed that people from servitude.

The contrast between the monotheism of Deuteronomy and the polytheism of Mesopotamia is in part the subject of the next chapter. In the course of the analysis to be given in this next chapter, this contrast will also become even clearer, and the difference which it makes will become even clearer. It is to this analysis that we now turn.

II

The Near Eastern Analogues

Having looked at the shape and language of the release-laws themselves and the way they work upon their audience, we would do well to turn elsewhere for means of comparison before delineating the place which the release-laws occupy in the sequence of laws in Deuteronomy and in the ideology of social justice present in those laws. The purpose of this comparison is to draw a portrait of the ideology of social justice found in the release-laws and in the other laws in Deuteronomy more clearly and more carefully by comparing that portrait with other portraits.

Two sources of comparison offer themselves to this task, being close enough in cultural and geographical space to Deuteronomy to provide helpful comparison. These are the cuneiform documents of the ancient Near East and the other collections of laws of the Old Testament. We will examine the first of these sources in this chapter and will then examine the second in the chapter following.

What we are after in both cases is not so much evidence of influence but means of comparison. That is, we are less concerned with tracing out lines of influence than in comparing the ways in which these various sources responded to analogous problems, the social problems which proceed from the existence of poverty and debt. How do the documents from Mesopotamia to be enumerated below deal with those who, because of their socio-economic status, stand in special need of care? *This* is the question which concerns us here.

Preliminary Comments

M. Greenberg has termed the level of legal discourse which we have available to us "the theoretical postulates of the law systems."[1] This means that throughout this chapter we will be operating to a great extent inter-textually, that is, comparing the documents of these two cultures on a theoretical level with the aim of seeing the similarities and differences in the way in which they deal on this theoretical level with very real social problems.

In seeking analogies, a complication arises in that the text at hand (i.e., Dt 15) contains two laws which need not have a direct connection outside of that provided by Deuteronomy itself. One should note in qualification that both are, at a fundamental level, economic—that is, both debt release and slave release have *economic* and not just moral consequences.

One notes too that the social realities which they represent are bound, both within Deuteronomy and in the Near Eastern sources to be described below, by a common vocabulary—dependence, oppression, need, release, freedom. In the case of the deuteronomic text, this common vocabulary is more apparent in the way we talk about the two parts of the text than the way in which it itself speaks.

In the case of the Near Eastern analogues, however, certain common words span the two kinds of concerns. *Andurārum*, *mīšarum*, and others weave themselves throughout this material so thoroughly that it is hard to see too precisely where each begins and ends and how we are to construe them in relation to one another. To be sure, this study will attempt to draw these items into focus, to make distinctions between what is public and what is private, what actual and what merely rhetorical, what personal and what pecuniary. One needs also to draw distinctions among the contexts in which these various precedents are found, since their context will determine to some extent the manner in which they can be brought to bear on the text in Deuteronomy.

---

[1] 1. M. Greenberg, "Some Postulates of Biblical Criminal Law," in *Yehezkel Kaufmann Jubilee Volume*, ed. M. Haran (Jerusalem: Magnes, 1960), 18, n.25 and within the essay. See more recently his "More Reflections on Biblical Criminal Law," in *Scripta Hierosolymitana 31*, ed. S. Japhet (Jerusalem: Magnes, 1986), 1-17.

But drawing those distinctions even imprecisely does not, in and of itself, completely illumine the text at hand. It does, however, at least in a qualified manner, enable us to see better what it is about these two laws of release which drew them together in the mind of the one who compiled the deuteronomic corpus.

Consequently, this chapter will not proceed along the lines one might expect, that is, with the analogies pertaining to the law of debt release described and analyzed first, followed by those having some relation to the law of slave release. Rather, the intermingling of these types of release in the mind of the Deuteronomist and their intermingling in Near Eastern legal and economic documents force us to treat the material in a more topical or thematic manner. After describing the various documents, the sources of our comparison, then, we will attempt to draw them together in some sort of synthesis in order to make comparisons on the theoretical level on which we are operating.

To return briefly to the matter of what the present study intends, what is intended is not the establishment by *tour de force* of a line of influence from Babylon or Nineveh or Larsa to the Israel of the Deuteronomist with respect to these two pieces of legislation. Rather, the intention is to draw upon a larger body of material and a wider frame of social reference for analogies to Deuteronomy 15 so that interpretation can proceed with a better understanding of the social needs being addressed by this text and the practices which it establishes to meet those needs.

This procedure is aided by the fact that the two terms of the comparison are known: we are not reconstructing "release-law in Israel" by means of Near Eastern material. This mitigates somewhat the ambiguity of the relationship between the two terms of the comparison (Dt 15 and its ancient Near Eastern analogies).

The material which will be drawn upon in this undertaking is of a variety of genres and content. Material is amassed according to interest: several things from disparate contexts can be of interest because of a common subject which cuts across differences in genre. Posed at the beginning as a question, the subject-interest that draws this material together is "Is there something about the nature of debt in ancient Near Eastern societies which created a group or class of people in special need of care?"

Obviously, what is of interest in these disparate documents is their bearing on Dt 15. This is not to say, however, that this is the only guiding principle in their selection. Also at work are questions which arise from the material itself—for instance, the nature of the various social classes alluded to in the ancient Near Eastern manumission material and the difference those social classes make in the treatment of the slave in question.

Because many of the documents to be drawn upon are not readily known by all, some indication of the nature of the larger groups of material to be drawn upon for the discovery of analogies to the release laws in Dt 15 is in order before proceeding to the topical ordering of those analogies. This is the step we mentioned as being descriptive. It is to be followed by an appraisal of this material in a synthetic manner so that comparison can be made along the lines of the topics which that material raises.

The order of discussion of the initial descriptive section will be the *mīšarum* edicts, the *andurārum* acts, and the Law Codes.

The Nature of the Evidence

The Mīšarum Edicts

Put simply, the *mīšarum* edicts were royal proclamations intended to release private debts and some forms of public taxes. These edicts can readily be seen as a fruitful means of comparison to the release-laws of Deuteronomy, especially when one notes that the one complete text also includes the release of slaves, though all of this in a limited geographical region.

The information we have concerning the *mīšarum* edicts comes from three sources: extant copies of these edicts (one complete and one partial), references to the edicts in royal year-date formulae, and references to edicts in contracts.

References to *mīšarum* edicts occur as early as the Third Dynasty of Ur in the last part of the third millennium, using the Sumerian term *nig.sí.sá*.[2] *Mīšarum* edicts are also referred to in year-date formulae from

---

[2] The Ur-nammu law code refers to the action of the king in establishing equity in the land (cf. lines 112-113; line 41 also refers to equity, *nig.sí.sá*, but there it is in parallel with *níg.gi.na*, truth [=Akk. *kittim*], and thus carries its more general connotation of equity in the sense of one of the two ordering principles of just society—see S. Paul, *Studies in the Book of the Covenant in the Light of Cuneiform and Biblical Law* (Leiden: E. J. Brill, 1970), 4. For the Ur-nammu code, two texts are extant: Text A, published by S. N. Kramer, "Ur-Nammu Law Code," *Or* n.s. 23 [1954], 40-48 and Text B, O. R. Gurney and S. N. Kramer, "Two Fragments of Sumerian Laws," *AS* 16 [1965], 13-19. These texts have been integrated and translated by J. J. Finkelstein in *ANET3*, 523-525). Another reference from this same period occurs in a religious text in which Ur-

the kingdom of Isin in the first two centuries of the second millennium B. C. E.[3] As will be discussed in more detail below, the greatest concentration of extant references to *mīšarum* edicts are grouped in the reigns of the Old Babylonian kings. Other possible occurrences are at Eshnunna[4] and Hana,[5] roughly contemporary with the Old Babylonian period. The *mīšarum* edicts themselves, then, are clustered in the last centuries of the third millennium and the first centuries of the second. There are also tag phrases which may be oblique indications that this practice was known in the Middle- and Neo-Babylonian periods.

The *mīšarum* edicts were normally proclaimed in the first year of a new king's reign. Examination of the year-date formulae of various Old Babylonian rulers bears this out. The list of year-date formulae for the reign of Hammurabi makes reference to a *mīšarum* act in the second year of his reign.[6] This reference is a bit misleading temporally, as it appears that Hammurabi in fact proclaimed the *mīšarum* in the first year of his accession, though the year-date formula for that first year was reserved for the accession formula.

A complicating factor is the time of year in which the preceding king died, which if late in the year would push the reform-act into the second year of the following king.[7] This would appear to be the case, for instance, with Ammiditana, who dates the second year of his reign by the propagation of the *mīšarum* act.[8] The edict of Ammiṣaduqa almost certainly occurred in the first year of his reign,[9] giving credence to the supposition that the Babylonian kings of the First Dynasty proclaimed this reform as soon after their accession to the throne as possible.

An examination of private documents leads one to believe that this type of edict was proclaimed at other times in the king's reign as well. Contracts from the period of the reign of Rim-Sin of Larsa reveal that this

---

nammu congratulates himself on bringing justice to the fore (text and translation in G. Castellino, "Urnammu: Three Religious Texts," *ZA* 53 [1959], 106-132; see esp. 119 and 132, l. 38).

3 See F. R. Kraus, *Ein Edikt des Königs Ammiṣaduqa von Babylon* (Leiden: E. J. Brill, 1958), 196 (text no. 1), 198 (no.4), and 200 (no. 7).

4 See Kraus, *Ein Edikt*, 230 (nos. 49 and 50).

5 See Kraus, *Ein Edikt*, 232-233 (nos. 54-57; the full text of no.56 is found in F. J. Stephens, "A Cuneiform Tablet from Dura-Europas," *RA* 34 (1937), 183-190).

6 *ANET3*, 269. Cf. J. Finkelstein, "Some New *Misharum* Material and Its Implications," *AS*, 16 (1965, Fs. B. Landsberger), 243.

7 J. J. Finkelstein, "Ammiṣaduqa's Edict and the Babylonian ʿLaw Codes,'" *JCS* 15 (1961), 93.

8 See *Ein Edikt*, 228, no. 41.

9 F. Kraus, *Ein Edikt*, 229, nos. 43 and 44.

king enacted such a measure at least three times during his tenure.[10] The year-date list of Ammiditana of Babylon shows an additional edict also,[11] as does that of Hammurabi in a veiled form (year-date 22).[12] F. Kraus catalogs the likely occurrences of *mīšarum* edicts in the period of the First Dynasty as follows (with additions as noted):[13]

Hammurabi, year 1.
(Hammurabi, year 12).[14]
(Hammurabi, year 22).
Samsuilani, year 1.
Samsuilani, year 8.
Abiēšuḫ, year 1.
Ammiditana, year 1.
Ammiditana, year 20.
Ammiṣaduqa, year 1.
Ammiṣaduqa, year 9.
Samsuditana, year 2.

This evidence forces us to draw the conclusion that the only certain time in which a *mīšarum* act could be expected was shortly after the accession of a new king. On the basis of this evidence we cannot assign a set cycle for the occurrence of this type of act. In this, then, the *mīšarum* edicts differ significantly from the release-laws in Deuteronomy. We will return to this point in the second major section of this chapter, the evaluative section below.

The *mīšarum* edict, then, is well attested in Babylon in the Old Babylonian period and in neighboring states even earlier. The character of the *mīšarum* edict is known only through the one complete extant text we have, that of Ammiṣaduqa, dated as we have seen to the first year of his reign, ca. 1646 B.C.E. In the broadest strokes, the structure of this text consists of a brief Preface[15] and the Terms of the Edict.[16]

---

[10] Cf. *Ein Edikt*, 203-209.

[11] *Ein Edikt*, 229, no. 42.

[12] *ANET3*, 270.

[13] F. Kraus, "Ein Edikt des Königs Samsu-ilani von Babylon," *AS* 16 (1965), 229.

[14] See "Some New *Misharum* Material," 243f, where Finkelstein cites a legal suit as evidence for a *mīšarum* edict in Hammurabi's twelfth year, though this edict is not referred to in the date-list.

[15] Corresponding to par. 1 in the text published in *ANET3*, 526-528. This text is a combination of that published by Kraus in *Ein Edikt* and a brief portion of another copy published by J. Finkelstein in "The Edict of Ammiṣaduqa: A New Text," *RA* 63

The structure of the edict has been outlined by at least two scholars.[17] For our purposes, a more general description of the contents of the edict would be more helpful.

The contents of the edict are surprisingly varied. Much of the edict is taken up with material which accords well with its basic purpose, namely, the remission of public taxes and private debts, the first at the cost of the state, the second to the detriment of private investors.[18]

A clear example is par. 13 of the edict: "The arrears of the porter(s) which had been assigned to the collecting-agent for collection are remitted; they will not be collected."[19] Here the intent is clear and conforms to the central purpose of the edict. Most of the material with this close affiliation with the basic purpose of the edict contains as a motive clause the phrase "because the king has invoked (or established) the *mīšarum* for the land."

Yet there is other material as well. Some of it has little or nothing to do with the basic purpose of the edict. This other material instead appears to establish social rules which are to be in effect from then on or to restate principles apparently being honored in the breach. These precepts are formulated apodictically. An example would be par. 18, which, though obscure, clearly intends to address an abuse which is not necessarily in the purview of the edict itself: "A taverness or a merchant who [. . .] dishonest weight shall die."[20] That an edict of punctiliar nature (that is, it is intended to have an effect now and not from then on) such as the *mīšarum* edicts should also contain material of a more permanent nature moves us in the direction of a Law Code. This connection will be explored more fully below (pp. 60-61).

Finally, the edict addresses issues which, as we shall see, are directly related to debt but not necessarily to the remission of debt. These sections are those which deal with the manumission of debt slaves. Ammiṣaduqa's edict takes care to give freedom to those who have

(1969), 45-64. All paragraph numeration will be according to the integrated text in *ANET3*.

16 See *ANET3*, 526-528, for a copy of Ammiṣaduqa's Edict.

17 By Kraus in *Ein Edict*, 182-188, and by N. Lemche in "*Andurārum* and *Mīšarum*: Comments on the Problem of the Social Edicts and Their Application in the Ancient Near East," *JNES* 38 (1979) 11-13.

18 *Ein Edikt*, 190.

19 *ANET3*, 527.

20 *ANET3*, 528.

become enslaved because of debt, their own or someone else's,[21] and yet to restrict the area and the circumstances in which that freedom can occur.[22] What is noteworthy is that these issues are addressed in a supplemental fashion. It is as if the edict were saying, "While these matters are not part of the economic functions covered by the edict, they are clearly intended to be a *consequence* of the edict; those enslaved because of their debt should not be left out or forgotten."

Several observations concerning the social and economic ramifications or purposes of this type of act can be made from the foregoing description.

It is certainly evident that the *misarum* edict was a frequent and well-known feature of the life of this society, as attested to both by its presence in the royal date-lists and by references to it in contractual and personal documents of the period. It is also evident that through these acts the king was very much a force in the private transactions of the day.[23] This intrusion was felt in both rural and urban areas (as evidenced by the geographical notations within the edict and the occupations of those covered by its terms). The *mīšarum* edict did not, at least in this instance, encompass trade (since par. 8 specifically exempts commercial loans from remittance, though the paragraph which follows covers interest accrued upon an advance).

In addition, Ammiṣaduqa's edict did take into account enslavement as the result of foreclosure but did not free those born into slavery, as we have noted. It also condemned in the strongest terms and with apparently permanent intent the forced hiring-out of subordinates by their superiors (the subject of the final section, par. 22).[24]

The combination of the frequency of these acts and the range of activities which they covered leads us to the conclusion that such an act did not cause the office of creditor to be entirely unprofitable—apparently

---

21 Par. 20: "If an obligation has resulted in foreclosure against a citizen of Numhia, a citizen of Emutbalum, a citizen of Idamaras, a citizen of Uruk, a citizen of Isin, a citizen of Kissura, or a citizen of Malgium (in consequence of which) he [placed] his own person, his wife or his [children] in debt servitude for silver, or as a pledge—because the king has instituted the *mīsharum* in the land, he is released; his freedom is in effect." (*ANET3*, 528.)

22 Par. 20 itself limits the granting of freedom only to the citizens of certain territories, and the following paragraph makes it clear that this granting of freedom does not apply to those in a state of permanent slavery.

23 *Ein Edikt*, 239.

24 *Ein Edikt*, 190-191. For the last see also Finkelstein's note (no. 9) on 528 of *ANET3*.

the population began amassing debt and their creditors exacting repayment with interest immediately after these periodic attempts at setting the ship of state on an even keel.

Finally, these *mīšarum* edicts were considered by the king to be among his most important accomplishments, as evidenced by their inclusion in the date-formulae, but the lack of mention of them in the Law Codes shows that they were not considered matters of permanent effect, though they surely must have been popular measures for most of the population. Certainly, they contributed to the portrayal of the king to his subjects as *šar mīšarim*.[25]

In addition, as is evident in the text before us, these edicts (that is, the written outgrowth of the act itself) did contain permanent "reform" measures and these measures were in some cases perhaps included in the Law Codes (e.g. the similarities between par. 15 of this edict and law no. 15 of the Eshnunna Code), which presented the claims of the kings "to the gods and to posterity of having achieved true justice," for all their being "pious hope and moral resolve."[26]

As with the *andurārum* acts and the Law Codes to be described in turn, so too at this point with the *mīšarum* edicts we will withhold comments of an evaluative nature for the latter section of the chapter. The intent at this point is to introduce the evidence to those unfamiliar with it.

The Andurārum Acts

The *andurārum* texts are of a more problematic nature. In its most general sense, the word *andurārum* and the acts which employ it simply indicate release, whether that be the release of slaves or some other obligation.

---

[25] For examples of this designation, cf. *LUGAL misarim* in CH col. xxivb:77, xxvb:7, xxvb:95-96, xxvib:13 (reading in Driver and Miles, *The Babylonian Laws, vol I*, 96, 98, and 100). This self-designation survived the OB period. Cf. in MB, Nebuchadnezzar I who calls himself *šar mēšari* on a boundary stone (the text is found in W. J. Hincke, *A New Boundary Stone of Nebuchadrezzar I*, BERes. 4 [Philadelphia: University of Pennsylvania, 1907], 146, col. II:23), and in NB, a text from Nebuchadnezzar II: "I, Nebuchadrezzar, am the king of justice (or the just king)" (text in S. Langdon, *Die Neubabylonischen Königsinschriften* [Leipzig: J. C. Hinrichs', 1912], 172, l. 26). Finkelstein makes this point in "Ammiṣaduqa's Edict," 102. K. W. Whitelam talks more generally about *šar mīšarim* in *The Just King* (JSOTSup 12; Sheffield: JSOT Press, 1979), 19-24, as does S. Paul in *Studies in the Book of the Covenant*, 25-26. See also E. A. Speiser, "Early Law and Civilization," in *Oriental and Biblical Studies* (ed. J. J. Finkelstein and M. Greenberg; Philadelphia: University of Pennsylvania, 1967), 550-551.

[26] "Ammiṣaduqa's Edict," 101-102.

The particular act of granting freedom to slaves is linked to the *mīšarum* edicts by its appearance in pars. 20 and 21 of Ammiṣaduqa's edict, as we have noted. The apodosis of par. 20 reads: "because the king has established the *mīšarum* for the land, he [i.e. the debt-slave] is released, his freedom is established."[27] In par. 20 of Ammiṣaduqa's edict the connections between debt, slavery, and freedom are clear. The sequence is 1) a debt is taken on; 2) the debtor cannot repay the debt; 3) the debtor places himself or his wife or children in debt slavery; and 4) this debt slavery is annulled by the *mīšarum* edict, presumably along with the annulment of the debt.

But *andurārum* does not only come with the *mīšarum* edict. Texts referring to *andurārum* by royal fiat occur from the twenty-fourth century B.C.E. in Lagash[28] to the seventh century B.C.E. in Assyria.[29] In terms of fitting these texts into an evaluation of the nature of debt and poverty and the issues of social justice which arise therefrom, the problem with the texts containing the term *andurārum* is that they are unclear in many cases as to whether the act has general compass or if it concerns only the freeing of a single individual. The exact nature of the act itself is also often unclear.

Certainly in the case of Ammiṣaduqa's edict both nature and intention are clear. The edict intends throughout the cited territories to establish the freedom of those enslaved because of their debt.

Similarly, the reference to *andurārum* in the Law Code of Hammurabi is reasonably clear. Laws 117, 188, and 280 of CH carry no qualifications as to the intended geographical scope of the manumission. Inasmuch as it can be assumed for the whole of the law code, the country-wide scope of these laws spelling out the terms in which freedom is granted or withheld is certain. One should qualify this by noting that these laws have to do with manumission of individuals one at a time, on a routine basis,

---

27 *Ein Edikt*, 40, ll. 32-35.

28 The "reform" of Urukagina. The text is in M. Lambert, "Les ʿReformes' d'Urukagina," *RA* 50 (1956), 169-184.

29 Several documents are extant: Neo-Assyrian slave sale contracts which give conditions for repayment in the case of an *andurārum* (cited by Lemche in "*Andurārum* and *mīšarum*," 21); a portion of an inscription by Esarhaddon commemorating the rebuilding of the Aššur temple which mentions the establishment of *andurārum* on this occasion (text in R. Borger, *Die Inschriften Asarhaddons Königs von Assyrien*, AfO Beiheft 9, Graz: Weidner, 1956; transliteration and translation in J. N. Postgate, *Taxation and Conscription in the Assyrian Empire* [Rome: PBI, 1974], 132). Others will be cited in the course of the study.

rather than the freeing of debt-slaves throughout the country all at once as in the *mīšarum* edict.

On the other end of the scale stand texts such as a slave document which deals with the manumission of a female slave.[30] Here the term *andurārum* refers to a private act undertaken by the owners of the slave in question.

Between these two points of clarity stand a host of texts which are unclear either as to the scope of the act or its provisions or both.

An example of this ambiguous type of reference is that of a year-date formula of the king Samsuiluna[31] which reads "king Samsuiluna, favored by the great gods, established the freedom of Sumer and Akkad." Here the nature of the act is uncertain. Its parallels with the year-date formulae of kings such as Hammurabi would lead one to think that something like a *mīšarum* edict, with its provision of the freeing of debt-slaves, is being referred to. Some confusion arises when one notes that the language of *andurārum* may also refer to the annulment of certain kinds of taxes[32]—that is, the act is of a more limited and fiscal nature. In the case of the year-date formula of Samsuiluna, one wonders why the language of the *mīšarum* edict, so prevalent in other Old Babylonian date-formulae, was not employed here if this is the activity being referred to. Perhaps some less inclusive act lies behind the year-date in this case. In our presentation of the evidence of the year-dates above, we cited this date as an occurrence of a *mīšarum* edict upon the accession of Samsuiluna. While this is probably the case, some doubt must be admitted.

Andurārum, then, does not refer necessarily to a specific type of royal proclamation but is a more general term which covers several different kinds of acts having to do with freedom or release.[33] It is this ambiguity

---

30 The text and translation of this document is in Y. Scheil, "Notules," *RA* 14 (1917), 151-152, no. 30. Cf. *CAD* A/2:115-116.

31 Text and translation in B. Landsberger, "The Date List of the Babylonian King Samsu-Ditana," *JNES* 14 (1955), 146, vii:2.

32 Lemche cites a text which he says deals with the exemption in one city of taxes on dates ("*Andurārum* and *Mīšarum*," 17), though CAD translates differently, that is, as debts payable in dates (CAD A/2:116). The text itself reads "the release of dates is established in KA.KA.si (but) not established in Babylon." This text is cited in *Ein Edikt*, 230, no. 47; Kraus declines to offer comment on this enigmatic passage.

33 On the ambiguity and range of usage for the term *andurārum*, see M. T. Larsen, *The Old Assyrian City-State and its Colonies* (Copenhagen: Akademisk Forlag, 1976), 63-80. The specific case Larsen discusses is that of Ilusuma (see E. F. Weidner, "Ilusumas Zug nach Babylonien," *ZA* 43 [1936], 114-123, with whom Larsen disagrees), but his

of usage which will force us in the evaluative section below to spell out in some detail the nature of the evidence when an *andurārum* text is cited.

The Law Codes

It has become a commonplace to note that the Law Codes which have been unearthed thus far are not referred to in contemporary court records.[34] While this observation must be tempered somewhat in light of more recent studies,[35] it is nonetheless still safe to say that these documents come to us as disembodied voices. They must be handled with care, then, when we try to glean from them some understanding of the nature of debt and the creation of people in need.

For the purposes of this introductory description, two sets of questions must be considered. The first has to do with the nature of the evidence—of what exactly do the Law Codes consist? Is there any analogy to them in our legal system? The second has to do with intention—what is it that this setting down of hundreds of lines of text means to accomplish? Are the Law Codes meant to be reformatory; that is, does this document represent a change in practice instigated by the king? Or are they meant to be a compilation of notable decisions made during the king's tenure? Need they have a single purpose?

These are the questions of nature and purpose, respectively, and they are obviously intertwined. In dealing with these questions, we have a host of theories on which to draw, but for the sake of brevity they can be

---

comments encompass the meaning of the term in other instances as well. See also the entry in *CAD*.

34 Cf. originally B. Landsberger, "Die babylonischen Termini fur Gesetz und Recht," *SDIOP II* (Fs. Koschaker), 221-222.

35 Most notably the study by Jacobsen ("An Ancient Mesopotamian Trial for Homicide," in *Toward the Image of Tammuz*, ed. W. L. Moran [Cambridge: Harvard, 1970], 193-214) of a Mesopotamian murder trial whose verdict appears to establish a new point of law concerning the culpability of an accessory, a decision which bears striking similarity to CH law 153, though the connection between the two cannot be determined. W. F. Leemans has collected instances where the king has ruled in a case by deciding a "point of law," thereby demonstrating the king's role as promulgator of law as well as judge (See W. F. Leemans, "King Hammurapi as Judge," *Symbolae David* II (Leiden: Brill, 1968), 107-129, esp. 114-117). An example is one in which the plaintiff informs the king that his paternal estate was taken by the local authorities. Hammurabi decides that if the property is indeed of a perpetual estate (*eqlum dūrum*), then the field should be returned. This text is found in F. Thureau-Dangin, "Correspondance de Hammurapi avec Šamaš-Ḫâṣir," *RA* 21 (1924), 15-16, no. 16. The relationship between the apodictically formulated sections of the *mīšarum* edicts and similar points in the Law Codes has already been noted and may serve as another hint that some connection existed between legal practice and the Law Codes.

classed into three groups: 1. the Law Codes as addendum to or revitalization of common law; 2. the Law Codes as enumeration of case decisions around a series of themes with the purpose of serving as a guide to judges (the Law Codes as practical application of legal theory); and 3. the Law Codes as the self-justification of the king to posterity concerning the just character of his reign (the Law Codes as royal apology).

The first broad group of theories (the Law Codes as addendum to common law) is exemplified by Driver and Miles in their commentary to the Hammurabi Code. They characterize the laws of Hammurabi as a series of amendments to the common law of Babylon.[36] The Hammurabi Code does not exhaustively catalog existing law but instead accepts most of the commonly held legal assumptions of the day and amends or restates parts of that set of assumptions.

Driver and Miles compare it to British "Statutes of the Realm": "They do not wholly take the place of existing law but are a series of amendments to that law, much in the same way as English statutes amend the common law and sometimes codify it in part."[37]

J. Klima approaches this conception when he says that the laws (as opposed to the poetic Prologues and Epilogues) were formulated by legal practitioners according to instructions handed down to them by the monarch or the appropriate organ of state.[38]

The trouble with this characterization of the Law Codes is the difficulty already mentioned of tracing any firm connection between these documents and the documents of legal practice. Presumably, any reform of common law, if it is meant to serve as a precedent for future decisions, would then be cited in the cases which follow. Except for a few obscure examples,[39] this is not the case. Certainly this is an argument from silence and so cannot be the final word. There is something of the self-evident in this theory which makes it especially attractive: why else write down these laws if not to serve as a guide in making judgments?

F. R. Kraus deviates from this position somewhat without departing from it entirely when he characterizes the Hammurabi Code as a collection of judgments.[40] That is, the Law Code is not forward-looking in the

---

36 G. R. Driver and J. C. Miles, *The Babylonian Laws,* vol. 1 (Oxford: Clarendon, 1952), 41.

37 *The Babylonian Laws,* vol. 1, 48.

38 J. Klima, "Gesetze," in *Reallexikon der Assyriologie,* 244.

39 See n.35 above and also the texts cited by F. R. Kraus in "Ein Zentrales Problem des Altmesopotamischen Rechtes: Was ist der Codex Hammurabi?" *Genava* 8 (1960), 292.

40 "Ein Zentrales Problem," 287-288.

sense of laying out amendments to common law which are to be followed from then on. Rather, they are backward-looking in their inception; that is, they represent judgments which the king has made during his reign in his function as judge. Their consequent authority is implied by their source. In going this far, Kraus places himself in the second group of theories, the Law Codes as practical application of legal theory.

Further examples of this second group of theories (the Law Codes as practical application of legal theory) about the nature and purpose of the Law Codes may be cited.

W. F. Leemans gives important nuance to this conception when he notes that the choice of "codification or collection of judgments" or "reforms" is too simple.[41] Since the king in ancient Mesopotamian society was both the source of law in his role as maintainer of justice on behalf of Šamaš and the dispenser of legal decisions and hence justice in his role as highest judge, there was no practical distinction between the judgments of the king and laws promulgated by the king.[42] "The king could give his judgment according to the customary law; in that case the ‹law' has the character of codification; but the king could also give his judgment according to his own insights of justice; then the ‹law' has the character of a reform."[43] In other words, in this society the king held the executive, legislative, and judicial functions of government all three, making the distinction between codification (a function of the judiciary in our understanding) and reform (a function of the legislative) moot.

This leaves open the question of nature and purpose, however. Kraus compared the Law Codes to the omen series, seeing in both the scientific arguing from cases which marks the work of the scribal schools.[44] R. Westbrook characterizes this view as concluding that the Law Codes in the end are a work of pure science in which the scribe rings the changes on legal decisions with little thought of application.[45] Westbrook pushes the analogy with the omen series even further by saying that, like the omen series, these collections of lists of legal decisions were then "to act as reference works for the royal judges in deciding difficult cases."[46] Unfortunately, the evidence he cites is inconclusive as to whether decision given (in this case by Hammurabi concerning redemption from

41 "King Hammurapi as Judge," 107.
42 "King Hammurapi as Judge," 108.
43 "King Hammurapi as Judge," 108.
44 "Ein Zentrales Problem," 288-290.
45 R. Westbrook, "Biblical and Cuneiform Law Codes," *RB* 92 (1985), 253.
46 "Biblical and Cuneiform Law Codes," 257-258.

temple funds of a captured soldier) served as precedent for or an application of the analogous section of Hammurabi's Law Code (CH 32).[47] Westbrook cites biblical passages as evidence that there is the same sort of progression from incident to decision to generalization to creation of a code based on academic variation to referral in a subsequent incident.[48]

Westbrook's characterization of the Law Codes as practical application of particular cases with an eye to providing a guide to future decisions is not functionally different from the "Law Codes as addendum to common law" theory of Driver and Miles. In both cases the Law Code is to function as a guide for judges. It is the inception of these judgments which is different. In the case of the first theory discussed, the king as judge departed from or felt the need to reassert common law assumptions in a particular case. These departures and restatements were then set down. In the second theory, it is with the understanding that the king is both the originator and promulgator of law that Westbrook traces the development of the Law Codes from particular decisions to the creation of scientific reference works for difficult cases. The judgment itself is but the first stage in a cycle of development whose end is these reference works, the Law Codes.

But as S. Paul notes, the king was not regarded in ideological terms as the source of law; he is rather the conduit of justice which has its origin in the meta-divine order of things.[49] Both these theories, then, must be altered somewhat to fit this ideological framework.

To take the second (in my view, the more precise) theory, the analogy to the omen texts becomes even stronger, since in both cases it is the assumption of an underlying order, a correspondence between what goes on in the realm of modes of being and the visible world, which enables the insightful person (such as the king to whom insight is given)

---

47 "Biblical and Cuneiform Law Codes," 260-261.

48 "Biblical and Cuneiform Law Codes," 261-264. His last example (Lev 24:10-23) is the most complete. In it, a case is presented (10-13); the sentence is served (14); application on a general level is made (15-16); academic variation on the subject of unlawful injury or death, a minor aspect of the case in question, cf.10, is undertaken (17-21); and the subsequent authority of the decision is asserted (23, in lieu of a subsequent reference to the code which is ruled out by the narrative context).

49 *Studies in the Book of the Covenant*, 5-7. See a text from Mari in which Šamaš is said to have been granted *kinatum* as a gift (G. Dossin, "L'inscription de fondation de Iaḫdun-Lim, roi de Mari," *Syria* 32 (1955), 4, ll.4-6). Cf. also M. Greenberg, "Some Postulates of Biblical Cuneiform Law," 9.

to see this underlying order and to make decisions based on it.[50] This is the king who, though he is judge, is also "the wise king".[51]

The third theory, the Law Codes as royal apology, also accords well with this view of the place of justice in the order of reality. This theory begins with the *mīšarum* edicts and the observation that they contain apodictically formulated injunctions, a phenomenon we noted above.

The path from the *misarum* edict proper to the Law Codes can be traced in several steps. First was the *mīšarum*-act itself, which consisted primarily of debt-remissive proclamations with no durative value. Included in this phase, either alongside of or shortly after the enactment of the missions itself, were general pronouncements of a more permanent character. Afterwards, a written text was created, of which the Ammiṣaduqa text is an example, preserving the provisions of the *mīšarum* edict. This was not the proclamation of the act itself, but was in some sense already retrospective.

Representing an intermediate stage, the Eshnunna Code contains casuistic (*šumma*) provisions interspersed within provisions of an apodictic style, as is the pattern in the Ammiṣaduqa text. While this cannot be described as a *mīšarum* edict (it lacks the very remissive provisions which define the genre), neither can it be directly related to the Law Codes, strictly defined, because of this structural similarity to the edict.

The Law Codes themselves represent a final stage in this process. Retrospective in nature, the Law Codes recount for religious and apologetic purposes the just character of the king's reign. The *mīšarum*-acts were recalled at this time (as reflected in the description of the king as having caused justice to prevail in the land—cf. the prologue to CH, i:31), and some of their permanent reformatory measures were incorporated into the codes.[52]

The purpose of the Law Codes was to show the king as having faithfully carried out the office with which he was entrusted, the creation and maintenance of a climate of justice. Doing so earned the king the appellation *šar mišarim,* the just king. The source of this justice was not the king, nor even the gods, as we have noted. Rather, the king was also subject to these truths which were eternally valid and merely entrusted to the king. The Law Codes were therefore an account of the degree (and it was always a high degree) to which the king's reign was marked by

---

50 Cf. "An Ancient Mesopotamian Trial for Homicide," 208.

51 See, for instance, the Prologue to CH, ii:21, iv:9.

52 This progression is that outlined by Finkelstein in "Ammiṣaduqa's Edict," 102-103.

the observance of this order. One of the ways in which the king effected such an adherence to a just order was the *mīšarum* edict.

It is plain that Hammurabi's Code, with its elaborate prologue and epilogue trumpeting the triumphs and gracious acts of his reign, is at least among other things a royal apology.[53] The same can be said of the Ur-Nammu and Lipit-Ishtar Codes which predate it and which share its form. These are texts which are made to have several functions: the casuistic format of the "laws" themselves fits the function, accorded to them by Westbrook and others, of practical application of notable cases, while their prologue-epilogue framework places the work as a whole within a different genre, the apology.

In this complication of genre-identity, if in no other, they are comparable to the book of Deuteronomy, taken as a whole. This is not to say that Deuteronomy functions as an apology, royal or otherwise.[54] It is to say that in the case of Deuteronomy, as in the case of these three Law Codes which are more complex in their form and function than others, to impute to the work one and only one intention or ordering principle is far too simple. These are all works of quite sophisticated compositional history, authored (inasmuch as one can employ such an anachronism in this context) with great skill and not a little degree of self-awareness.

To state the point in terms of Deuteronomy, for instance, one sees on the level of intention a desire to portray itself as repristinating and recharging a set of understandings of right behavior handed to the community at its inception. Stated on the level of form, this self-portrayal works itself out through the casting of the book as three speeches by the authority figure of the nation's beginnings, Moses. But there is also the intent to state this understanding of the just community in such a way that loyalty is demanded and demanded again and again to a community whose present day is perpetually receding from the view of that purported original moment in which Israel was challenged to bind itself to God. On the level of form, the parallels (by now generally accepted) with the international treaties as well as certain rhetorical refrains serve to drive this point home.

And yet Deuteronomy is also self-evidently a collection of laws. This fact is not negated by observing that the deuteronomic legal corpus rests

53 Westbrook, generally not satisfied with this characterization of the basic purpose of the Law Codes, concedes this much—see "Biblical and Cuneiform Law Codes," 251.

54 Cf. "Biblical and Cuneiform Law Codes," 250.

a bit uneasily within its framework, any less than it does in the case of Hammurabi's Code.[55]

There appears, however, to have been a settling down of the understanding of the Law Codes onto one of the aspects apparent in the Codes of Hammurabi, Lipit-Ishtar, and Ur-Nammu,[56] if indeed the more complex form ever existed outside of central Mesopotamia.[57] Later Law Codes which lack the prologue and epilogue, at least in extant examples, downplay the element of apology.

Yet the observation that there is the potential for genre complication—even with something as straightforward as these lists of judgments and their logical corollaries—serves to remind us, as we enter into evaluation, of the unspecialized nature of Mesopotamian society, as did the examination of the role of the king in their production. The taking up of what in our culture and time could serve but one purpose and placing it in a "historical-poetical-religious"[58] setting for the purpose of self-justification not only to posterity but also to the meta-divine realm which underlies reality is but one example of what will become apparent in the pages to follow—that relationships between discrete aspects of this culture are at one and the same time less compartmentalized than our own, and so less given to an analysis which looks at only one part of the culture, and more complex, and so more difficult to trace out completely with no remainder.

In addition to drawing upon these three large classes of documents, the following evaluative section will make use of public and private documents of a more personal nature—loan contracts, bills of sale, manumission declarations, etc. These will be identified when cited.

The Nature of Debt and People in Need

The section to follow will seek to enumerate a set of social conditions in which the documents described above make sense, indeed in which they are necessary. To put this in terms of the question posed in the introduction we might say "Is there something about the nature of debt in this society, stable to a great extent over a millennium and a half,

55 M. Weinfeld acknowledges this multiplicity of form and purpose on a lesser level in his *Deuteronomy and the Deuteronomic School,* especially in the section "Law-Code Versus Treaty," 146-157.

56 *Studies in the Book of the Covenant,* 11 n.5.

57 "Biblical and Cuneiform Law Codes," 250.

58 The wording is that of S. Paul—*Studies in the Book of the Covenant,* 12.

which created a group or class of people in special need to which these documents, in whole or in part, are a response?"

But this question has a second edge to it, which says "To what extent can the release-laws of Deuteronomy be seen to serve this same function, to respond to this same need, in Israel's society?" Obviously, an assumption underlies this side of the issue, namely that Israelite society and the societies of Mesopotamia from which our documents come are similar enough to warrant comparison on the level of social function in this regard. This assumption will have to be shown to be accurate enough to be helpful.

In the context of this evaluative or topical presentation, such language raises a further question, "If the release-laws fit a similar social function, to what extent do they do so in an analogous manner?" That is, operating purely or partially inter-textually, do the Mesopotamian documents provide us with analogies for more fully getting at the social situation being addressed by the release-laws and the way in which these people in need are being cared for by the release-laws?

To start at the point at which our discussion of the Law Codes left off (that is, with the observation that this is a society less highly specialized and so more tightly interwoven than our own) we note the variety of activities in which ancient Mesopotamian merchants were engaged. They traded in commodities, they bought and sold real estate, they bought and sold slaves, they loaned money.[59]

The significance of this observation is that it demonstrates the personal interconnections between commerce, debt, land, and slavery. Another telling point of interconnection appears in Hammurabi's Code, 117-119, which spells out the limits of servitude for those who have been sold into slavery because of their own debt or the debt of another. CH 118 and 119 specifically mention the merchant (*tamkārum*) as holder of the

59 I. Mendelsohn, *Slavery in the Ancient Near East*, 4-5 and nn. 29 and 30. Mendelsohn cites examples from Larsa at the time of Rim-Sin, and mentions others in "Ancient and Neo-Babylonia, as well as Assyria," 5. Examples of three of these activities are found in J. Kohler and A. Ungnad, *Assyrischen Rechtsurkunden* (Leipzig: Eduard Pfeiffer, 1913)—money lending: 117-118, no. 153; trading in slaves: 291, no. 461; and trading in real estate: 279, no. 444. These examples all deal with one Rimani-Adad of Assyria whom Kohler and Ungnad date as active around 671 B.C.E. (cf. 55, no. 65; 303, no. 482). One example of slave trading by Mendelsohn's exemplar, Balmunamḫe, a *tamkārum* of Larsa, is found in E. Grant, "Balmunamge, the Slave Dealer," *AJSL* 34 (1917), 199-204. W. F. Leemans discusses the range of occupations in which the *tamkārum* could be engaged in his *The Old Babylonian Merchant*, 6-21.

loan and recipient of the enslaved. Thus one person can be both creditor to another person and, in foreclosure, owner of that person.[60]

Indeed, there are any number of documents in which the pledge for a loan is the borrower himself or herself, or a close relative.[61] Additionally, W. F. Leemans cites a text in which people sold themselves to one Balmunamḫe and thereby paid off their debt.[62] On the other side of the debtor-creditor relationship, then, a single person can very easily be both borrower and enslaved, either serially or simultaneously.

In this manner we see the difficulty in trying to unravel the very complex and yet unspecialized manner in which debt and need are intertwined. Nevertheless, we have already observed the process at work. In tracing the connection between the *mīšarum* edicts and *andurārum*, we noted a four-fold sequence from debt to release: 1) a debt is taken on; 2) the debtor cannot repay the debt; 3) the debtor places himself or herself or a dependent in debt slavery, thereby paying off the debt; and 4) this debt slavery is annulled by the *mīšarum* edict or some other mechanism whereby *andurārum*, release, is effected.

At every stage of this sequence, the relationships created or fostered are marked by dependence. F. C. Fensham uses the term "the weak" to describe this class of people.[63] This term is not adequate. In the case of the indebted and subsequently enslaved, a position of "weakness" within the social hierarchy of Mesopotamian society is incumbent upon their already having entered into a relationship of dependence. They are dependent, and hence subject to oppression, abuse, manipulation.

The term "weak" also makes a value judgment which should be avoided. These are people who find themselves in the state they are in for economic reasons and not through a moral failing on their part. Likewise they can not alter their status by dint of hard work or moral uprightness. "Dependent" is the preferable term.

---

60 This is expressed proverbially in an omen text: "If in a field is a trapezoid, he shall enter the house of debt, a *tamkārum* will be his master." See S. Langdon, "Assyrian Grammatical Texts," *RA* 13 (1916), 27ff; and C. J. Gadd, "Forms and Colors," *RA* 19 (1922), 153.

61 Cf. J. Kohler, A. Ungnad, and P. Koschaker, *Hammurabi's Gesetz* (Leipzig: Eduard Pfeiffer, 1913), 23, no. 1481 (pledge of self); and 25-26, no. 1474 (pledge of son).

62 *The Old Babylonian Merchant*, 17. See *Assyrische Rechtsurkunden*, 38, no. 43, for a bill of sale in which Ahat-abisa, the daughter of Isdi-Asur, is given to Zabdi in place of her father's loan payment.

63 F. C. Fensham, "The Widow, Orphan, and the Poor in Ancient Near Eastern Legal and Wisdom Literature," *JNES* 21 (1962), 129-139, *passim*.

This relationship of dependence might well exist before the debt is taken on, but certainly the structure of debt and interest in this society serve to foster a dependent relationship. Already lacking in income and hence requiring a loan, those lacking in resources now face the added burden of high interest rates. The going rate in Old Babylonia, according to Hammurabi's Code, was twenty percent.[64]

Whether or not this rate was enforced or merely represented "pious hope and moral resolve" is an open question. Certainly there are documents in which the rate of interest is stated in language similar to that of the Code itself such as "according to the decree of the king" or "the interest rate of Šamaš."[65] In Babylon it appears that the twenty percent rate was honored.[66]

In Assyria even this high fixed rate was not honored. Kohler and Ungnad rehearse documents in which the rate of interest from seedtime to harvest varies from this twenty percent to well over one hundred percent.[67] Mendelsohn publishes a document from Nuzi in which the rate of interest is fifty percent—twelve *minas* of lead lent and eighteen to be returned.[68] Certainly it is not surprising that the partial dependency of the borrower on the lender often becomes absolute when the loan with its interest comes due.

The right of the creditor to bodily seize the holder of a loan which has become overdue is generally recognized by the Law Codes[69] and, as we have already seen, private documents bear out the practice of this right. In fact, the private documents already cited show that the debtor or a dependent of the debtor can enter into servitude as a condition of the loan in the first place. And once bound into servitude, the Law Codes prescribe and proscribe the behavior of the owner toward the debt-slave.[70] One assumes that these injunctions are intended to curtail abuse

---

64 Cf. CH 88 and the note in *ANET3*. The following laws, 89 and 90, fix this rate and prescribe penalties for exceeding it. The Eshnunna code sets the rate at around this same twenty percent (CE 18A, though on the enigmatic nature of this paragraph, see R. Yaron, *The Laws of Eshnunna*, 11 n. 36).

65 *Şimdat LUGAL* and *sibat* ^{d}*šamaš* respectively; cf. CH 89 for the former and unpublished text cited by Mendelsohn in *Slavery in the Ancient Near East*, 24-25, l. 2 for the latter.

66 See *Assyrischen Rechtsurkunden*, 459 n2.

67 *Assyrischen Rechtsurkunden*, 460 and the texts cited there.

68 *Slavery in the Ancient Near East*, 25-26.

69 Cf. by implication CE 22 and 23; CH 114-119, 151-152; MAL 39, 44, and 48.

70 See most directly MAL A:39, 44, and 48.

of the pledged or the debt-slave at the hand of an owner, and so one can reckon that actual practice was worse rather than better.

This, then, is the social need being met through these extraordinary measures. By extraordinary we mean that their very existence shows some cultural awareness of a need of such particular force that some solution had to be found which stepped outside or beyond the normal operation of social commerce and that some means had to be effected which could break this cycle of dependence, if only temporarily or for a few.

That this type of occasional measure made itself felt throughout this cycle of dependence is apparent in the clause attached to several bills of sale in which a seller wants to express the intention that upon his acceptance of the "full price" he relinquishes any claim on the property once and for all—the field is said from henceforth "not subject to (claims arising from) a remission of debts."[71]

As in Deuteronomy, with its repeated exhortations to remember the widow, the orphan, the enslaved (and in the case of the last to do so using the most evocative phrases of the people's internal history)—all those who have no ready system of support[72] —so too in these "theoretical postulates" is there special concern for the dependent.

We have already noted the way that this works itself out in the extant *mīšarum* edict: while the situation of these dependents is not immediately addressed by the terms of the edict, they are taken care of in a manner which highlights them as a special concern of the act.

---

71 So *CAD* A/2:116. J. Lewy discusses this and similar texts from Hana in his "The Biblical Institution of *D^e^ror* in the Light of Akkadian Documents," *Eretz Israel* 5 (1958), 23ff. On the issue of the phrase "full price (*ana šîm gamer*)" see esp. p. 26. On the other side of the line, a text from the Old Babylonian period translated in Kohler and Ungnad, *Hammurabi's Gesetz*, vol. 3 (Leipzig: Eduard Pfeiffer, 1909), 212 and discussed by Lewy on p. 27 speaks of the return of a house and an orchard because the king established the *andurārum*. See also the Assyrian documents cited above (n. 35).

72 72. See P. D. Miller, "Israel As Host to Strangers," *Today's Immigrants and Refugees: A Christian Understanding* (Washington: United States Catholic Conference, Inc., 1988), 1-19. D. E. Gowan remarks that while poverty is something that can happen to anyone, these are people whose poverty is of a particularly disadvantaged sort, since they are powerless for other reasons in addition to poverty ("Wealth and Poverty in the Old Testament," 343-344). See also F. C. Fensham, "Widow, Orphan, and the Poor in Ancient Near Eastern Legal and Wisdom Literature," 129-139, esp. his final point on 139 that these classes of people could be oppressed with impunity because they had no clear legal rights or personalities.

Compare this special attention with that accorded to the dependent in Deuteronomy 16:9-12:

> You shall count off seven weeks; start to count the seven weeks when the sickle is first put to the standing grain. Then you shall observe the Feast of Weeks for the Lord your God, offering your freewill contribution according as the Lord your God has blessed you. You shall rejoice before the Lord your God with your son and daughter, your male and female slave, the Levite in your communities, and the stranger, the fatherless, and the widow in your midst, at the place where the Lord your God will choose to establish God's name. Bear in mind that you were slaves in Egypt, and take care to obey these laws.[73]

Just as in the manumission paragraphs in Ammiṣaduqa's edict, this text in Deuteronomy calls to mind those dependent members of society who might ordinarily not partake of the benefits of the legislation. To be sure, these texts are from very different types of social contexts.[74] Still, the intention to include the excluded, the voiceless, the dependent, is unmistakable.

Likewise, this concern for the dependent is voiced in the Law Codes. In the Middle Assyrian Laws, for instance, special care is taken to preserve the marital rights of the indentured:

> A:48: If a man in whose house his debtor's daughter is living on account of (i.e., as pledge for) a debt asks her father, he may give her to a husband; but, if her father does not agree, he shall not give her.
>
> If her father is dead, he shall ask one of her brothers, then the latter shall speak to her (other) brothers; if a brother says, "I will redeem my sister within one full month", if he does not redeem her within one full month, the creditor, if he pleases, shall declare her quit (of all claim and) give her to a husband. . . .[75]

Two points can be derived from this quotation. First, one notices the desire of the text to exhaust all conceivable possibilities. This accords with a characterization of its fundamental purpose as a reference work

---

73 This translation follows that of *Tanakh* (New York: JPS, 1985).

74 Though as we have seen, the gap between law and liturgy is not so broad as to be unbridgeable.

75 Driver and Miles, *The Assyrian Laws*, 416-419; the text becomes too fragmentary at this point to proceed usefully. However, the point of protection of the rights of the dependent can be made on the basis of this partial text. Cf. the translation in *ANET3*, 184.

derived from practical application of particular cases as outlined above in our discussion of the Law Codes.

The second point is that this law prevents the holder of the pledged daughter from taking unreasonable advantage of her dependent status. To be sure, the position of women in this culture is such that she herself has little choice in the matter. Still, within this context care is being taken that she is not completely severed in this matter from her natural family, even though divorced from that family physically and economically.

The concern to prevent the holder of the enslaved from taking unreasonable advantage of that slave finds echoes in Dt 15. In both portions of the release-laws, particular attention is paid to the response of the one who holds the advantage, as we have noted at some length (Dt 15:7-11; 18). While the feelings of the slaveholder are not mentioned in the Middle Assyrian Laws, the strict circumscription of the behavior of that slaveholder toward at least this class of slave-dependent corresponds functionally to that section of the release-laws. In both cases, the one in a hortatory and evocative manner, the other matter-of-fact and precise, attention is given to preserve the rights of the dependent to at least a modicum of care. Thus those who have no resources of their own to protect their rights to care are given such by these documents which set forth current understanding of right behavior.

In some cases, too, there is a hierarchy within the ranks of the dependent. In the sections of Hammurabi's Code dealing with debts and slavery, distinction is made between those who enter into an indentured status having been free previously and those who are given as pledge for debt having already been enslaved:

> 117: If a liability has come due against a man and he sold his wife, his son, or his daughter or (they are) given over[76] into service, they shall do

---

[76] On the passive form of this verb, see T. J. Meeks's translation in *ANET3* and the footnote there. Meeks applies this verb to the one whose debt comes due—that is, in addition to the possibility of the obligee selling close dependents, that one can also sell himself. Driver and Miles also admit the possibility of a passive rendering at this point, though they apparently read the persons previously listed (the wife, the son, or the daughter) as a collective subject of this verb, apparently in parallel with the following sentence which has two types of masters ("has sold"-"is given into servitude"//"the one who bought"-"the one who takes into servitude"). I. Cardellini also makes a distinction between the status of the indentured who is "sold" *ana kaspim* and the one who is "bound over" *ana kiššatim* (*Die biblischen "Sklaven"-Gesetze*, 79-81). Leemans (*The Old Babylonian Merchant*, 17) cites texts which speak of two ways of giving security corresponding to these two phrases which have the same "economic value." While it is certainly possible, as noted already, for people to sell themselves in

work in the house of the one who has purchased them or has taken them into service for three years; in the fourth year their freedom shall be established.

118: If a male slave or a female slave has been given over into service,[77] the merchant shall let the (term of the loan) expire (and then) he may sell[78] (them); he may not be reclaimed.

119: If a liability has come due against a man and he sells[79] his female slave who bore him children, the (original) owner of the female slave may repay the money which the merchant has given and (so) he may redeem his female slave.[80]

It is important to notice the sequence here: 1) the situation which occurs when the free dependent of a debtor is given as payment for a loan by whatever means; 2) the situation which occurs when a slave is given as payment *ana kiššatum*; 3) the apparently exceptional situation which occurs when a slave who has borne children to the debtor is given as payment *ana kaspim*.

One significance of this logical outworking or practical application of a legal principle is that it shows some attempt at making regular practice what is clearly an extraordinary event in the case of Ammiṣaduqa's edict: the release of certain types of slave-dependents (the debt-slave), though not others (the slave by birth, accident of war, or those who became enslaved by some means other than debt forfeiture). This is an attempt to break the cycle of dependence systemically, that is, to divorce the limitation of debt-slavery from a royal act which was occasional.

---

order to pay off a debt, the fact that the two following laws play out the logical possibilities of the situation in terms of the slave handed as pledge in each of these two forms (though in different scenarios) tips the scales in favor of two different types of security, the distinction between which is not clear, being treated here.

77 I.e., *ana kiššatum*.

78 *Ana kaspim*—that is, after the term of the loan runs out, the status of the transaction changes from *ana kiššatim* to *ana kaspim*.

79 *Ana kaspim*.

80 A similar type of hierarchy is implied in MAL A:44 if one allows the interpretation of Lewy ("The Biblical Institution of *D^eror* in the Light of Akkadian Documents," 26*) that the phrase "full price" refers to acquisition of absolute property and thus ownership which cannot be voided by such acts as *andurārum*. Lewy cites C + G:3 which distinguishes between the sale of pledges to a buyer in another country (a practice prohibited by the law) and sale of slaves bought at full value (which can be sold to a buyer in another country). This interpretation seems eminently logical in light of these two texts and the presence of such a hierarchy in CH.

In this respect, then, the release-laws in Deuteronomy, particularly Dt 15:12-18, are functioning in much the same fashion as this portion of Hammurabi's Code. In response to a systemic tendency toward the creation of a class of people whose dependence is such that it requires special attention or extraordinary measures, the Deuteronomic corpus has attempted to break this cycle of dependence by circumscribing limits around the length of that servitude.[81]

Both this portion of Hammurabi's Code and paragraphs 20 and 21 of Ammiṣaduqa's edict also share with the release-laws in Deuteronomy an eye wide open to distinctions within the ranks of the dependent. CH and Ammiṣaduqa's edict distinguish between those who become slave-dependents on account of their debt and those who become slaves by some other means. Deuteronomy distinguishes between the foreign and the kin.

A wide-eyed awareness of the likely reaction of those in whose power the dependent finds herself or himself is also a theme which connects Deuteronomy to the *mīšarum* edicts. Dt 15:7-11 counters any reluctance on the part of the lender to continue to lend in the face of likely debt erasure. With a similar prescience, Ammiṣaduqa's edict attempts to anticipate abuses of debt collection.[82] The picture one gets is that the edict is aware that a lender, knowing that a *mīšarum* edict is approaching, will attempt to call in outstanding loans before the edict can be promulgated or that the lender will attempt to circumvent the intention of the edict by other fraudulent means.

An interesting confirmation of this interpretation is gained when one notices the reference to a "royal decree (*ṣimdat šarrim*)" in par. 5 of the edict. This phrase does not serve as the functional equivalent of the general motive clause of the edict.[83] Rather, this refers to standing legal custom which has been royally endorsed.[84]

Thus while the immediate trigger for such an offense was the *mīšarum* edict, the mechanism for the identification of this behavior as out of bounds and worthy of extreme punishment was already in place. Finkelstein puts it this way:

---

81 On the connections with Exod. 21:1-11, see chapter 3 below.

82 Cf. Ammiṣaduqa's edict, par. 5. This interpretation is based in part on a reading of the phrase *siman šadduttim* as referring to the season of the settlement of debts. Finkelstein argues this persuasively in "A New Text," 56-58. Par. 6 can also be interpreted as having this anticipatory quality.

83 I.e., "because the king has established the *mīšarum* in the land."

84 On the meaning of *ṣimdat* generally and *ṣimdat šarrim* in particular, see M. de J. Ellis, "*Ṣimdatu* in the Old Babylonian Sources," *JCS* 24 (1972), 74-82.

> [T]he penal statement as it now stands must be understood as applicable to such illegal attempts at premature collection of debts in any year; that the rule is included in the Edict suggests that Ammiṣaduqa was well aware that the impending *mīšarum* could trigger an inordinate number of such violations as compared with other years.[85]

It is similar with the comparable section in Dt 15. While the ideal is stated in 15:4, 15:7-11 counters with a bracing dose of reality, showing an awareness that even extraordinary measures will not completely break the cycle of dependence which is to the advantage of those who would join house to house and field to field (Isa 5:8). Thus the need to command an open hand and a willing heart.

Conclusion

To return at last to the matter of comparison, ample points of comparison to the release-laws have been found in these Mesopotamian texts. These points of comparison will not be repeated here. More needs to be said about one of them, however.

As with some of the Law Codes, the release-law legislation has been altered drastically by placing it in a context other than the simplest required for legal and moral intention to be communicated. Still, certain similarities in intent and social function have been discovered which justify our calling these analogues of Deuteronomy 15. The reader of Dt 15 can look upon them as filling an analogous social function and operating with a similar intent to order society along the lines of a justice which yet lies beyond the power of even the monarch to define it. In this sense at least the release-laws of Deuteronomy fulfill a humanizing function in the ideal society, as do the analogous documents from the ancient Near East.

It is perhaps ironic, however, that the oft-noted "humanizing" or "democratizing" tendencies in Deuteronomy which exceed those of the ancient Near East are the result of the taking of this conception of justice away from a meta-divine realm beyond the reach of any despotic ruler to define it. Deuteronomy places it instead in the hands of a potentially arbitrary deity, subject from a practical or jaundiced point of view to the whims of the interlocutors of the divine.

That this ideological alteration has been made is apparent in the phrase in Dt 15:2 which prohibits deviation from the ordinance "because

85 "A New Text," 59.

the release belonging to YHWH has been proclaimed," a phrase we have called a divine warrant. This phrase is resonant with the motive clause in the *mīšarum* edict, "because the king has established the *mīšarum* for the land." It is functionally parallel to the *mīšarum* phrase, as both serve as justificatory or authority-granting phrases.

Coupled with the severing of the act from royal accession or the occasional act of the king and the placing of it on a fixed cycle,[86] this phrase puts YHWH in the position of guardian of justice and the people as a whole (the "you" addressed by the text) in the position of the ones who see to its enactment.

The role of the king in the establishment of the just society is thus split in Deuteronomy, giving to YHWH the responsibility for instituting the ordinance and seeing that blessings fall from its being carried out and giving to the nation the responsibility of carrying it out. It is in the transcendence of YHWH even above the meta-divine springs of "justice and truth" that the roots of a social justice no longer dependent on a benign ruler for its accomplishment are found.

This observation is particularly of moment as we turn next to examine the biblical parallels to the release-laws since, as we shall see, it is the way in which the various codifications of an ideology of social justice in legal form appeal to God and characterize the principals involved which form the greatest area of comparison between the laws of the Covenant and Holiness Code and the laws of Deuteronomy. In this at least they stand together in contrast to analogous material from the ancient Near East: only one God is acknowledged as demanding loyalty and obedience. The significance of this statement is often lost in its being obvious. At this point of transition from the social realm of ancient Mesopotamia to that of the Old Testament, it needs to be restated with vigor. In the chapter which follows, one should not lose sight of this area of commonality in drawing contrast between the release-laws of Deuteronomy and their biblical parallels.

---

86 This in contrast to CH 117 which only deals with the release of the debt-slave and not the remission of debts—only one of the consequences of the *mīšarum* edict is so treated in Hammurabi's Code.

III

The Biblical Parallels

Just as similar material in related cultures can provide analogies in a study of the release-laws of Dt 15, so too can biblical material, especially the related passages in Exod and Lev. The comparison between Dt and other legal sections of the Old Testament will be both simpler and more complex than that between the release-laws of Deuteronomy and the cuneiform material. Simpler, because the social and cultural relatedness of the materials is unquestioned. More complex, because while the fact of cultural relation is unquestioned, the exact lines of relationship are all the more blurred because of their being in such close proximity.

The wisest course to take is to approach the matter afresh. This is something of an empty boast given the degree to which this ground has already been worked. Still, a fresh approach, though not necessarily an uninformed one, is possible.

The means by which a new vision can be had of the relationships temporal and ideological which these texts have to one another is by stepping outside of the normal terms of the discussion (viz., the assigning of texts to particular hypothetical writers, strands, redactors, compilers, or whatever and thence the placing of them in a particular order one to another) and approaching them by means of the method which relates most closely to the overall subject of the study, namely, the shape of Deuteronomy's system of social justice.

This goal is aided most strongly by comparing the ways in which problems of social justice were responded to, as we did in chapter 2. This means that questions of dating, etc., though germane to the task at hand, are less important than a careful examination of the particular response to problems of social justice on an ideological level. Because this course is somewhat different from that ordinarily taken in comparing parallel examples of biblical laws, some preliminary comments are necessary in order to further explain what the analysis with which this chapter will conclude is all about.

Preliminary Comments

An examination of the varied biblical responses to problems of social justice on an ideological or systemic level is possible, even necessary, due to the looseness with which any particular piece of law is attached to its framework. As in the case of Hammurabi's Code, so too the biblical laws are material which have been made to serve more than one function. They are not simply law or compilation of law or even practical application on a general level of the verdict of particularly difficult or unusual cases for the benefit of future reference. They are "value-laden and intensely theological."[1] These collections of laws represent law of the type which enjoyed general currency in ancient Near Eastern culture brought under the control of tradition which provided theological command and exhortation.[2] J. L. Mays calls the synthesis which ensues "rules of righteousness."[3]

---

[1] J. L. Mays, "Justice: Perspectives from the Prophetic Tradition," *Int* 37 (1983), 13.

[2] "Justice," 12-13. On the role of motive clauses in the creation of this theological control, see B. Gemser, "The Importance of the Motive Clause," 50-66 and J. Levenson, "The Theologies of Commandment in Biblical Israel," 17-33, though the presence of motive clauses in quasi-legal documents such as the *mīšarum* edicts no longer allows us to say with Gemser that "[t]he motive clause is clearly and definitely a peculiarity of Old Testament law" ("The Importance of the Motive Clause," 52).

[3] "Justice," 12-13, though I disagree with Mays's characterization of the legal custom which Israel shared with neighboring cultures as "secular and neutral, free of terms of value or appeal to faith, simply statements of what had been established as the accepted way to settle cases" (*Ibid.*). As we have seen, this picture does not do justice to the (in their minds) theological and ideological underpinnings of Near Eastern law. Still, his overall point, that the placing of legal material in the various contexts of the Pentateuch alters its social, ideological, and theological intent, is to be preferred over simple equation of this material with that of Mesopotamian legal corpora (as in R. Westbrook, "Biblical and Cuneiform Law Codes," 247-248).

To put this matter another way, when seeking means of comparison by which a sharper definition of the system of social justice found in Dt 15 can be had, just as in the issue of ancient Near Eastern comparisons, so too in the case of biblical parallels interpretation is not finished just because one can answer to a reasonable degree of satisfaction the questions "Where did this come from?" or even "Which of these texts is the oldest?" In part, the obscurity of what might (by analogy with New Testament studies) be called "synoptic" comparison in the Pentateuch has its basis in the slipperiness of the term "original."

In judging among various possible reconstructions of the "original" law, what set of criteria is to be preferred? Is that which hews most closely to observable (though ultimately hypothetical) norms of construction or that which departs from those norms the more original? Is it that which is most pertinent to its present context—most pertinent and hence most likely to have guided the selection of the editor? And in the case of texts which bear the marks of the grafting together of two or more sources, these become even harder to judge since questions of form and pertinence can now be worked from several antecedent directions.

Another dimension of this problem surfaces when one takes seriously the very looseness-to-context which has already been mentioned. Recent comments by several scholars have undermined the confidence which one can attach to the assignment of a text to any particular Pentateuchal stratum.[4] In the case of legal texts, the situation is even more precarious. S. Kaufman puts it this way:

> The importance of oral transmission . . . has been a primary contributor to the formation of the current mini-consensus among biblicists that regards the strict application of the Documentary Hypothesis to narrative materials as highly tenuous at best and the assignment of literary relationships between prescriptive ("legal") texts and purely narrative pericopes as

---

4 See especially the trenchant comments of R. Rendtorff in "The ʿYahwist' as Theologian? The Dilemma of Pentateuchal Criticism," *JSOT* 3 (1977), 2-10. In the end, Rendtorff's essay is more successful in its calling into question what had become unexamined assumptions in Pentateuchal criticism. His constructive suggestions are less convincing. See also less pointedly and more helpfully S. Kaufman, "The Temple Scroll and Higher Criticism," *HUCA* 53 (1982), 29-43, where Kaufman describes, on the basis of the Qumran Temple Scroll's use of its sources and the degree to which we can determine how those sources have been reworked, the limits under which Pentateuchal studies must labor in identifying source-relationships without the benefit of those sources themselves.

fruitless speculation.[5]

Kaufman goes on to express qualified confidence with regards to comparisons among the major blocks of "prescriptive" compilations (the Covenant, Deuteronomic, and Holiness Codes) as wholes and between specific parallel subsections of any pair of them. What Kaufman in the end calls for, and to which we may assent, is greater clarity regarding the particularity of any one text in comparison with its parallel text in another block of laws.

One can see this point most clearly by example. A fairly recent study by S. Japhet attempts to contradict the classical formulation of the temporal sequence of the Pentateuchal sources (JE first, D second, P last). She undertakes an analysis of the manumission laws in Exodus, Leviticus, and Deuteronomy and concludes from her study that P (in this case, the Levitical Holiness Code formulation of manumission legislation) predates D.[6]

Her analysis rests primarily on two conclusions. The first is that the relationship between the manumission laws of Lev and Dt is the primary one in determining the order in which the manumission laws were composed. The relationship between the manumission laws in Exod and Dt is secondary. She arrives at this conclusion by eliminating the usual arguments in favor of resolving the syntactical difficulties present in these three texts which are normally resolved by emending them on the basis of the Exod-Dt relationship. This opens up the possibility of explaining the syntactical difficulties present in these three laws by means of the Lev-Dt relationship. The similarities between the two pieces of legislation are significant enough to believe that some line of influence exists between them.[7] The question then is, "In which direction does the line of influence run?"

---

5 S. A. Kaufman, "A Reconstruction of the Social Welfare Systems of Ancient Israel," in *In the Shelter of Elyon: Essays on Palestinian Life and Literature in Honor of G. W. Ahlstrom*, W. B. Barrick and J. R. Spencer, eds. (JSOTSup 31; Sheffield: JSOT Press, 1984), 277.

6 S. Japhet, "The Relationship between the Legal Corpora in the Pentateuch in Light of Manumission Laws," in *Studies in Bible* (*Scripta Hierosolymitana* 31), ed. S. Japhet (Jerusalem: Magnes, 1986), 63-84. The description of Japhet's argument will not make further reference to this article as it follows the line of reasoning of the article as a whole.

7 Chief among these correspondences are the presence of the definite subject "your brother (*ʾāḥîkā*)," the identity of the buyer in the second person, and the passive use of *mkr* to indicate the transfer of property ("The Relationship Between the Legal Corpora," 73-74).

The second principal observation in Japhet's analysis follows from the first one. After establishing the strong linguistic bond between the Dt and Lev versions of the manumission laws, Japhet moves to determine their relative antiquity. Chapter 25 of Lev, she notes, has, as a whole, to do with the concern for the impoverished Israelite who is distinguished from the foreigner through the use of *ʾāḥ*, which use represents the transfer of a familial or tribal term into the national sphere. The use of "brother" in the manumission law in Lev is crucial to the basic postulates of the law; in the Dt version, "brother" is used as in Dt generally and not as an organic part of this particular law. This being the case, Japhet concludes that the manumission law in the Holiness Code must be the older law, part of an integrated series of postulates concerning the treatment of the penurious, which law Dt blended with the opening formula of the Covenant Code to create a law intended to supplant both. She substantiates this conclusion with the point that the reference to the slave as hired servant (Lev 25:40; Dt 15:18) makes sense in the Holiness Code's enumeration of the laws concerning the impoverished as part of the distinction between the status of the poor Israelite who will be freed in the Jubilee Year, and so not regarded as a slave permanently, and the foreigner enslaved for a lifetime. In Dt it is a secondary concern, part of the homiletical rationalization characteristic of Deuteronomy. The Dt version of the manumission law, Japhet says, is in fact a polemic against the Holiness Code version, refusing to grant the existence of non-Israelites as slaves in the land.

This analysis can be critiqued on two levels, the particular and the theoretical. On the level of the particular, one can find fault with both of her principal observations. While it is manifestly the case that the opening clauses of the laws in Dt and Lev are closely related,[8] it is less obvious that the direction of influence must run from Lev to Dt.

As S. Kaufman notes,[9] the passive form of the verb in the protasis of both opening clauses has several parallels in Dt;[10] it is unique in Leviticus. In addition, Japhet's citation of *ʾāḥ* as being primary in Lev and sec-

---

8 Dt: *kî-yimmākēr lĕkā ʾāḥîkā hāʿibrî ʾô hāʿibrîyā(h).*
Lev: *wĕkî-yāmûk ʾāḥîkā ʿimmāk wĕnimkar-lāk.*

9 S. Kaufman, "Deuteronomy 15 and Recent Research," 275. Kaufman is responding to Japhet's Hebrew article from which "The Relationship Between the Legal Corpora" was translated.

10 Kaufman cites Dt 15:19, 17:12, 17:8, 21:1, 22:6, 22:22, and 24:7. He might also have drawn attention to 12:22, though here the context is not exactly the same. Still, *yēʾākēl* serves as the protasis to a further clarification of the command given in 12:20—syntactically it is functioning as is *yimmākēr* in 15:12.

ondary in Dt founders on the observation that Leviticus (the Holiness Code) prefers to use *ʿam* when referring to a fellow Israelite.[11] In Dt, of course, *ʾāḥ* is widely used in this sense.

Further, that ch. 25 of Lev contains an integrated series of postulates concerning the treatment of the poor is merely to say that it shares with the ancient Near Eastern Law Codes the quality of scientific listing from cases or creation of sequences around a theme which we noted in the previous chapter.[12]

Also on the level of the particular is S. Kaufman's argument that Lev 25 must be the later of the pair, and not Dt 15, because of the primacy of the concept of Sabbath in Lev 25 (and the sabbath of Sabbatical years, the Jubilee), which joins together the older concepts of the fallow year, the tribal *yōbēl* (cf. Num 36:4), and the practice of issuing proclamations of freedom (as in Dt 15). That this joining together of sabbatical and release concepts is thought to be later rests on the speculation in Lev 26 that the Exile is a result of failure to observe the Sabbatical year, thus firmly tying the Holiness Code legislation to a date during or after the Exile.[13]

On the level of the theoretical, one can question Japhet's first point, that having failed to establish an acceptable emendation of the Exod law on the basis of its Dt parallel one must then turn to the version of the law in Dt and say that it is not "the original."

---

[11] "Deuteronomy 15 and Recent Research," 275. See within the Holiness Code Lev 17:9, 19:8, and 23:29, where the distinction made between being counted as kin and being cut off from that relationship is quite clear.

[12] See pp 58-59 above and bibliography cited there. See also "Deuteronomy 15 and Recent Research," 275; S. Kaufman, "The Structure of Deuteronomic Law," 115; S. Paul, *Studies in the Book of the Covenant*, 106; and in a qualified manner, R. Yaron, *The Laws of Eshnunna*, 52-55.

[13] S. Kaufman, "A Reconstruction of the Social Welfare Systems of Ancient Israel," 283. On the subject of the *yōbēl* mentioned in Num 36, see N. P. Lemche, "The Manumission of Slaves—The Fallow Year—The Sabbatical Year—The Jobel Year," *VT* 26 (1976), 55, who, like Kaufman ("A Reconstruction," 285 n10), notices that this *yōbēl* stands in contradiction to the one found in Lev 25, the subject here being acquisition of land by tribe to be apportioned by lot in the *yōbēl* as opposed to the returning of property to its original owner as in Lev. Kaufman and Lemche use the same criterion (the contradiction in intent of the jobel in Num 36 and Lev 25) to argue opposite conclusions: Kaufman that the Num text is an earlier, tribal practice ("A Reconstruction," 280) and Lemche that the mention of *yōbēl* in Num is a secondary insertion. I find Kaufman to have the better of the two arguments, since the citation of the *yōbēl* custom is the trigger which raises the issue of which the passage as a whole is concerned—the permanent transferral of property from one tribal inheritance to another. It can hardly be secondary. See also R. North, *Sociology of the Biblical Jubilee* (AnBib 4; Rome: PBI, 1954), 35.

Here again, one runs afoul of the term "original." If one can show that both versions are "original" to their context in the sense of fitting into the logical sequence established by that context,[14] then it becomes extremely problematic to say that either version is "original" in the other sense of being untouched by that context and hence providing a window onto a source underlying both versions.

To take the issue of the puzzling second-person verb form with which the manumission law in Exod 21 begins, Japhet finds it difficult to believe that Dt would change this opening verb in every particular (verbal root, person, and voice), especially since Dt otherwise emphasizes the activity of the second person addressee in the remainder of the passage and, indeed, in the book as a whole.[15] Thus if one cannot suppose an "original" third person formulation behind the Exod text ("original" here in the sense of being present in the source available to the compiler of the Covenant Code before its insertion into its present context) from which the third-person opening of the Dt version can be derived, then the "originality" of the Dt version with only Exod as an antecedent is called into question, and one must look elsewhere for the "origin" of Dt 15:12a.

Yet this analysis fails to take account of the wider context and the overall intent of the texts in question. The Exodus 21 version, on the one hand, is not "unoriginal" to the Covenant Code for its beginning in the second person. While it is true that this section of the Covenant Code employs the third-person indefinite subject (with the exception of the displaced participial laws in 21:12-17), this is not universally true of the whole of the Covenant Code. Most tellingly, Exod 22:21-24 and 25-27, which again deal with the relationship between the powerful and the dependent, employ the second person.[16]

---

[14] That is, the "original" formulation of the compiler of the Covenant Code and the "original" formulation of the compiler of the Deuteronomic Code.

[15] "The Relationship Between the Legal Corpora," 70-71.

[16] Since we are at this point trying to establish the relationship between parts of the Covenant Code as a whole in order to determine their relationship each to that whole we may disregard for this purpose the oft-asserted divisions within the Code itself. This may be done for three reasons: first, since the question at issue here is that of whether or not Exod 21:2 is anomalous within the Covenant Code and so questionable in its present form, it is appropriate to cite other parts of that Code as evidence pro or con; second, if the compiler of the Code (as opposed to the editor of Exod) has altered the person of the verb *qnh* in 21:2 then that compiler might well have done so in order to bring this piece of legislation in line syntactically with other similar laws in the Code and so to relate them to one another in the sequence of laws, a possibility which could well have repercussions for how the reader is meant to

In fact, the use of the second person in the first piece of legislation in the Covenant Code, a law dealing with the treatment of the dependent slave, is deliberate and revealing. The person who sells self or is sold into slavery has no further capacity to act on his or her own behalf. She or he has traded that capacity for a relationship of dependence. CH 117, though it follows the casuistic third person impersonal form, in effect acknowledges this when it says that the indentured shall "be freed." Exodus (the Covenant Code) makes the point more explicitly: the onus to act on behalf of the dependent is placed at the feet of the one who still has the power to act, the "you" who buys the slave. This is not negated by the fact that the passage continues by talking of the conditions in which others attached to the slave are freed. In fact, the conditions which limit release further substantiate the point that the legislation is written from the perspective of the owner (the "you" of the passage).

The Deuteronomy 15 version, on the other hand, is not "unoriginal" to the Deuteronomic Code for its placing the verb of the protasis in the third person. The Deuteronomic shaping of this legal concept (manumission) is in fact an example of the "humanitarian" thrust of the Deuteronomic corpus. This is particularly apparent when one translates the N of *mkr* in Dt 15:12 reflexively[17]: "If your kin, a Hebrew man or

---

construe the collection as a whole (that is, does this "alteration" then signify that we are meant to understand the quality of the legislation here arranged in light of the laws formulated in the "mixed" casuistic-apodictic form); and, related to this second point, third, if these and other laws can be said to be of a recognizable type, then it becomes problematic to alter one of them on the basis of a different, supposedly governing, type even if that other type is more prevalent in the immediate textual area (cf. A. Jirku's largely superceded categories in *Das weltlich Recht im Alten Testament* [Gütersloh: Bertelsmann, 1927], 41, for an example of one who labels the hybrid form we find here the "Wenn-Du" formula; Jirku sees this as a combination of the what has come to be called "casuistic" form [the "If-then" form] and the "apodictic" [Jirku calls it the "you-should"] form. See also more recently H. W. Gilmer, *The If-You Form in Israelite Law* [SBLDS 15; Missoula: Scholars, 1975], 46-56.). On the divisions within the Covenant Code, see B. Childs, *The Book of Exodus* (OTL; Philadelphia: Westminster, 1974), 453-458, and Lemche, "The Manumission of Slaves," 42. For an example of one who sees in the "If-you" form a clue to the structure of the Covenant Code, see H. Cazelles, *Etudes sur le Code de l'Alliance* (Paris: Letouzney et Ané, 1946; the copy available to me was on microfilm from the Yale University Photographic Services, 1980), 109. See also *The If-You Form*, 49.

17 As also with *nmkr* in Lev 25:39, 47, 48, 50; Jer 34:14; Neh 5:8 (so BDB, 569), all in the context of selling oneself into slavery. Other examples of *mkr* in the N with reference to persons which BDB translates as a passive do not really contradict this usage. Lev 25:42 should be translated "they shall not sell themselves" when one understands that a distinction is being made here between the foreigner who may enter

woman, sells self to you. . . ." This makes it clear that the one who sells self is giving up the power to act due to the poverty which remains (the interconnecting feature which ties this law to the previous *šĕmiṭṭāh* law).

The intent of the law is that all should go out, and, like the Covenant Code legislation, the onus is placed on the master to let the slave go free. Unlike the Exodus version, however, not just bare freedom is offered to the slave. Rather, the newly freed slave is given a stake with which to begin again. Thus while the onus to act is all on the owner, the focus of care throughout the law is on the slave. It is thus natural that the law would begin from this perspective, that is, from the perspective of the one who sells self.

Thus neither version can be said to be "unoriginal" on the basis of apparent tension to their respective contexts (that is, the particular expression of the legal concept of regular manumission). Exodus draws our attention to the power of the one who owns to set free and enumerates the various theoretical conditions in which that setting free is to be restricted; hence, the second-person verb which addresses the buyer is appropriate. Deuteronomy deals at heart with the manner in which the freed slave is to be cared for upon release (or with that one's ability to refuse to accept the gifts of freedom and endowment); hence, the third-person verb is appropriate. Neither *requires* emendation, and the directness of the link between them is called into question.

This is not to say that grammatical tensions do not exist in these texts.[18] It is to say that it does not necessarily follow from the fact that these tensions exist that one or more of the terms in the synoptic comparison must therefore be "unoriginal" and stand in need of correction.

Of equal or greater interest and of greater utility in the bringing into focus of our particular legal text (Dt 15) is the project of using parallel material to define the social context in which the text before us arose and

---

into permanent servitude and so be considered a "slave" and the Israelite whose possible term of servitude is limited, hence who is to be thought of as a "hired servant" rather as a "slave." The Israelite therefore may not sell him- or herself into permanent slavery. Isa 52:3 can also be read as reflexive. Other texts cannot. Exod 22:2 (MT) deals with the same subject, the selling of a person because that one cannot make restitution for (in this case) a stolen item. The difference is not in action described but in actor—the community replaces the individual as seller because of the criminal nature of that which led to indebtedness, hence the passive is appropriate. See also Isa 50:1, Est 7:4, and Ps 105:7 where context makes the passive preferable.

[18] The tension between the buyer addressed as "you" in Exod 21:2 and "his master" in the remainder of the passage, for example, is unavoidable.

the social problem which it sought to ameliorate. This comparison will be done by taking up the two collections of laws, the Covenant Code and the Holiness Code, in turn. In each case, those laws which deal with the problems arising from the existence of poverty will be singled out and discussed. Comparison with the release-laws in Deuteronomy will then follow.

The Covenant Code

For our purposes the net must be cast wider than the narrowly defined parallels ("manumission laws," for instance) of other studies. Stated first in terms of the Covenant Code (Exod 20:22-23:33[19]) set of laws, the matter can be expressed as a desire to determine the constellation of factors (ideology, theology, social mechanics, etc.) through which the text reveals its system of social justice and its means of caring for people in need.

In the broadest sense, of course, one must take the measure of the Code as a whole in order to gain the sense of this system. However, isolating those texts dealing directly with the care of people in need, dealing with the alleviation of oppressive situations, carries with it the advantage of allowing us to look most closely at material analogous to the release-laws in Deuteronomy.

With this in mind, the texts bearing directly upon the issue we have posed for ourselves are Exod 21:2-6, 22:20, 22:21-23, 22:25, 22:26-27, 23:6, and 23:9. This list corresponds to that which H. W. Gilmer labels "Humanitarian Formulations Dealing with the Treatment of the Oppressed,"[20] which he defines as "those people who had neither strong

---

[19] These limits are those defined by the narrative transitions at 20:22 and 24:1. See n16 above and the bibliography cited there on the issue of subdivisions within the Code. See also S. Paul, *Studies in the Book of the Covenant*, *passim*, and M. Noth, *Exodus* (trans. J. Bowden; OTL; Philadelphia: Westminster, 1962), *loc. cit.*, for discussions of the divisions within this text. Obviously the focus of what follows will be on the legal corpus proper, but, given the scope of the enterprise and the discussion above, I see no reason to exclude pertinent elements of the "moral and sapiential exhortations and the cultic calendar," Exod 22:18-23:19 (*Studies in the Book of the Covenant*, 43), since it is precisely the level of moral awareness and social responsiveness with which we are concerned. Another way of expressing this is to say that we are dealing with the Covenant Code as a *text* indicative of certain theological and ideological attitudes, which attitudes we may then compare to their counterparts in the Deuteronomic corpus.

[20] *The If-You Form in Israelite Law*, 47.

family nor adequate finances for their security (the poor, the slave, the sojourner, the widow, and the orphan),"[21] a definition similar to that arrived at in the last chapter. To Gilmer's list we may add Exod 21:7-11, which, though casuistic in form and not hortatory in flavor, yet deals with an oppressed or dependent class (the female slave in concubinage).

In a similar vein are Exod 21:20-21 and 26-27. These are pieces of legislation which are part of the outworking of the law concerning injury inflicted upon another. Thus while they are in one sense not independent, still their subject is the application of the legal principle of restitution to the case of injury inflicted against the slave, and so they fit within our area of interest. We shall also add Exod 23:10-11 and 12, whose present intent at least is expressed in terms of care for the oppressed (the poor, the child of the female slave, the sojourner).

Our working text is thus

Exod 21:2-6	the manumission of the Hebrew slave
:7-11	treatment of the concubine
:20-21	death of the slave at the hands of the owner
:26-27	injury of the slave
22:20-22	prohibition against oppression of the sojourner (*gēr*), widow, or orphan (Eng. 21-23)
:24	prohibition of lending at interest to the poor (Eng. 25)
:25-26	restoration of the pledged garment (Eng. 26-27)
23:6	prohibition against perversion of justice toward the poor
:9	prohibition against oppression of the sojourner
:10-11	the fallow year
:12	the seventh day rest for beasts of burden, child of the slave, and alien.

Excursus on the Term "Hebrew Slave"

A preliminary exegetical comment is in order before evaluating the complex of laws as a whole. This has to do with the designation "Hebrew slave" (*ʿébed ʿibrî*) in the first law of our working text, Exod 21:2. The literature on the subject is extensive and the lines of discussion are well known.[22] N. Na'aman explicates the meaning of the appellative *ḫabiru*, which is related to O. T. *ʿibrî*, as uprooted immigrants who would live for a time as foreigners in another country, often banding together, and who

[21] *The If-You Form in Israelite Law*, 48.

[22] See most recently N. Na'aman, "*ḪABIRU* and Hebrews: the Transfer of a Social Term to the Literary Sphere," *JNES* 45 (1986), 271-288, which has a brief overview of the issue and extensive bibliography.

were eventually absorbed into their new environment.[23] In the Old Testament, Na'aman finds a close parallel in the figure of David fleeing from Saul. David gathers a band about him, and together they live as uprooted persons living on the margins of society.[24]

As the term "Hebrew (*ʿibrî*)" found its way into literary spheres in the O. T., its usage became more specific. While applying generically at this point to any member of the Israelite community, the term "Hebrew" refers to those members either in their status as aliens who have migrated to a foreign country (Joseph in Egypt, the Israelites staying in Egypt generally) or in their status as slaves.[25]

In the combination of these two references, the exegetical point should be made that the association with the Egyptian bondage means that the designation here of the slave as "Hebrew slave" is meant to evoke the experience of slavery in Egypt (cf. Exod 2:11, 13), as we have intimated already in chapter 1.

In the Covenant Code, this is spelled out in 23:9 where the motivation for the prohibition against oppressing the sojourner is that of the calling to mind of the Egyptian sojourn. Just as the sojourn in Egypt allows the ones addressed to locate within themselves knowledge of the "heart of the sojourner," so the designation "Hebrew slave" allows the purchaser of that slave to resonate with the enslaved Israelite. That is, one designated "Hebrew slave" in Exod 21:2 is not only to be thought of in this context as an Israelite who becomes a slave but as one who, because that one is a slave, is to be thought of as a Hebrew "just as we were Hebrews in Egypt."

But this point has more than critical consequences. It in fact brings us back to the point with which the present chapter opened, namely that in comparison with the Near Eastern material, the most striking feature of these sets of laws is the greater role given to matters of motivation, justification, and drawing out the theological consequences for not obeying (that is, the theological valuation given to these laws).

While it is the case that this type of material (the motive clause) is less prevalent in the Covenant Code than in the Deuteronomic or Holiness Codes,[26] nevertheless the presence of motive clauses in the

---

23 "*ḪABIRU* and Hebrews," 271-275, esp. 273.

24 "*ḪABIRU* and Hebrews," 280-281.

25 "*ḪABIRU* and Hebrews," 286.

26 B. Gemser establishes the percentages of paragraphs containing motive clauses as seventeen percent for the Covenant Code, sixty percent for the Deuteronomic Code and sixty-five percent for the Holiness Code ("The Importance of the Motive

Covenant Code and more particularly their distribution provides us with a provocative entry into the working text we have established.

The Motive Clause

Of the eleven passages which we isolated as our working text, five of them are equipped with motive clauses.[27] This is a concentration of motive clauses which exceeds that of the Covenant Code as a whole. One notices two motive clauses at 23:7 and 8 attached to the injunctions concerning the ensuring of equitable justice which, though not directly of the same subject matter as the verse isolated for our working text (v 6, dealing directly with justice toward the poor), is still of the same subject matter in a general sense and of the tight set of laws on the subject of equitable justice.

In fact, of the nine motive clauses Gemser found within the Covenant Code, only two have no relation to laws concerning the creation of social justice for those in special need. One is in the preliminary section to the Code proper warning against the use of hewn stones in altar building (20:25) and one is at 23:15 in the law of the feast of unleavened bread.

In addition to the motive clauses strictly defined, one must add as well the rationales attached to the laws of fallow year and sabbath (23:11 and 23:12).[28] Thus only two of the laws in our working text are set forth without any motivation attached: the law concerning manumission of the Hebrew slave and the law dealing with setting free the injured slave on account of that injury.

As B. Gemser notes,[29] this concentration of motive clauses providing rationale or exhortation for laws directed toward treatment of the dependent in the Covenant Code has in the Deuteronomic and Holiness Codes been expanded so that they are attached to legislation with other

---

Clause," 51-52). Using a more sophisticated statistical method, R. Sonsino (*Motive Clauses in Biblical Hebrew*) determines the percentage of motivated laws as sixteen percent for the Covenant Code (*Motive Clauses*, 88), fifty percent for the Deuteronomic Code (*Motive Clauses*, 93), and fifty-one percent for the Holiness Code (*Motive Clauses*, 91; see also the chart on 102 of Sonsino's book).

27 Exod 21:8, 21; 22:21, 27; 23:9.

28 While many scholars have emphasized the cultic aspect of these laws (see Noth, *Exodus*, 189; Weinfeld, *Deuteronomy and the Deuteronomic School*, 233n1; and Sonsino, *Motive Clauses*, 88), the addition of the motive clause providing a humanitarian rationale brings it within the sphere of our study, as was noted above (and in C. Wright, "What Happened Every Seven Years in Israel?" *EvQ* 56 [1984], 130-131; Lemche, "The Manumission of Slaves," 42; and L. Epzstein, *Social Justice in the Ancient Near East and the People of the Bible*, trans. J. Bower [London: SCM, 1986], 132).

29 "The Importance of the Motive Clause," 63.

subjects as well. While this can be taken as evidence of the greater antiquity of the Covenant Code,[30] more importantly for our study it certainly indicates a perception of these laws by the compiler of the Code as in some respect different from the others within the Code in a way in which the other two Codes do not so perceive them.

The content of these motive clauses reveals this as well. These can be grouped into four types:

1) economic rationale,
2) moral rationale,
3) theocentric rationale, and
4) historical rationale.

1) Economic Rationale

There is only one example of the first type, strictly put. This is the notice at 21:21 that in the case of the slave who does not die immediately upon receipt of the injurious blow, the subsequent death of that slave does not result in punishment of the assailant (who is the owner of the slave) "for the slave is his money." Here it is painfully clear that the Covenant Code, whatever its intention toward the ordering of society in a just manner, still regards the slave in the end as property. This is a commonplace observation, of course, but one which bears repeating and which is a point of connection with the other pieces of slavery legislation in our working text. Exod 21:2-6, 7-11, and 26-27, like 21:20-21, are dealing at base with economic matters, that is, the conditions under which property is to be given up.

The importance of repeating this commonplace is that it reminds us that the slave exists in a web of relationships, relationships which have economic dimensions, and so the slave is not simply a member of a social class with no consequent relationship with the rest of society. Stated another way, this is the same distinction as that made in the previous chapter between "weak" and "dependent." The slave is not weak in the sense of having, as an intrinsic aspect of his or her character or circumstances, a deficit which can be corrected upon application of sufficient will or ingenuity. Rather, the slave is dependent in the sense of being completely reliant upon the will of another or the collective intent of society toward him or her. With respect to the motive clause at 21:21, the

---

30 So that a progression can be seen from Covenant to Deuteronomic to Holiness Code based on the growing expansion of the use of motive clauses.

law is decidedly with the one who has control over the fate of the dependent.

2) Moral Rationale

The second type of motive clause is also an appeal to those who have some control over the dependent, but in this case with different results. Of the type we have labeled the "moral rationale" for the law to which the motive clause is attached, there are three examples, 21:8, 22:27, and 23:8.

To call this type of motive clause "moral" is in some sense misleading since there is no appeal made to a system of ethical reasoning of any complexity. Rather, the appeal to those addressed by the Code is simple and direct.

Exod 21:8 provides an example: here the female slave designated as concubine who is not pleasing to the one who bought her is made to be redeemed with no possibility of sale abroad, "since he has dealt faithlessly with her." The level of moral appeal is quite direct: displeasure is not sufficient grounds for placing the woman outside the bounds of the society of her kin. Thus in a manner analogous to the MAL A:48,[31] the dependent woman, though she is not able to choose her fate for herself, is yet given some measure of protection by this injunction, a protection which receives the sanction of direct moral appeal. Some provision is made to prevent the owner from taking unreasonable advantage of the dependent, and the collective intent which expressed itself as favorable to the owner in the previous example receives a degree of tempering.

Of a similar nature is the law prohibiting the taking of a bribe in a legal context, "for a bribe blinds the officials, and subverts the cause of those who are in the right." (23:8) As with the example cited above, the appeal is such that its force is taken as self-evident. The importance of clear-sighted officials,[32] often apparently honored in the breach (cf. for instance Am 5:12), is given particular emphasis by the addition of the self-evident appeal to reason. Its significance for our study lies in the implication that justice which can be bribed is justice for the rich. This explains the close textual link between this law and its heading-law concerning justice for the poor. At base they are addressing the same concern. The poor are in a position of special need with respect to the courts,

---

[31] This law was discussed in chapter 2 above, p. 67.

[32] The term is *piqḥîm*, literally "clear-sighted ones" (BDB, 824). Thus the inclusion of the qualifier "eyes" found in the LXX (*ophthalmous bleponton*) and other texts is redundant.

which are easily swayed by the blandishments of those in positions of social privilege.

This concern expressed for the poor in their dependent relationship with those who have power over them is evident in the final example of this type of motive clause, the one at 22:27 appended to the prohibition against keeping the poor neighbor's garment overnight "for that is his only covering; in what else shall he sleep?" In this case, the direct appeal to the moral sense of the community is reinforced in the following phrase by reminder of the compassion of God at the sound of a cry.[33]

We note too the reference to the neighbor (*rē[a]ᶜ*). While the use of "neighbor" in the Covenant Code is not obviously restricted to the fellow Israelite,[34] the specification here is to "[one of] my people, that is, [one of] the poor among you."

In other instances the neighbor is one person in opposition to the principal actor. Therefore since in many cases the Covenant Code uses "neighbor" as a neutral term, the use of "neighbor" in reference to the poor borrower must mean that the poor here is being *defined* as "neighbor" when from another perspective the borrower could be seen as something other than neighbor, as a group within society to whom the full weight and protection of the law need not apply; instead, the borrower is given the same status as the one attacked by another in a fit of rage (21:14) or the one from whom goods are stolen (22:7-8).

Thus the poor who must borrow does not become any less a "neighbor" with full status under the law for having done so; that one is no less a "neighbor" than are those referred to as *rē(a)ᶜ* elsewhere.[35]

3) Theocentric Rationale

There is but one example of a motive clause which can be defined as strictly theocentric in nature. This is the occurrence at 23:7 of direct divine address in reference to dispensation of justice. As with the direct moral appeal made in the following law, equitable justice is being

---

33 See the study by R. Boyce cited in chapter 1, p. 18 n24 on this dynamic.

34 The occurrences are Exod 21:14, 18, 35; 22:6, 7, 8, 9, 10, 13, and 25 (all MT). In many of these instances, the reference is clearly generic legal terminology: for instance, 21:14, "If persons dispute and one hits the other (lit., his neighbor). . . ."

35 We are of course aware that the change in terminology and specific concern (lending at interest, what happens to the pledged garment) can be taken as evidence of a seam in the editing at this point. Again, in determining the attitude of this text, the Covenant Code, toward the dependent, we are putting these questions to one side.

singled out as of such importance that it warrants an appeal to the character of the deity.

As with the direct moral appeal in the case of bribes in the law at v 8, discussed above, the close connection with the law at 23:6 concerning justice to the poor underscores the fact that it is the dependent, the disadvantaged, who are most likely to suffer miscarriages of justice. In this respect it is similar to the inclusion within the *mīšarum* edicts of specific measures to counter abuse of the indebted at the hands of the creditor and, as we have seen, the note in the release-laws (Dt 15:7-11) which takes great care to counter the reluctance of the lender in the face of the release of debts. In all three cases, law anticipates abuse of law.

4) Historical Rationale

Of those clauses which are formal motive clauses, the final group makes appeal to historical memory and internal identification as rationale for observance of the injunction to which it is attached. The two examples of this group are really one, the doublet prohibiting oppression of the sojourner "because you were sojourners in the land of Egypt" (22:21 and 23:9).[36] We have already mentioned in connection with the term "Hebrew slave" the connotative powers of this phrase. These connotations are rendered explicit by the insertion of an emotional note in the second occurrence of the prohibition, "you know the *népeš* of the sojourner." This is an example of what H. Richard Niebuhr calls *internal history*, "the story of what happened to us, the living memory of the community."[37] The distinction which Niebuhr makes is between history as the succession of events observable to an external spectator and history as lived and apprehended from within.[38] In the latter case, this is history which is owned by the community and so which has a power over it.

To say that the sojourner within the community has the same identity as members of the community themselves had at one point of their

---

[36] On the nature of the "sojourner" (*gēr*), see F. Spina, "Israelites as *gērîm*, 'Sojourners,' in Social and Historical Context," in *The Word of the Lord Shall Go Forth* (Fest. Freedman, ed. C. Meyers and M. O'Connor; Winona Lake, IN: Eisenbrauns, 1983), 321-335. Though Spina settles on the translation of *gēr* as "immigrant," I am continuing to use the archaic term "sojourner" because "immigrant" suggests to the modern reader a process of willful migration and assimilation into the society to which the immigrant moves, a process not present in the case of the Old Testament *gēr*.

[37] H. Richard Niebuhr, *The Meaning of Revelation* (New York: Macmillan, 1941), 66.

[38] *The Meaning of Revelation*, 44f.

own history (a point which has powerful connotations for the identity of the community) is to bring the sojourner within that community in an emotional sense even if the sojourner is still outside of it in a political sense.

The motive clause attached to the prohibition against oppressing the sojourner is thus a personal and emotional appeal of the most fundamental sort. It functions to include within the community's moral and emotional sphere one who could otherwise be seen as outside of it.

This tendency toward inclusion of those who stand in some danger of exclusion we have already seen with respect to the poor one forced to borrow who is defined as neighbor and to the female slave who is in danger of sale outside of the community because of the attitude of her owner. The tendency toward inclusion is continued in the case of the other example of the law of the sojourner at 22:21, which is followed by an injunction not to afflict the widow or the orphan. Again we are dealing with members of the community who have been cut loose from the normal moorings of support and so who stand in danger of being excluded or overlooked by the community. In this instance the intent of the law is underlined by the reiteration of the character of God as one who hears the cry of the afflicted[39] and who responds to that cry by overturning the governing social systems so that those who formerly enjoyed a full set of supports are made to become as those whom they had oppressed, namely widows and orphans (cf 22:24b).

The willingness to ground inclusion by appeal to the character of the deity as one who responds to the cry of the oppressed thus occupies a small portion of the Covenant Code legislation. Another example already cited is Exod 22:27b which deals with restoring the neighbor's garment taken in pledge. This one has recourse to the cry to God just as the widow and the orphan do. It is, moreover, implied in the "internal history" of the people which we have discussed already, since it is the response of God at the cry of those in Egypt which has led to their being in a position to care for the sojourner with whom they are akin in having been a stranger (22:21 and 23:9). The two are intimately bound up with one another—inclusion on the basis of internal history and an appeal to the character of the God who hears the cry of the oppressed. Both are implied in the characterization of the slave as *ʿibrî*, which as we have

39 As with the term "Hebrew slave" and the explicit reference to the sojourn in Egypt, this is a reference on the level of internal history of the situation of the community in Egyptian bondage (cf. Exod 2:23-25 and 3:7-8 for examples of this).

seen is a means of connecting that one to the experience of Egyptian servitude.

In sum, then, two main streams of intention are expressed in the laws which seek to care for those in special need. These are the tendency toward inclusion and the willingness to ground that tendency by appeal to the character of the deity. Of the two pieces of legislation with functional, though not formal, motive clauses (the fallow year and the sabbath), the first of these intentions is clearly expressed by the clause which functions as rationale or suasion toward compliance. The poor, the slave, the sojourner, even beasts of burden are identified as those whose inclusion is central to the intent of the law.

Of the two passages in our working text which are without motive clauses, the tendency toward inclusion must govern our reading of them. In the first instance, Exod 21:2-6, the policy of inclusion is directed to the one who buys, as we have noted already. We have also noted already the connotative dimension of the reference to the slave as "Hebrew slave," which places that slave within the community by appeal to its internal history. In addition to these observations, the implication of the general tendency toward inclusion with respect to the dependent one on whom the action of the owner falls is that neither of the choices available to the slave, freedom or permanent servitude, can issue in exclusion from the community—even the slave for life is to enjoy many of the benefits of life in the community (cf. 23:12) though this cannot be said without qualification (cf. 21:21). Indeed, the laws concerning slaves tend to err on the side of humane treatment and the granting of freedom (cf. 21:8). This is also expressed in the final passage of our working text, which grants freedom in the case of disfiguring injury (21:26-27).

The Holiness Code

In the case of both of the main streams present in legislation of the Covenant Code which display concern for those in positions of dependency, the Holiness Code has transformed them in significant ways. For the purposes of determining the specific manner in which this transformation has been worked in the arena of social justice and care for those in need, we will limit our observations to those texts which bear directly upon this issue, just as we did in the case of the Covenant Code. These texts are

Lev 19	:9-10	the law of gleanings
	:13a	prohibition against oppressing the neighbor
	:13b	the wages of the hired servant
	:14	prohibition against ill treatment of the sense-impaired
	:15	equity in dispensing justice
	:16	prohibition against slander
	:17-18	prohibition against hatred of neighbor
	:32	honor for the elderly
	:33-34	love of the sojourner
	:35-36	just weights
23	:22	the law of gleanings in the context of the festival of first-fruits
25	:1-7	concerning the sabbath for the land
	:8-17	concerning the jubilee year
	:25-34	cases dealing with redemption of patrimony
	:35-38	lending to the poor
	:39-46	treatment and manumission of the debt slave
	:47-55	provisions for Israelite sold to the sojourner

In the case of the Holiness Code, while one could mount an argument in favor of a statistical determination of the ratio of laws with and without motive clauses,[40] it is clear that the laws stand in a different relation to those motive clauses than they do in the Covenant Code. In the case of the laws found in Lev 19, for instance, while not every one of them stands in immediate relation to the phrase "I am YHWH your God," the refrain-like nature of that clause places it in a justificatory or sanctioning stance with regard to all the laws in which it is interspersed. It is more properly called a refrain than a motive clause, the former term being more descriptive of the liturgical nature of the Code. The repetition of the law of gleanings in Lev 23 is followed by the refrain as well.

The situation is different with the laws found in Lev 25. Here the refrain does not appear as often or with as strict a liturgical relation with the whole of the chapter.[41] Many of the laws have attached to them motive clauses of a more familiar sort.[42] Even among those laws which

---

[40] Gemser ventures the figure of sixty-five percent with motive clauses for the Holiness Code as a whole ("The Importance of the Motive Clause," 51. Sonsino puts the count at fifty-one percent (*Motive Clauses*, 91).

[41] It is found only at 25:17 after the initial explanation of the Jubilee and 25:38 with an expansion calling to mind the sojourn in Egypt (similar to the one found at 19:37 and at 19:34 in reverse order).

[42] E.g., 25:42 in reinforcement of the distinction between the indentured Israelite as "hired servant" and slaves bought from the nations round about: "for they are my servants, whom I brought forth out of the land of Egypt."

contain no formal motive clauses, however,[43] the setting forth of the law is so saturated with theological valuation and rational explanation that its observance can hardly be said to be motivation-free.

Thus the presence or absence of motive clauses in the case of these laws extracted from the Holiness Code does not provide us with the exegetical entry into the text which it afforded us in the case of the Covenant Code. Another point of entry needs to be found. We have established a characterization of the (earlier) Covenant Code's main theological and ideological bases for the care of the dependent. The next step to take, then, is to compare these bases which the Covenant Code exhibits to those bases which the Holiness Code makes use of when dealing with similar issues. This comparison will provide us with a point of entry into the Holiness Code and the way in which the Holiness Code deals with the dependent.

The Holiness Code and the Covenant Code

With respect to the Covenant Code, we found that the particulars of this system of care could be subsumed under the broad headings of a policy of inclusion or a tendency toward inclusion and the willingness to appeal to the character of God for confirmation of the justness of this position (Exod 22:27b: "And if he cries to me, I will hear, for I am compassionate").

The Appeal to the Character of God

To deal with these in reverse order, we have already noted the refrain-like quality of the oft-repeated "I am YHWH" or "I am YHWH your God." The attached clause has no direct bearing on the subject at hand except to sanction it in a general way. The law of gleanings, for instance, receives no additional moral urgency for its being brought into proximity with this refrain; certainly no more than other laws which have no direct implications for the care of the dependent (such as the prohibition against consulting a medium, 19:31). The character of the deity has become a sanction for law in general (in the form of the Holiness Code) rather than a particular feature of theological sanction for those laws protecting the dependent from abuse or exclusion.

43 E.g., the law of the sabbath for the land, 25:1-7.

The Tendency Toward Inclusion

The tendency toward inclusion has likewise undergone transformation. To be sure, many of the particulars of the Covenant Code legislation are still present: the inclusion of the sojourner, the concern for equity in dispensing justice, provisions for lending to the poor, though each in a different guise; still, the relationships which the actors have to one another has been brought into sharper focus in the Holiness Code. If the overarching tendency in the Covenant Code's provisions for the dependent can be said to be inclusion, then that of the Holiness Code is definition—definition of the actors involved, definition of the relationship which they have to one another, and definition of the action owed to each.

The Tendency Toward Definition

This tendency toward definition is clearly evident in the laws of manumission with which we began our discussion. As Japhet notes[44] and as we have noted ourselves, the key to understanding the paired laws concerning manumission is the distinction made between native slaves and those purchased from the nations round about. Here it is the identity of the actors in the view of the manumission law which receives definition.

To be sure, in certain instances the tendency toward definition or greater focus causes responsibility to be laid upon those whose relationship to the law was ambiguous in the Covenant Code,[45] in which case it is the relationship among the actors which is in view, since the relationship the actors have to the law of the community to a great degree defines their relationship to one another. The Holiness Code cannot be said to be less ethical or more exclusive for its insistence on greater definition of relationships. Still, this tendency has undeniable implications for the way in which social justice is practiced, as witnessed by the manumission laws just discussed.

---

44 See above, p. 77.

45 For instance, the status of the sojourner who is included in many of the laws of the Holiness Code as explicitly responsible for their observance (see for example the laws in Lev 17 concerning sacrifice and the avoidance of eating the blood of the slaughtered animal). The Covenant Code deals with the relationship which should obtain between the people of Israel and those who are resident foreigners in their midst. It does not spell out the other end of the equation, namely the relationship in which the sojourner is to stand with respect to native legal custom.

Another case in point is that of the fallow year, here transformed into the sabbath year of rest for the land which belongs to YHWH and so responds to YHWH's will for its fecundity (Lev 25:1-7, 20-22). One notices the definition of those who are to be provided for by the greater productivity of the land in the sixth year (25:6: "yourself, your male and female slave, your hired servant, and the sojourners dwelling with you"). This is a significant and telling departure from the law of the fallow year in Exod which mentions only "the poor" (Exod 22:11).

On the one hand, this reflects a different understanding of the point of the fallow year. For Exod, the fallow year serves to provide sustenance for the poor. For Lev, that sustenance the poor are to glean for themselves (Lev 19:9-10, 23:22). The fallow year, rather, is an assertion of the primacy of YHWH's ownership (25:23-24).[46]

On the other hand, however, the concern to spell out the identity of those to be fed by the plenty of the land is in line with the general tendency toward definition in the sense that it says that it is *this* collection of social classes which is to enjoy that plenty.

This is not to say that definition and the circumscribing of those who are covered by the law is unique to the Holiness Code, merely that there is a greater tendency in this direction here than in similar legislation in the Covenant Code. This phenomenon in both cases reflects the desire for exhaustiveness which we observed in the case of the Mesopotamian Law Codes.

It also discloses a society to whom greater definition among its various classes is of greater concern. The sojourner who resides within the community as opposed to the foreigner without, the one who is still included as a member of that community as opposed to the one who on account of some action is meted the punishment of exclusion from the community, the native debt slave who is granted freedom at the jubilee as opposed to the foreign slave who remains in service for perpetuity—these are but some of the oppositions set out in the Holiness Code.

In terms of the significance of the tendency toward definition for a system of social justice, one must repeat that this tendency does not in and of itself cause the system to be regarded as less ethical or moral. In many cases the opposite is true. It does create a trajectory toward limitation of responsibility, in this instance responsibility toward those outside

[46] It reminds one of the closing of private streets for a token day each year in order to maintain legal claim to the right of way; without this token assertion of right of way by briefly denying it to others, the right of way falls into the hands of the public.

the immediate orbit of the community and a greater constriction of one's responsibility toward those within the community.

Conclusion

The result of this analysis is that we are given two points (the Covenant Code and the Holiness Code) which, along with the preceding analysis of comparable Mesopotamian material, will provide necessary orientation for our location of the release-laws of Deuteronomy upon a spectrum of possible responses to the social problem of care for people in special need. The issues of the tendency toward inclusion, the character of God as sanction for the laws providing care for those in need, and a desire for definition, in addition to the specific content of the various laws dealing with the dependent, will surely provide helpful handles by which to grasp the Deuteronomic material.

The first of these issues is the tendency to include those who stand in some danger of exclusion. This issue finds resonance in the release-laws of Dt 15, and in much the same terms. In the Covenant Code, the tendency toward inclusion was found in such motive clauses as in the case of the injunction to give true justice to the sojourner, which has as its motivation "because you were sojourners in Egypt." This phrase, of course, finds its counterpart in the manumission law, though there the subject is the slave rather than the sojourner. Like the manumission law, the Covenant Code at this point is willing to call upon the central, most evocative experience of Israel's history to ground the claim of one who might, in the normal course of things, be excluded from the normal course of justice in Israel's society.

The second of these issues is the willingness to ground the push to inclusion by appeal to the character of the deity who hears the cry of the oppressed. While there was only one direct example of this willingness to so appeal to the character of God in the Covenant Code (i.e., Exod 23:7), such a tendency represents a clear connection with the release-laws. Those release-laws similarly allow the oppressed a court of appeal in God (Dt 15:9).

In the case of the third main issue, we observed a tendency to define the actors involved, the relationship which they have to one another, and the action owed to each. In this too, comparison can be made with the release-laws in Deuteronomy, which, though they define the relationships within the community encompassed by the laws in the widest possible terms, yet also define those relationships over against those relationships which obtain outside of the community. The tendency toward inclusion in Dt 15 is tempered by a desire to give priority and a special character to the kinds of relationships which exist within the community. In consequence, a contrast is set between those relationships within the community and similar relationships without.

IV

The Context of Deuteronomy 15

Summary and Introduction

In the first chapter we explored the rhetorical dimension of the text—that is, we attempted to make explicit and tangible the strategies used by the text to manipulate the response of its audience. In that part of our study, it became apparent that this text employs several very effective strategies designed to elicit the desired response in its audience, the response of assent and compliance.

Among those strategies was the skillful presentation of material at the several levels of abstraction on which we studied the structure of the text. With the structural strategies of evocation in our view, we discovered that the release-law setting forth the *šĕmiṭṭāh* law was given using a highly developed pattern of presentation calculated to lead the audience through its argument, thereby highlighting certain points crucial to the law, its implementation, and the attitude which it is intended to engender.

In the case of the manumission law, the pattern of presentation was less highly developed but nonetheless displayed a surprisingly similar structure when viewed at levels of abstraction higher than the method of argument employed in individual sections. This structure in both cases served to anticipate and foreclose grudging response to the law and in both cases grounded its persuasive system of presentation in a basic pattern of law and consequence which emphasized the blessing which would follow from observance. All of this was done in order not only to *influence* but to *overwhelm* those elements of society most capable of seeing that the intention of the release-laws could be put into practice.

This same audience is the target of the emotionally pregnant language chosen with the purpose of undergirding the evocative structure of the release-laws. When examining this aspect of the text, we divided our study into two parts, one dealing with the somatic imagery employed by the chapter and the other looking at its relational vocabulary, rather than looking at the two laws in sequence.

In the case of the somatic imagery, we noticed how the set of words "hand," "heart," and "eye" served primarily to delineate the attitudes present in or anticipated by the legislation. In the *šĕmiṭṭāh* law, the open hand and the heart which gave without seeing evil in so doing were contrasted with the closed fist, the hard heart, and the eyes which saw no good reason to give. Similarly, in the manumission law the eye of the master was not to see hardship in the freedom of the slave.

The relational vocabulary in consort with the other aspects of the text's rhetoric addresses the issue of the identity of the characters of this legislation. In particular, the relational terms used by Dt 15 define those characters in the widest possible terms: the ones to whom care is owed are to be thought of as "kin," "neighbor," "*ʿibrî*", while the ones who are to give care in being confronted by this sort of relational definition in the broadest, most evocative terms are defined as anyone willing to see kinship in the one who needs care.

In the second chapter, we compared the ideology of social justice revealed in the passage's rhetoric to analogous documents from the ancient Near East. After describing the nature of the material to be examined, we looked at that material with a particular question in mind, namely, "Is there something about the nature of poverty and debt in this society that created a group or class of people in special need of care to which these documents are a response?"

As countermeasures against the reality of a cycle of debt and enslavement, the *mīšarum* edicts, the *andurārum* acts, and certain portions of the Law Codes contain measures to break this cycle of debt and enslavement in which the dependents in this society found themselves. In the case of the Law Codes, some attempt was made to make this special concern for the dependent a regular feature of society, for example through laws which, like the manumission law in Deuteronomy, released the debt slave individually on a routine basis.

Another feature of this material which finds a parallel in the release-laws is that in many instances (in the *mīšarum* edicts, for example) abuse of law and attempts to undermine the intention of the law are anticipated. While the law or the edict sets forth its intention in clear terms, it also takes some pains to anticipate how this intention can be undermined in actual practice.

Finally, we noted the fundamental difference between these documents from the ancient Near East and the release-laws of Deuteronomy, namely that Deuteronomy insists on the singularity of YHWH and YHWH as the sole source of the law. On the other side of things, Deuteronomy places the burden of implementing the law on the people of YHWH. Its rhetoric addresses the need to see to the law's being carried out to the "you" (the audience). This stands in contrast to a Mesopotamian view of the matter which saw both the gods (chiefly Šamaš) and the king together attempting to make manifest the underlying order of reality in the social and legal practices of society.

In the third chapter, we extended the means of comparison to the biblical parallels to the release-laws. In doing so we did not restrict the discussion to those laws which are direct parallels, but broadened the scope of comparison to include all those laws which show how the other two collections of biblical laws, the Covenant Code and the Holiness Code, addressed the problems which arose from the existence of poverty and dependence in society.

In the case of the Covenant Code, an examination of the kinds of motive clauses attached to these laws, to a degree disproportionate to the rest of the Code, revealed two main tendencies which the Covenant Code has toward those in special need of care.

The first of these tendencies is the tendency to include those who stand in some danger of exclusion. We saw this in the case of the injunction to give true justice to the sojourner "because you were sojourners in Egypt." Like the manumission law in Dt 15, so too the Covenant Code at this point is willing to call upon the central, most evocative experience of Israel's history to ground the claim of one who might, in the normal course of things, be excluded from the normal course of justice in Israel's society.

The second of these tendencies is the willingness to ground the push to inclusion by appeal to the character of the deity who hears the cry of the oppressed. While there was only one direct example of this tendency in the Covenant Code (i.e., Exod 23:7), such a tendency represents a clear connection with the release-laws which similarly allow the oppressed a court of appeal in God (Dt 15:9).

In the case of the laws in the Holiness Code which give special attention to the dependent, the main tendency we observed was a tendency to define the actors involved, the relationship which they have to one another, and the action owed to each. In this too, comparison can be made with the release-laws in Deuteronomy, which though they define the relationships within the community encompassed by the laws in the widest possible terms, yet also define those relationships over against those relationships which obtain outside of the community.

Having come this far, we are now in a position to look beyond the release-laws themselves and see how they fit in the broader scheme of Deuteronomy's system of social justice. Does the sort of attention afforded the dependent in the release-laws conform to that found elsewhere in Deuteronomy? Do the comparisons and contrasts we made between Dt 15 and our two means of comparison (the analogous documents from the ancient Near East and the biblical parallels) work out in the rest of the book?

We will carry out this placing of the release-laws within the larger scheme of Deuteronomy's system of social justice in two stages.

First, we will examine the place which Dt 15 holds in the sequence of laws in the Deuteronomic Code. In this way, a sense of the relative importance of the passage can be gained. In this way, too, a glimpse can be gained of the structuring role played by issues of social justice in the laws of Deuteronomy.

Second, once this sense of relative importance is gained, we will examine the degree to which it has influence on or conformity to the other laws in Deuteronomy dealing with issues of social justice.

The end point of this analysis will be a description of the system of social justice, and the ideology that underlies it, which is found in the corpus of laws in Deuteronomy.

The Place of Deuteronomy 15 in the Structure of Deuteronomic Law

Excursus on the Views of the Sequence of Laws in Deuteronomy

The pattern which underlies the order of the laws in Deuteronomy has been seen in many different ways. For the purposes of description, these approaches can be divided into three rough groups, each group defined according to the way its members view the structure of the Deuteronomic legal corpus rather than the particular description each member gives of it—that is, the examples within each group may bear little resemblance to one another in every other way but agree on the level of the general assumptions or findings each has about the manner in which the Deuteronomic Code has been arranged (or not arranged). These groups can be presented along a line from those who see a relatively high degree of *disorder* in the arrangement of the laws to those who see a relatively high degree of *order* as perceived by another observer. Obviously, as with any paradigm, any one exemplar will not fit precisely into any one of these categories but nonetheless can be taken for the purposes of systematization to fit more comfortably into one group than the next.

The first of these three rough groups, then, is the one which holds that there is no overarching order to the Deuteronomic laws, or at least that what order there is exists in only small subsegments of the laws and that the transition from one subsegment to the next is lacking or is opaque.

In a sense, this group can claim that the Deuteronomic Code in this respect bears a great deal of resemblance to the Law Codes of the ancient Near East which take up one subject and treat it in as exhaustive a manner as possible, winding their way through that subject on the basis of catchwords and subject associations, sometimes wandering far afield in so doing. The next subject taken up may follow from this wandering, but then again, it may not.

One example among the commentators of this view of the arrangement, or more precisely, the lack of arrangement, of the sequence of laws in the Deuteronomic Code is A. D. H. Mayes. Mayes has an extensive treatment of the structure of the book in the "Introduction" to his Commentary[1] yet concentrates his attention on the framework which surrounds the legal corpus.

---

1 *Deuteronomy*, 29-55.

When he turns in his discussion to "the original Deuteronomy," however, it is clear that Mayes's view of the growth of the book is of a core of material which has been expanded and added to. While there can be discerned certain characteristics to the "original Deuteronomy,"[2] still, the laws as we have them in their present form bear the marks of several hands.

Mayes even goes so far as to say that at whatever stage of redaction one takes as a standpoint (and his reader presumes that he would include the final form of the book under this umbrella statement), the impression one gets is of "an unfinished mixture of material of varied origins which has not had a uniform history or a systematic and polished presentation."[3]

Mayes is of course not the only student of the book to have taken such a stance, and his own discussion is rife with allusions to others who work with a similar view of the creation and present internal logic of the Deuteronomic Code. Indeed it would seem that the burden of proof is on those who would see some consistent sequence within the laws which can explain the logic behind the moving, for instance, from the subject of the manumission of the Hebrew slave in 15:18 to the treatment of the firstlings in 15:19.

Examples can be multiplied of such seemingly illogical juxtapositions. Still, other students of the book assert just such a consistency, either of a general nature (the grouping together of laws of a particular subject) or of a particular nature (in which every law has its own place in a generated sequence based on observable principles of association). These two positions correspond to the second and third rough groups respectively.

The second rough group bears some resemblance to the first in that it admits within its system a certain amount of disorder in the arrangement of the laws. Given this internal disorder, however, those who fit to one degree or another within this rough group discern on a higher level of abstraction certain divisions within the Deuteronomic Code, generally on the basis of observed tag phrases or transitional formulae.

Among this second group is N. Lohfink. The most accessible source for Lohfink's thinking on this issue is a pair of articles on the subject of the distribution of official functions in the Deuteronomic Code.[4] Here

---

2 *Deuteronomy*, 48.

3 *Deuteronomy*, 49.

4 "Distribution of the Functions of Power," in *Great Themes from the Old Testament*, 55-75; and "The Deuteronomists and the Idea of Separation of Powers" (Unpublished

Lohfink outlines in some detail a compositional scheme which, like the first group we examined, calls upon the Law Codes of the ancient Near East to provide an analogy.

In Lohfink's view, the Law Codes (both those from Mesopotamia and the one found in Deuteronomy) proceed through their laws by moving from one law to the next under the influence of catchwords and subject associations. He cites the Deuteronomic laws concerning officials as an example of one subject intruding into the exposition of another in the sequence A, B, A2.[5]

More particularly, the laws concerning officials represent a logical sequence in themselves, inserted as a "constitution" by post-exilic deuteronomistic editors[6] into a series of laws dealing with the judicial system which breaks off at 17:13 and resumes at 19:1.[7]

In Lohfink's view as it can be derived from these two sources, then, the present form of the Deuteronomic Code is the end product of a rather complicated editorial history with the sequence of laws (in at least one instance) interrupted by self-contained blocks of laws. These self-contained blocks of laws are on subjects related to those upon which they intrude in the mind of an editor subsequent to one who earlier had strung together those other laws.

Such a view does admit of some organization within the Deuteronomic Code, at least in the case of certain identifiable blocks within the sequence. Still, such a view can only be placed toward a midpoint on the spectrum from randomness in the sequence of laws in Deuteronomy to a high degree of order.

Another example which should be placed somewhere in this middle area but which edges closer to a higher degree of overall order is that of S. D. McBride, Jr., who groups the laws in the Deuteronomic Code into coherent blocks.[8]

Any detailed order within the sequence of laws, McBride thinks, is "beyond the reach of critical analysis to demonstrate."[9] Still, McBride sees five large groupings within the legal corpus: 12:2-28 (the single sanctuary), 12:29-17:13 (corporate institutions, rites, and judicial procedures),

---

paper read at the Los Angeles International Congress of Learned Societies in the Field of Religion, 1972).

5 "Functions of Power," 65-66.

6 "Separation of Powers," esp. 13-16.

7 "Functions of Power," 65-66.

8 S. D. McBride, Jr., "Polity of the Covenant People: The Book of Deuteronomy," 239-243.

9 *Ibid.*, 239.

17:14-18:22 (the officials of the nation), 19:1-25:19 (social policies centered around the sanctity of life and the worth of the individual), and 26:1-15 (celebration of public theology).

There is even a coherent sequence winding through these divisions. This sequence runs from the single sanctuary which gives Israel a corporate identity, through delineation of structures and obligations binding that nation together, through a delimitation of social authority, through laws explicating social policy and individual responsibility, and finally full circle back to the institutional center of Israel.[10]

For our purposes, the important thing to note about this portrait is that the laws are grouped according to subject with only secondary regard given to sequence. That is, if the laws in group four were transposed with the laws from group three, say, this would cause little disturbance to the conception of the internal logic of the sequencing of the laws which lies behind this portrait. If the Deuteronomic Code had come to us in this order, its portrait might look different (that is, the alteration in sequence might cause us to say, for instance, that greater emphasis is being placed upon social policy as opposed to governing officials) but the *way* one goes about describing the structure would be the same. This portrait is descriptive (that is, it is based on an observation of what actually obtains in the text) to the extent that it observes large patterns or subject-groupings within the sequence of laws, but describing the sequence of laws this way implies that there is no inner compulsion to this sequence, no internal principles which necessitate that the sequence must fall out *this* way and no other. The authorial assumption is that a person or series of persons with a certain goal in mind (creating an ideal constitutional program for Israel) sat down with a given body of law which they modified according to their ideological preferences and grouped according to logical divisions. This is certainly a plausible conception, though not the only one.

The third rough group stands even further along the spectrum from disorder to order in the perceived arrangement of the laws of Deuteronomy. Those who can be placed to a greater or lesser degree within this group see not only a certain rough order in the divisions of the laws, but ordering principles in the presentation of those laws on even the smallest level.

Chief of more recent figures who can be placed among those in this third group are S. Kaufman and G. Braulik, both of whom revive the idea

[10] *Ibid.*, 242-243.

that the sequence of laws in the Deuteronomic Code follows the sequence of laws in the Decalogue, and in fact that there is a discernible logic to the sequence of laws which are present in each section, or "Word" (to echo the Decalogue's designation as the "Ten Words").[11] This logic is based on several principles, all derived from observation of the sequences within the words themselves, with the help of ordering principles discernible in the Mesopotamian Law Codes.

The gain which this conception gives the student of the Deuteronomic Code is that it gives that one the ability to see how any one law stands both within its own Word and within the sequence as a whole with a precision unavailable to those in the other two groups. In the case of the release-laws in Dt 15, the association of those laws with the Sabbath Commandment becomes more direct than the obvious connections (seven days—seven years; release from work—release from debt and servitude; the repetition of the phrase "remember that you were a slave in the land of Egypt"). This connection is in fact the very reason that these laws appear here and not elsewhere in the sequence—not even alongside laws with a similar intent. They fit here and nowhere else, not because of their happenstance position along a stream of catchwords and associations nor even because they occupy by dint of their subject matter a certain observable place in a constitutional program (a place which can be observed but not generated). Rather, it is the conceptual relation which these two laws hold to the Decalogue, the generative paradigm of the sequence, which says that they belong here.

It is in part the purpose of the analysis which follows to lend some credence to this last view of the degree of order in the Deuteronomic Code (the one with the highest degree of order) by tracing out the ties which bind the portion of the sequence of which the two release-laws are a part to the Sabbath Commandment. Should this prove convincing and helpful, then the perspective represented by Kaufman and Braulik as a whole is given greater weight.

The Release-Laws and the Sabbath Commandment

According to Kaufman and Braulik, the release-laws are part of a section which is tied to the Sabbath Commandment. This section extends

---

[11] S. Kaufman, "The Structure of Deuteronomic Law" and G. Braulik, "Die Abfolge der Gesetze in Dtn 12-26," in *Das Deuteronomium. Enstehung, Gestalt und Botschaft* (ed. N. Lohfink; BETL 68; Leuven: University Press, 1985).

from Dt 14:28, the tithe of the third year, to 16:17, which ends the enumerating of the festivals. This section appears at this point in the sequence of laws in Dueteronomy because on the broadest level it shares with the Sabbath Commandment the conceptual connection of a perpetually recurring cycle—the Sabbath cycle ending on the seventh day which is vested with sacred significance and the cycles of release and of the festivals which hallow their repeated functions.[12]

The implication of this in terms of a larger Deuteronomic conception of social justice (at least in terms of the social-political-economic relations defined by these two laws) is that the release-laws are deemed of such crucial, society-constituting nature that they are given the eternal, perpetual quality of the cycle, as opposed to the conceivably random, event-subject quality of the *mīšarum* and *andurārum* edicts of the ancient Near East. It is as if to say that *these* relationships *must* be given the same sort of regular pattern as the yearly festivals which define the people's ongoing, perpetual (and perpetuating) relationship with YHWH. G. Braulik appropriately calls this phenomenon a "holy rhythm" ("*heilige Rhythmus*").[13]

The connections between the Sabbath Commandment and this set of laws can be observed on a verbal level as well. We must note at the outset the repetition of the motive clause, "Remember that you were a slave in the land of Egypt." The verb *ʿābad* (which appears at 15:12 and 18) is another tie between the Sabbath Commandment and this block of laws.

This common verb is used in several different senses in Deuteronomy. Most commonly it is used to refer to serving other gods, either by Israel or the nations.[14] Once it is used ironically in this sense with reference to the enemies of Israel.[15] Other times, *ʿābad* is used to refer to the proper relationship of serving YHWH.[16] Once it is used in the agricultural sense of "working" one's vineyard (28:39). Once it occurs to describe what to do with those who inhabit the land and who capitulate to the entering Israelites—that is, to make them serve (20:11). Only in the Sabbath command and in our chapter does it refer to "working" in a general

---

12 "The Structure of Deuteronomic Law," 131-132.

13 "Die Abfolge der Gesetze in Dtn 12-26," 259, 263.

14 Dt 4:19, 28; 7:4, 16; 11:16; 12:2, 30; 13:7, 14; 17:3; 28:14, 36, 64; 29:17, 25; 30:17; and 31:20.

15 That is, if you don't "serve" YHWH you will "serve" your enemies—Dt 28:48.

16 Dt 6:13; 10:12, 20; 11:13; 13:5; and 28:47.

sense—the work which is done during the six days between Sabbaths (5:13) and the work rendered to the owner by the slave (15:12, 18).

This is a link forged along the central concerns of both the Sabbath Commandment (the cyclical cessation of labor) and the manumission law (the cyclical cessation of the labor of the slave by setting that one free). Indeed, the manumission law repeats this verb at either end of the law (vv 12 and 18), bracketing the legislation with an identically worded phrase.[17]

In its first occurrence, this phrase appears with the conjunction which places the action of the sentence in the future (that is, the verb is a "converted perfect").

In its second occurrence at the end of the manumission law, this phrase describes the labor which the slave *has done* at a rate beneficial to the owner.[18]

This phrase serving as an *inclusio* to the manumission law thus names the limit of the slave's service (the length of time which the slave *shall* serve), the nature of the slave's wages in economic (wage) terms (since that one has served at half wages), and the persons involved in the relationship (owner, slave).

Further, *ʿābad* serves as a link to the following law, the law of firstlings which are consecrated (15:19-23). These animals are not to be worked.[19]

S. Kaufman has noted the transitional position which 15:19-23 occupies.[20] Of the laws linked to the Sabbath command, the law of firstlings stands between those laws having to do with social welfare (the tithe of the third year [14:28-29] and the two release-laws of 15:1-18) and those laws having to do with the festivals (Passover [16:1-8], the Feast of Weeks [16:9-12], and the Feast of Booths [16:13-17]). With the latter, the law of firstlings shares the Passover themes of the firstborn (cf. Exod 13) and the specific types of livestock to be used in the observance of the Passover. With the former, the law of firstlings is linked by *ʿābad*.

---

17 15:12: *waʿăbādĕkā šēš šānîm.*
15:18: *ʿăbādĕkā šēš šānîm.*

18 The meaning of the phrase *mišneh śĕkar śākîr* has not been resolved convincingly. Even without knowing the semantics of the phrase exactly, the clear sense of the passage emphasizes the benefits to the owner of the slave's service.

19 The phrase is *lōʾ taʿăbōd bibkōr šôrekā.*

20 "The Structure of the Deuteronomic Law," 132.

To these connections must be added the ones mentioned in passing (seven days—seven years; cessation of labor—cessation of debt and servitude).

All of these connections with the Sabbath Commandment of the Decalogue on a conceptual and a verbal level bind the two together so that the concerns and sequential position of one must be seen in light of the concerns and sequential position of the other. Because of this, we must trace out the relative importance accorded to the Sabbath Commandment in its deuteronomic version as a way of gaining some perspective on the relative importance to be attached to the block of laws associated with it in the Deuteronomic Code. The chief source for this task is N. Lohfink.

Lohfink's observations concerning the shape of the Decalogue by the one who placed it in Dt 5 show that in this version, the opening commandments concerning exclusive worship are highlighted by their length and by their position at the head of the list.[21] But alongside this "Chief Stipulation," the Sabbath Commandment has been brought to the fore. This has been done in several ways.

First, the Sabbath Commandment has been bracketed by two verbs of command (*šmr* and *ʿśh*) which are closely linked in Deuteronomy and which place brackets around it in order to give it some sense of unity and separateness.[22]

Second, the commandment is structured in a chiastic fashion around certain key terms.[23]

Third, the Sabbath Commandment provides links at two points to either end of the Decalogue: Deuteronomy's version of this command-

---

21 N. Lohfink, "Zur Dekalogfassung von Dt 5," *BZ* 9 (1965), 26-27.

22 *Ibid.*, 21-22.

23 *Ibid.*, 22. Lohfink outlines the text this way:

5,12 Beobachte den Sabbattag
12 wie dir Jahwe, dem Gott, geboten hat
14 Jahwe, deinem Gott
14 und dein Sklave und deine Sklavin
14 damit (als Wendemarke des Textes)
14 dein Sklave und deine Sklavin
15 Jahwe, dein Gott
15 darum hat dir Jahwe, dein Gott, geboten
15 den Sabattag zu halten

That Lohfink must excise so much of the text in order to display this structure blunts the force of his analysis somewhat. That criticism aside, however, Lohfink's analysis does show the skill with which the Sabbath Commandment has been arranged, using language familiar to readers of Deuteronomy.

ment gives as a motive clause the reminder of slavery in Egypt, a clause which hearkens back to the historical prologue (the First Commandment in some traditions) of the Decalogue; and this version of the Sabbath Commandment adds the phrase "your ox and your ass," a phrase which anticipates the list of coveted things in the Tenth Commandment.[24]

Fourth, the Decalogue in Deuteronomy has been altered structurally by the stringing together of the last five commandments with conjunctions. This has the effect of structuring the commandments of the Decalogue into five blocks of unequal but regularly varying lengths:

Block 1: The Worship of YHWH—5:6-10 (long)
Block 2: The Name of YHWH—5:11 (short)
Block 3: The Sabbath—5:12-15 (long)
Block 4: The Elders—5:16 (short)
Block 5: The Ethical Prohibitions—5:17-21 (long).

Such a structure places the Sabbath Commandment at the center of the Decalogue and gives it a weight formerly reserved for the lengthy stipulations concerning allegiance to YHWH (Block 1).[25] The Sabbath is "not simply one on the list, but is the pivotal longer statement at the center."[26]

It would follow, then, that the particular ordinances associated with the Sabbath Commandment receive through this association an added weight as well. Lohfink thinks that this version of the Decalogue (which he calls the "Sabbath Decalogue"[27]), laden with characteristically deuteronomic vocabulary, comes to its position late and replaces a form of the Decalogue which stood there before,[28] one whose contents must have differed from the present one but which contained the same stipulations.

As Kaufman notes, however, and as our exploration of the manifold ties between the Sabbath Commandment and the block of laws contained in Dt 14:23-16:17 confirms, the sequence of laws in the Deuteronomic Code hearken back not just to the Decalogue, but to the Decalogue as it appears in Dt 5:6-21. Lohfink is certainly correct in pointing out that the

---

24 *Ibid.*, 23-24.
25 *Ibid.*, 26-27.
26 Miller, "The Human Sabbath," 84.
27 "Zur Dekalogfassung," 30.
28 *Ibid.*, 28-29.

Decalogue in Deuteronomy assumes an earlier pronouncement of its contents.[29]

Such a calling to mind of the Decalogue before Moses rehearses it in Deuteronomy need not be a reference to an earlier version of the Decalogue *in Deuteronomy,* now replaced. The phrase "as YHWH your God commanded you" (Dt 5:12, 16) can, for instance, be more readily explained as part of the literary setting of Deuteronomy, which here, where it has Moses re-presenting the Decalogue on the plains of Moab to the new generation, hearkens back to its original presentation by YHWH on Mount Horeb. It is part and parcel of the literary scheme of Deuteronomy, namely that Moses is recalling to the minds of the people of YHWH as they stand at the edge of the Promised Land that covenant which had already been consummated. It is a covenant which had included the Decalogue.

In any case, the ties between the block of laws of which Dt 15:1-18 is a part and the deuteronomic version of the Sabbath Commandment are clear. They place the release-laws of Dt 15 and the tithing law which precedes them at the center of Deuteronomy's concern for those in special need of care. They are programmatic of this concern in the same way in which Dt 12 (tied to the First Commandment) is programmatic of the worship of YHWH and Dt 16:18-18:22 (tied to the Fifth Commandment) is programmatic of the structuring of leadership in Israel.[30]

Even the laws concerning the firstling and the festivals are given under the aegis of this program. In each case, no opportunity is lost to reinforce the intention (akin to that which we observed in the previous chapter dealing with the release-laws alone) that these sacred functions are celebrations in which the *whole* community participates, including the servants of the household (cf. Dt 15:20 [the whole household]; 16:4 [the whole territory]; 16:11 and 14 [the dependents of the community]). In each case, rejoicing, remembrance, and rest from work are named as the content of the festival or the purpose of the sacrifice, with blessing as the result.

Altogether, the special tithe for those with no portion, the twin laws of release, the law of the firstlings, and the laws concerning the three festivals paint a beatific portrait of the community where everyone is cared for, where economic or physical enslavement can only be temporary, and where the whole community gathers to rejoice and to receive

---

29 Note Dt 5:12 and 16 which reinforce the Sabbath and Elder Commandments with the phrase "as YHWH your God commanded you." "Zur Dekalogfassung," 29.

30 On this threefold program in Deuteronomy, see Miller, "The Way of Torah," 22.

the blessing of YHWH. In this way the requirements, the intention, and the remembrances of the Sabbath Commandment are given specificity. The association of the Sabbath Commandment with these laws in turn imparts to them a centrality and an underlying commonality of intended relief and blessing.

We have mentioned the significance of the cyclical nature of each of the laws within this block and of the Sabbath Commandment. We might note, too, that this placing of these laws in the realm of the "holy rhythm" of the community means that at weekly, annual, triennial, and septennial points the linear progression of life in Israel is brought to a halt and a fresh start is made.[31] The repeated recollection of the experience of slavery in Egypt and of redemption from slavery in Egypt in both the Sabbath Commandment and in the block of laws associated with it emphasizes that this fresh start is akin to that original fresh start which God provided at the beginning of Israel's history as a nation.

The Release-Laws and the Deuteronomic Code of Laws

If these laws are at the center of Deuteronomy's concern for those in need of care, then they should stand in some relation to other laws which deal with this concern. This is not to suggest that the program established in Dt 15 and the block of laws in which it is located has a controlling relationship to these other laws, as does the order of the commandments of the Decalogue to the sequence of laws in Dt 12-26. It is to say that we expect to find these laws, though far from Dt 15 in the sequence, to be consistent with the release-laws in spirit and in intention.

In the previous chapter, we found that the release-laws by the structure and vocabulary of their presentation stressed several things:

First, they stressed the obligatory nature of the legislation. The two laws are explicitly addressed to those who have the capacity to effect change. Concerning these, the laws are careful to structure their argument so that the force of the law, its divine warrant, the positive and negative consequence which result from compliance or noncompliance, and the community-wide nature of the problem which the law addresses and of the consequence which proceeds from compliance are all unmistakable. The high concentration of emphatic verbal phrases (in particular, the unique concentration of infinitives) also underscores this point.

---

31 Miller, "The Human Sabbath," 94.

The obligatory nature of the release-laws is reinforced by the language of the passage, specifically by its relational terms which names as "kin," "neighbor," and "*ʿibrî*" the one on whose behalf the law is given and therefore to whom the action which the laws demand is owed. The law is thereby placed in the sphere of the personal, and the obligation to comply is also placed on that level. One is not merely to act in compliance to a "law" in the abstract, or even to divinely warranted command, but to do that which profoundly affects the quality of life which one's kin can enjoy.

Second, in addition to instilling a sense of obligation, the structure and vocabulary of the laws push that sense of obligation to its widest possible compass. The one to whom compliant behavior is owed, the scope of society which feels the effect of compliance, the emotional connections of internal history and relational connection—in all of these things, both of the release-laws refuse to draw the circle any more tightly than the whole of the people of YHWH. This broadening of compass is even more apparent when the drama of poverty is cast onto the stage of the divine where the poor find redress and whence comes the abundance which gives provision to the poor and the slave. This broadening of the area of impact to include the realm of the divine is, of course, not unique to Deuteronomy and finds parallels in the other legal systems we have examined. Yet it should be noted that the divine too is encompassed in the sphere of action of these two laws.

To these observations we have added several more concerning the place of these laws in Deuteronomy's program when the associations they hold with the Sabbath Commandment are brought into relief.

First, the structural and conceptual connections between the block of laws of which the two release-laws are a part and the Sabbath Commandment underscore the rhythmic, cyclical nature of the laws. This is a phenomenon we noted first in contrast to the punctiliar nature of release in the ancient Near East. There we noted that in the deuteronomic release-laws (as in the laws concerning the terms of debt-slavery in Hammurabi's Code) an attempt has been made to make release from the pattern of debt and slavery a regular occurrence as opposed to an extraordinary one. The associations with the Sabbath Commandment we noted give greater import to this regularity. The release-laws, like the festivals, are to be seen as the "holy rhythm" of the community; that is, as those regular occurrences by which the community's relationship with YHWH is given reality in time. The several implications of this quality of "holy rhythm" have already been mentioned.

Second, as with the rhetoric of the release-laws, so too with this Sabbath association, the clear intention of the legislation is that the whole community participate in the relief of one type addressed explicitly by the Sabbath Commandment (relief from labor) and of other types by the corresponding block laws in the Deuteronomic Code (relief from hunger [Dt 14:28-29], relief from debt and enslavement [15:1-18], and relief from exclusion from the public enjoyment of the divine blessing [15:19-16:17]).

Thus the emphases we have uncovered from both of these perspectives can for the sake of convenience be given the rubrics "obligation" and "inclusion."

The latter rubric, "inclusion," is self-evident from the comments on the rhetoric of the release-laws themselves and on their associations with the Sabbath Commandment just summarized.

The former rubric, "obligation," is evident with regard to the Sabbath Commandment associations when one considers the obligatory nature of "holy rhythm." The purpose of the "holy rhythm" of Israel as we have explicated it with respect to the release-laws is twofold. First, release from the pattern of debt and slavery is made regular as opposed to dependent on the goodwill of the ruler. Second, these regular occurrences are to make manifest the temporal reality of YHWH's rulership over Israel. Both of these purposes require a sense of obligation, the first in order to insure that willful (that is, arbitrary) application of amelioration is not exercised, and the second in order to ensure that YHWH's rulership is not compromised.

Having established these rubrics (and having access to the discussions which lie behind them), we are now equipped to see the extent to which this attitude toward the justness and well-being of the ideal society corresponds to the tendencies and attitudes which play themselves out in other legislation of a similar subject.

As with the examinations undertaken of the Covenant and Holiness Codes, this spinning out elsewhere in the Deuteronomic Code of a system of social justice exemplified and adumbrated in Dt 15 will have to be representative rather than exhaustive. The representative laws to be compared and contrasted with the two release-laws will be selected in part because of a related subject matter (loans, slavery) and in part because of a similar concern for the dependent or marginalized (e.g., the gleaning laws).

The bulk of these representative laws touching on a concern for social justice which can be placed beside the release-laws in large part come from the last part of the Deuteronomic Code, specifically that portion of Deuteronomy usually discussed under the heading of "Various Laws"—Dt 22-25.

In between these laws and Dt 15 and its surrounding block of Sabbath Commandment legislation stand sections dealing with the Fifth and Sixth Commandments (Authority and Homicide[32]). They are woven into those Words which, in the Decalogue as it is found in Deuteronomy, are connected by the conjunction. This is that block in the Decalogue which Lohfink calls "Ethical Prohibitions," a block which begins with the Sixth Commandment.

Since even in the Decalogue these prohibitions are apparently viewed as to some extent of a piece, it is little wonder, then, that a reader giving a cursory glance to the content of these laws within the Code itself which correspond to them in the sequence of Deuteronomic legislation would see little interconnection and so would title them "Various Laws."

The particular interconnecting logic of these laws and their relation to the Decalogue need not be our concern here.[33] Our concern, rather, is the extent to which their own content and manner of dealing with the particular social inequities which they address correspond or fail to correspond to that which we have unearthed thus far with respect to the release-laws of Dt 15.

Some of the laws to be selected as representative of the manner in which the Deuteronomic Code of laws deals with issues of social justice are self-evident. Dt 23:16f (Eng. 15f), dealing with the fugitive slave, and 23:20f (Eng. 19f), prohibiting lending with interest to a fellow Israelite, show an obvious connection in subject matter and content with the release-laws. So it is too in a slightly less direct way with such pieces of legislation as 24:6 (taking a millstone in pledge), 24:7 (stealing and enslaving an Israelite), 24:10-13 (the manner in which one takes and keeps a pledge), or 24:14f (paying the hired servant), all of which deal with issues central to the release-laws, namely, the interlocking issues of loans, debt, and slavery.

Dt 24:17f, protection of the sojourner, orphan, and widow from abuse, which when viewed as a piece of social legislation would appear to be somewhat truncated, can be viewed as a reprise in the midst of these "Various Laws" of the very internal history called upon to give

---

32 The titles are Kaufman's, "The Structure of Deuteronomic Law," 113.

33 The reader is referred for this information to the articles by Kaufman and Braulik already cited and, in addition, a more recent piece by Braulik which deals with the intervening sections of laws at some length, "Zur Abfolge der Gesetze in Deuteronomium 16,18-21,23. Weitere Beobachtungen," *Bib* 69 (1988), 63-92.

warrant and to evoke a sense of obligation to the content of the release-laws. These three are also the subject of the law on gleanings (24:19-21), which will accordingly be discussed along with 24:17f.

Several laws which could be discussed in terms of the ideology or system of social justice evident in Deuteronomy will not be taken up—principally the laws having to do with good treatment of animals considered either as the property of one's neighbor (22:1-4), as wildlife (22:6-7), or as one's own working stock (25:4). So it is too with the laws dealing with just punishment (25:1-3) and just measures (25:13-16).

To make this distinction is not to say that these laws have no bearing on attitudes toward social justice—indeed they do, particularly as they are expressed in Deuteronomy. It is rather to restrict our focus to a selection of laws the analysis of which will adequately serve to provide a portrait of the ideology of social justice which prevails in the Deuteronomic Code of laws. The laws which will be discussed have been selected for the closeness of their connection with the release-laws, and the foregoing analysis must therefore be taken as suggestive rather than exhaustive.

Specific Laws and the Release-Laws

To take these various laws in order from their being closely or less closely connected to the language and subject matter of the release-laws, we start with those laws having an immediate connection in content to the two release-laws, namely, the escaped slave, Dt 23:16f (Eng. 15f.) and loans on interest, 23:20f. (Eng. 19f). We shall deal with these in the order in which they are found in Deuteronomy rather than take them up in the order in which their subjects are dealt with by the release-laws.

The Escaped Slave (23:16f): Obligation

In terms of the first rubric, "obligation," the piece of legislation dealing with the escaped slave bears similarity to the rhetoric of the release-laws in two ways: its vocabulary and its willingness to call upon deep evocative phrases to hook the audience into assent and compliance.

The first of the connections to be noted between the law concerning the escaped slave and the release-laws is one of vocabulary, though perhaps we should say more particularly of subject. This law shares with the manumission law the subject "slave." These are the only two laws dealing with the slave in the Deuteronomic corpus. The slave is mentioned at other points, often as one who is to participate in the life of the community.[34] Otherwise, the word "slave (*ʿébed*)" is used of Israel's experience in Egypt in such phrases as "the house of bondage."[35]

Having noted the uniqueness of this connection, however, it must be said that these two laws stand in some tension with one another, one (15:12-18) which while it provides for the end of service in the case of individual slaves still does not exclude slavery as a part of the economy of Israelite society, and the other (23:16f [Eng 15f]) which would seem to undermine the authority of master over slave.

This tension is made even more apparent when one takes into account the evocative language of the text. As has been noted by some of the commentators, the phrase which established the fugitive slave's right to choose that one's own portion in the land employs the same language as that which Deuteronomy normally reserves for God's choosing of the divine dwelling-place, namely "in the place which he shall choose" (23:17).[36] With the single exception of the escaped slave, only of YHWH is it said that the dwelling-place will be "in the place which he shall choose." Thus, the slave who is fleeing that one's master is the only person of whom it is said that that one has the right to choose a dwelling-place. This text thus makes the slave "like YHWH" in this crucial sense, that the slave also has the right to choose a dwelling-place. That is, the text gives the escaped slave YHWH-like powers in this respect.

---

34 Cf. 12:12, 18; and 16:11, 14 within the legal corpus. One notices incidentally that these references are confined to the First and Fourth Commandments—the chief stipulation and the Sabbath Commandment which the Deuteronomic Decalogue highlights. This is not as startling as may first appear, for these are also the points at which the law concentrates on the public worship of the whole community and its participation in the sacred sharing of the blessings of the land. It does, however, in an indirect way lend credence to the notion that the Deuteronomic Code is patterned not only after the Decalogue, but the Decalogue as it is found in Dt 5.

35 These references occur primarily outside of the legal corpus (e.g., 5:6; 6:12; 7:8; and 8:14), but there are a couple instances within the Code, namely at 13:6 and 11 [Eng 5 and 10].

36 Mayes, 319-320, though Mayes does no more than note the similarity in language and label it deuteronomic. The same phrase occurs of YHWH's choosing a place to dwell among Israel principally in chapter 12 (vv 5, 11, 14, 18, 21, 26). Another heavy concentration occurs, significantly, in the Sabbath section (the citations are 14:23, 24, 25; 15:20; 15:2, 6, 7, 11, 15, and 16)—see note 34 above for a suggestion about the significance of this dual concentration on the view of the ordering of the sequence of laws in the Code. There are other scattered citations in the legal corpus: 17:8, 10; and 18:6. This list of citations comes from Weinfeld's catalogue of deuteronomic rhetoric in *Deuteronomy and the Deuteronomic School* 324, no. II.1.

Thus just as in the manumission law, so here in the other law in the Code which deals with the treatment of the slave, a phrase of deep evocative power is called upon to buttress the law and evoke compliance by playing on the passions of the audience, in the one case on the passions which flow from that audience's internal history (remembering the experience of slavery in Egypt) and in the other on those which flow from the central concern of Deuteronomy (to safeguard the exclusivity of Israel's relation to God, in this case by asserting the divine right to choose a dwelling-place—the concern for "centralization").

To do so, however, heightens the tension which already exists between these two laws, one of which seems to bow to the normalness of slavery in this society even while setting limits upon it, the other of which undermines the ability of the master to count on the central feature of slavery, namely that the slave is property. The idea of the slave as property is undermined by this law because a slave who can flee without fear of being returned cannot be considered property in the same way that other possessions can whose return in the case of theft can be demanded.

The commentators almost without fail resolve this tension by saying that the slave under discussion here is the foreign slave who escapes from another country into Israel.[37] This is an interpretation of long standing, going back as least as far as Ibn Ezra and Rashi.[38] The law can be cited even with this qualification as evidence of the greater humanity of Deuteronomy over against the Law Codes of the ancient Near East.[39] And most likely this interpretation is correct.

Having said that, however, we should not gloss over the tension between these laws too quickly. Both call upon the deepest wells of Israel's experience of God to evoke assent and compliance (the activities governed by the rubric "obligation"). Yet they have a basically contrary view of the justness of slavery, even if the above interpretation of the fugitive slave law is correct. This is so because nowhere in the manumission law of Dt 15 is the *idea* of slavery undermined—only its term is limited. When the slave (even a foreign slave) can escape with impunity, then the very *idea* of slavery is indeed undermined. This kind of protec-

37 Schneider, *Das fünfte Buch Mose*, 221; Rennes, *Le Deutéronome*, 106; Steuernagel, *Das Deuteronomium*, 137; Ridderbos, *Deuteronomy*, 231; Reider, *Deuteronomy*, 217; von Rad, *Deuteronomy*, 147; Driver, *Deuteronomy*, 264; and Mayes, *Deuteronomy*, 320.

38 As Reider (217) notes.

39 Cf. Hammurabi's Code, pars 15-20, which metes out the strictest punishment for those harboring fugitive slaves.

tion and freedom anywhere calls into question the legitimacy of slavery everywhere, even within Israel.

And in fact the law concerning the escaped slave underlines this tension even more by relating the slave to YHWH by means of the granting to the slave a YHWH-like power to choose a dwelling-place, one which seems good to him (23:17).

Thus when Deuteronomy turns to issues of social justice, the result is not always a single, consistent perspective. Deuteronomy at these two points comes up with contradictory messages about slavery, regardless of the qualifications one places on the two laws themselves. There is tension here at a deeper level than the content of the two laws, a tension that cannot be undone.

It is a tension which is given the imprimatur of the most basic, most evocative phrasing which Deuteronomy has at its command. One can even say that in this case the deuteronomic phrasing inevitably leads Deuteronomy to this contradiction, since even in the manumission law to call upon the remembrance of slavery in Egypt (and redemption by YHWH) in order to underscore the justness of release is to call into question the justness of slavery. This contradiction is only brought out into the open by the law concerning the escaped slave, which again calls upon a "typical" deuteronomic phrase (though in this case in a highly atypical manner) to evoke assent.

Thus the language which Deuteronomy employs to address a central issue of social justice in this society in the case of the manumission law undercuts the very attitude which the text has toward that issue (slavery). The text "deconstructs" itself when its language is given full play. It does so especially when that language forces one not to relieve the tension between the manumission-law text and this text (i.e. 24:16f.) dealing with the escaped slave but rather to follow the tension between them into a conflict of values which can then be seen as having existed all along in the manumission law itself.

This set of observations leaves open the possibility of talking about "trajectories" here, "trajectories" in the sense of a thrust established by the manumission-law in comparison to earlier texts which allows subsequent interpreters of the law to build a case for a broader condemnation of slavery. What we have seen is that such a condemnation is present already, submerged in the language of the text, in the emotionally pregnant language with which it chooses to address this issue, and brought to the surface by other texts on the same issue. This submerged condemnation then forms a trajectory which forces the audience to pose justice questions which even the text is not willing to pose.

The Escaped Slave (23:16f): Inclusion

It becomes a relatively simple matter at this point to discuss this law in terms of the second of our two rubrics, namely, "inclusion." Inclusion in this case is the very point of the law, and again a contradiction opens up when this law is compared to other texts in Deuteronomy dealing with issues of social justice.

If the slave being spoken of here, the slave who escapes and who is given the right that only YHWH has otherwise (to choose a place), is indeed a fugitive from a foreign country, then the distinction made in the *šĕmiṭṭāh* law between the foreigner from whom one can demand repayment and the fellow Israelite to whom release is owed breaks down at least in terms of this one obligation.

Nor can this breaking down of the distinction between fellow Israelite and foreigner be said to be because of the fact that this one is a slave, since the manumission law implies this distinction when it frames the obligation to release in terms of the slave who is a Hebrew, presumably with ownership of slaves gained from, say, foreign conquest not being restricted to six years (as in the laws of conquest, particularly 20:10f).

Yet it is this very distinction (kin and foreign) which is at the heart of the law concerning loans on interest (23:20f. [Eng. 19f.]), the next law to fall in order in our discussion. Rather than close off our discussion of the escaped slave under the rubric of "inclusion," we will continue to explore the contradiction which it uncovers as we pick up the law concerning loans on interest. Therefore, the rubric "inclusion" will be the first we will take up with respect to this law.

Loans on Interest (23:20f): Inclusion

To a great extent, the law dealing with loans on interest (23:20f [Eng. 19f]) parallels the *šĕmiṭṭāh*-year law, particularly with regard to those features which fall under the rubric "inclusion." Both make a contrast between the economic behavior owed to the kin and that owed to the foreigner. Both employ the same terms to make that contrast, namely *ʾāḥ* and *nokrî*.

It is true that certain aspects of the two laws do not correspond, in particular the language they use to speak of the enterprise of loans and lending. None of this language—*nāgaś* (to exact), the denominative verb

ʿābaṭ (to give a pledge), and *nešek* (loan) along with its denominative verb *nāšak* (to make one pay interest)—is particularly widespread in the Old Testament.

Indeed, *ʿābaṭ* and the related noun *ʿăbôṭ* are found only in Dt 15 and in Dt 24:10-13 (to be discussed below).[40]

Similarly, the use of *nešek* and its verbal cognate is restricted to Dt 23:20f. (Eng 19f.) and parallel legal texts in Exod and Lev.[41] The only exceptions to this statement are interesting and provocative. The noun *nešek* occurs in addition to these legal texts in three discussions about the contrast between the just person and the unjust person—Ps 15:5, Prov 28:8, and Ezek 18:8 and 13. The connection between this text and these others which discuss just and unjust persons shows us that more is at stake, when the subject is lending at interest to one's kin, than simply economic gain at the expense of another—indeed, the Psalms passage places this activity in direct parallel with the taking of a bribe.

So it is too with *nāgaś*. The immediate meaning of the verb is "to press, drive, oppress, exact."[42] It is used relatively infrequently, and a closer examination of its occurrences reveals that the common thread running through all of them is the relationship between tyrant and tyrannized. In the G stem *nāgaś* is used to describe the nature of the tyrant: the driver of livestock (Job 39:7), the overseer of slaves or prisoners (as a substantive, Job 3:18; Exod 3:7; 5:6, 10, 13, 14; as a verb, Isa 58:3), the tyrannical or wayward ruler, whether native or foreign (Isa 3:9, 9:3, 14:2, 4; Zech 9:8; 2 Kgs 23:35), the one who demands repayment of a loan or payment of tribute (2 Kgs 23:35 again; Dt 15:2, 3; Dan 11:20). In the N stem it is used to describe the state of being tyrannized by another (Isa 3:5, 53:7; I Sam 13:6 and 14:24[43]).

The only exceptions to this use of the verb to paint the picture of the way the tyrant oppresses the tyrannized are Isa 60:17 and Zech 10:4, both texts having to do with the intervention of YHWH to overturn and transform the normal order of things and so texts which do not alter the general picture of the kind of relationship which this verb describes.

---

40 The only other occurrence (Joel 2:7) is disputed, and alternatives have been proposed by translators. See BDB, 716.

41 There is certainly evidence of lines of influence in this. Determining just how this influence runs is not the concern of the present discussion.

42 BDB, 620.

43 Though this last is disputed in the translations and among the lexicographers. See the apparatus *loc.cit.* in BHS and BDB, 620.

Thus in the case of both of these laws, the law concerning lending at interest in Dt 24 and the *šĕmiṭṭāh* law in Dt 15, more is at stake than a simple business transaction. What sorts of people will make up the nation and what sorts of relationships will obtain there? Will the people of Israel show themselves to be just or unjust as they deal commercially with one another (just as they may show themselves to be just or unjust as they deal with one another in the court, bribing or not bribing)? Will they act toward one another as tyrants or not? *These* are the questions which underlie these two laws, and not simply the question of what defines usury.

It is in this light that we should see the distinction between kin and foreigner. These two laws are addressing issues of the gravest consequence for the justness and unjustness of the members of the community and the quality of relationship which will predominate within that community. With the nature of the community of Israel under the rule of YHWH at the fore of Deuteronomy's constitutional system, it is of less concern that the relationships which exist between that community and those which surround it have the same quality as those which exist within the community itself.

Having given this nuance to the distinctions being made in these two laws between fellow citizen and foreigner, the tension with which we entered this discussion between the *šĕmiṭṭāh* law and loans on interest, on the one hand, and the escaped slave law, on the other hand, remains, since the escaped slave law, far from excluding the foreign slave, gives the foreign slave pride of place. This is a tension, a contradiction, which cannot be resolved. In this respect, the law concerning the escaped slave is unique in its inclusiveness. There is no latent or submerged universalism in the two laws concerning loans. And other texts are even harsher in their depiction of the treatment of the non-Israelite (e.g., ch. 20), as has long been noted.

If there is a capacity for these laws concerning loans to be extended beyond the realm of relations within the nation, it must be said to be nascent rather than submerged. What is meant by this distinction is that the capacity for extension beyond the borders of the nation is not something that resides in the phrasing or vocabulary of the text itself (as was the case with the manumission law and its play on the evocative phrases of Israel's internal history), but rather is something which the language used by the laws on loans allows one with a different frame of reference to take advantage of. The seeds are there, but in these texts themselves, those seeds do not find fertile soil. One must come from outside, from a different frame of reference, a more fertile ground, in order to effect this growth. "Brother" and "neighbor" in this more fertile soil can be said to cover relationships and the attitude which should hold within the circle of those relationships outside of as well as within the nation itself.[44]

For the purposes of determining and giving nuance to the ideology of social justice which holds in the laws of Deuteronomy, the tension which exists between the law of the escaped slave and these laws concerning loans must be allowed to stand without a final resolution other than this pointing to a way in which resolution can be found outside of the text itself. Inclusion as a principle of social justice must be said to be a limited principle, used in fact to exclude as well as include. The principle of inclusion operates within the nation and serves to define the relationships which should be found there as just and as non-tyrannical. In establishing this principle, however, there is built within the system a certain amount of over-againstness. That is, within Israel, *these* kinds of relationships should be found as over against those which are found outside of Israel or between Israel and its neighbors.

And yet the law of the escaped slave cannot be dismissed either, folded within this general principle. It sticks out. Stated in terms of the internal history which the other Deuteronomic law dealing with slaves draws upon, it may be suggested that the experience, the remembrance, of having been slaves once in Egypt is so strong that those from without the nation who share with its citizens the experience of slavery are allowed to slip through the limited principle of inclusion-within.

This suggestion is given more credence when one notices that the verb used to describe the flight of slave from master (*nāṣal,* here in the N) is the same verb which is used to speak of deliverance from Egypt (in the H, e.g., in prospect, Exod 3:8, and in retrospect, Exod 18:8) as well as deliverance in a more general sense.

We will have the opportunity to reflect on this tension further when we discuss the law dealing with the treatment of the dependents (that is, the sojourner, the orphan and the widow in 24:17f) which invokes this same internal history to evoke assent and compliance. For the present, we move on to discuss the law concerning loans on interest under the rubric of "obligation."

---

44 What I have in mind here is of course the transformation of the term "neighbor" from "one-to-whom-obligation-is-owed" to "one-who-acts-as-neighbor" in the parable of the Good Samaritan (Luke 10:25-37).

Loans on Interest (23:20f): Obligation

Like the two release-laws, the law concerning loans on interest follows the sequence "law-consequence." In this case, the consequence parallels that of 15:10 and 18: "that YHWH your God may bless you in all the enterprise of your hand." There are some slight differences among them, chiefly the phrase used to describe the object of YHWH's blessing—*mišlaḥ yādekā* in 23:21 (Eng 23:20), *maʿăśekā* and *mišlaḥ yādekā* in 15:10, and the relative clause *ʾăšer taʿăśeh* in 15:18—but in essence the phrase is the same.

The startling thing to note is that this is the only such motive clause in the group of the laws which we are dealing with.[45] There is some uniqueness here. The uniqueness works in the opposite direction as well: the phrase "that YHWH your God may bless you in all the enterprise of your hand" occurs in the laws only here and in the section which is associated with the Sabbath Commandment (that is, 14:28-16:17).[46]

In other words, only one blessing motive clause is found in the group of laws concerning social justice which we are examining. This motive clause is "that YHWH your God may bless you in all the enterprise of your hand" (and its variants). This one motive clause is found only here and in the laws associated with the Sabbath Commandment. It is as if the compiler of these laws, in wanting to draw a connection between these two groups of laws, chose to do so in part by employing this motive clause in only these two places, and only this one in the laws in the later portion of the Deuteronomic Code which deal with similar issues of social justice. The subject connection between the two release-laws and the law concerning loans on interest is thus reinforced on a rhetorical level by the phrasing of the positive consequence of obedience.

This observation might seem to be stretching a point somewhat, given the multitude of interchangeable phrases which Deuteronomy employs to make this point. A closer look at these phrases, however, reveals that they actually occur fairly infrequently in the laws themselves, and that the occurrences are clustered in two places: ch 12, which is associated with the "Chief Stipulation" of exclusive worship, and the Sabbath section.[47]

---

45 This phrase occurs at 24:19 (in the gleaning law) in addition to 23:21.

46 See the lists on "Retribution and Material Motivation" in *Deuteronomy and the Deuteronomic School*, 345-346. The particular citations in the Sabbath block of laws are 14:29, 15:10, 18, and 16:15.

47 The citations are

"in order that YHWH may bless you (and co.)": 12:7, 15:6,14, and 16:10;

A general pattern thus appears where the blessing of God upon compliance stated in these terms is restricted to the two laws which the Decalogue as it is found in Dt 5 takes care to highlight. That such a phrase appears here, where the law is dealing with a closely related matter further, substantiates the position that the Deuteronomic Code contains an ideology of social justice, since where the Code returns after some chapters' absence from social justice issues, it also picks up again the blessing theme expressed in these terms.

That the exceptions to this pattern found in the intervening chapters (honest judges [16:20], the humble king [17:20], cities of refuge [19:13], and leaving the nesting bird [22:7, with two different such clauses]) can be said to occur in laws with some bearing on issues of social justice or bearing some resemblance to them in attitude also strengthens this position.

What, then, about the pairing of the Sabbath block of laws and these other laws dealing with issues of some import for a system of social justice and the laws dealing with the "Chief Stipulation" of exclusive worship? In fact, this pairing of the Sabbath block of laws and the laws

---

"to bless the enterprise of": 14:29, 15:10,18, and 16:15;
"so that it may be well with you": 12:25,28;
"to rejoice before YHWH": 12:12,18, 16:11; and
"happy in all the undertakings": 12:7,18.

Several of the exceptions occur at transitional points in relation to these two sections or in material which is related to them in some way.

"In order that YHWH may bless you" occurs in 14:24 which deals with the tithe of the land, a text bordering on the third-year tithe for the poor which begins the Sabbath section. It also occurs in 26:15, the blessing which is to be said over the tithe of the third year.

"Bless the enterprise of," of course, occurs in the laws presently in view, 23:21 and 24:19.

"To prolong (one's) days" appears in the law concerning just weights and measures, 25:15. This occurrence can be said to be an exception to the pattern being suggested here, since while this law deals with the same ideological range of issues, it lacks the directness in connection apparent in either the law concerning loans on interest or even the law on gleanings.

The other five exceptions to this general pattern within the laws are "to prolong days," which appears in connection with the law of the king (17:20) and the law concerning treatment of the nesting bird (22:7). The law concerning the nesting bird also contains the phrase "so that it may be well with you" (22:7). A similar phrase occurs at 19:13 in the law about the cities of refuge. Finally, "to live (prosper)" occurs in the law dealing with appointment of honest judges (16:20).

These citations are derived from Weinfeld's tables in *Deuteronomy and the Deuteronomic School*, 345-346.

connected to the "Chief Stipulation" brings us back to the characterization we had made earlier about these texts occupying a pivotal position in Deuteronomy's constitutional scheme. Not only are they related in their several ways to their respective Decalogue commands, but they are also related to each other by this rhetorical pattern. Credence is thus given to the suspicion that at least these two areas of concern are fundamental to the Deuteronomic Code: the worship of God (ch 12), and the treatment of the dependent (ch 15).[48] Our thesis that the release-laws are central in exhibiting special concern for the dependent has thus been given surprising confirmation by stepping outside of them and noting how unusual it is for a phrase to appear elsewhere which they bear so easily.

In terms of an analysis of the law concerning loans on interest under the rubric "obligation," moreover, this unusual employment of a consequence-phrase which is more at home elsewhere only heightens the persuasiveness of the sequence "law-consequence" where that (positive) consequence is given the language normally restricted to those areas of fundamental concern dealt with at length elsewhere. The law concerning loans on interest, while it uses a different vocabulary to talk about this economic transaction, is closely bound to the *šĕmiṭṭāh* law both by its common subject (loans) and a common benefit of obedience.

Kidnapping, Pledges, and the Payment of Wages (24:7, 24:6 and 10-13, and 24:14f): Obligation

We will deal first with the rubric "obligation" in the case of the four laws (that is, kidnapping, 24:7; pledges, 24:6 and 10-13; and payment of wages, 24:14f) which by dint of their subject-matter have a more direct connection to the two release-laws than do the ones to follow.

Under the rubric "obligation," we notice first of all that as with the two release-laws, so too here the flow of obligation is clear. The laws are all four addressed to the one who has the power to effect justice in the community and serve to protect those who are dependent and so in some fundamental way in danger of being preyed upon. This is a truism that must be given some nuance.

---

48 P. Miller, Jr., suggests a third, as we have mentioned: the system and character of primary institutions and offices that govern the people ("The Way of Torah," 22). That two of the five exceptions to the overall rhetorical pattern we have been discussing lie within those laws having to do with this area of concern (and in the related Fifth Commandment) is certainly suggestive.

In the case of the one who is kidnapped into slavery (24:7), which is associated with the Eighth Commandment,[49] the obligation of the community to safeguard its members from forced enslavement is enforced by capital punishment.

Further, the motivation given for doing so, to "purge the evil from your midst," is a justification used to identify perversions of the social order: perversion of the sacral order by enticing to serve other gods (13:6, 17:7), perversion of the judicial order through judgment not carried out or through malicious witness (17:12, 19:13), perversion of the blood purity of the community by the spilling of innocent blood (19:13, 21:9), and perversion of the order of the household by insolent children, marriage under false pretenses, or adultery (21:21, 22:21, 22:22). The kidnapping of a fellow citizen in order to force that one into slavery is thus to be seen as a perversion of the social order on a similar level.

Order in society, whether one agrees or disagrees with the importance and shape of the aspect of the social order thus circumscribed, serves to provide security. To so motivate the law against kidnapping and forced enslavement is therefore to tag it as a prohibition designed to provide security, or to state the matter negatively, to enable people to live without constant fear of the violent disruption of their lives by abduction.

It is somewhat different with the two laws concerning pledges (prohibition of taking the millstone as pledge, 24:6, and the taking of pledges in general, 24:10-13). Here obligation is affixed to the audience by direct argument ("for that one has its life in the pledge" [24:6]; "that he may sleep in his cloak" [24:13]) and by appeal to the character of the deity (who grants the righteousness of obedient action [24:13]), methods which we are familiar with both in the release-laws and elsewhere in the biblical laws.

Also like the release-laws is the infusion of drama into the law by telling what happens when the law is obeyed or not obeyed.

In both the *šĕmiṭṭāh* law and the general law concerning pledges, moreover, the audience is reminded that the one whom the law intends to protect ultimately has the power to declare weal or woe on society by crying out to God (15:9) or by blessing the one who returns the pledge at

49 As are all the laws in the group which deal with the "unlawful taking or withholding of property rightfully belonging to another"—23:20-24:7 ("The Structure of the Deuteronomic Law," 139-140; see also "Die Abfolge der Gesetze," 260 where Braulik sees only 24:6ff as belonging undisputedly to this Commandment, with the others being transition from the Seventh Commandment).

nightfall (24:13). Again, the purpose of this dramatic reminder is not to inform the poor what course of action they may take should they be abused (presumably because they know it already), but to remind those who have the power to do justly toward them that the poor in fact have recourse to that power to bless or to cry out.

Further, like the case of kidnapping just discussed, there is an implicit sacral dimension to the law prohibiting the taking of a millstone in pledge. This dimension becomes explicit upon noticing the parallel to the law at 12:20-28 concerning the slaughtering of animals away from the sanctuary.

In the law about the millstone, part of the motivation not to take the millstone in pledge is because it would be "taking a life in pledge" (24:6). In the law about the slaughtering of animals away from the sanctuary, the legislation prohibits the eating of the blood of the slaughtered animal along with its flesh, "for the blood is the life" (12:23). It is as if at 24:6, we are told that the millstone is lifeblood to the borrower, as indeed it is in the case of the poor who must grind his or her own grain for daily bread.

These same two elements, direct argument ("for that one is poor and to it [that is, the wages] that one has set that one's heart" [24:15a]) and appeal to the character of the deity by means of a dramatic explication of the law (24:15b) are found in the law concerning the taking of pledges and need only be noted briefly. The second of these strategies serves as a link to the *šĕmiṭṭāh*-law with which it is related by subject matter, as it employs the same dramatic language of crying to God and disobedience reckoned as sin (*ḥēṭʾ*). Again, the one who is tempted to disobey is reminded that the oppressed find a ready ear in God who hears their cry.

Kidnapping, Pledges, and the Payment of Wages (24:7, 24:6 and 10-13, and 24:14f): Inclusion

In like manner, these four laws employ strategies similar to the release-laws to push the circle of those to whom obligation is due to the widest possible compass. While the law concerning the millstone as collateral simply uses the impersonal legal construction (in this case, *lōʾ yaḥăbōl*—24:6), the others draw upon the language of relationship familiar to the audience of Deuteronomy, "kin" (24:7, 14) and "neighbor" (24:10).

In addition, and in this sense with some similarity to the law of the escaped slave, the non-Israelite (here, the sojourner) is also explicitly covered by the law concerning prompt payment of wages to the working poor (24:14). Again the limited principle of inclusion-within is stretched at points to ensure that the outsider who resides within Israel (the slave who escapes, the sojourner who has been forced to leave another country and seek a livelihood in Israel[50]) enjoys a measure of protection from oppression and economic abuse. To bring up the subject of the sojourner, however, throws us into the next law to be taken up, the law which prohibits the perversion of justice due to the sojourner as well as to the orphan and widow (24:17f).

Sojourner, Orphan and Widow (24:17f): Inclusion

The status of these three groups of people has been discussed at some length in chapter 3 of this study. They are the dependents in Israelite society, without the social safety-net normally provided by kin or fellow citizen. Both the Covenant Code (in which we find a strong parallel to the law at 24:17f. at Exod 22:21-24) and the Deuteronomic Code make some provision for their protection from oppression and abuse, though the Holiness Code does not, which is in keeping with our characterization of its preoccupation in such matters with "definition" over against "inclusion."

When one looks for this triad of dependents in the Covenant Code and the Deuteronomic Code, however, it quickly becomes apparent that they are of greater concern to the latter than the former. The law cited at Exod 22:21-24 is the only place where these three are found together in the Covenant Code, while they are often so grouped in Deuteronomy.[51]

To look at the place of these three just within the Deuteronomic Code, then, one notes that they are protected in three areas: economic abuse, ability to sustain themselves physically, and place in the worship life of the community.

The signal text for the first of these three areas, protection from economic abuse, is the one before us, 24:17. The sojourner is mentioned as well in the law which we have just discussed, the payment of wages, which also falls within this category.

---

[50] This portrayal of the sojourner has been alluded to above in chapter 3, p. 89. The case for the *gēr* as a person who has abandoned that one's country of origin due to social and political upheaval is made convincingly in Spina, "Israelites as *gērim*," 323-325.

[51] The words "orphan" (*yātōm*) and "widow" (*ʾalmānā[h]*) are found only in a list with "sojourner" (*gēr*), while the last is found in some places by itself. As will become apparent below, even these exceptions occur within the general pattern of concern for these three.

The second of the three, protection of the ability to sustain oneself, is similar to the first, protection from economic abuse, in that it deals with the physical situation of the dependent. This area of concern is apparent in the law concerning gleanings (24:19-22), where the triad of dependents are named as the ones for whom the law is given.

In addition to this citation, however, the occurrences of this triad in the laws concerning the tithe of the third year (14:29) as well as the blessing which the Israelite is to say over that tithe (26:12,13) should also be mentioned.

The sojourner appears alone in texts associated with this topic as well, specifically in the law prohibiting the eating of animal corpses (14:21a), and in instruction concerning the proper disposal of the first fruits in 26:1-11 (the occurrence of *gēr* is at 26:11).

These last citations, while they function to give sustenance to the dependent, also edge over into the third area mentioned, the protection of the ability of the triad of dependents to participate in the public worship of the community. The sojourner, the orphan, and the widow are named along with others in a similar social situation (the slave, the Levite) in the laws outlining the celebration of the feast of weeks (16:11) and the feast of booths (16:14).

Thus with the exception of the sojourner in four cases,[52] the triad of dependents in Israel appear together in the Deuteronomic Code, and they appear together in texts dealing with specific issues of some import for social justice in Israel. This is not an earthshaking observation, perhaps, but it does underline the connection between the block of laws associated with the Sabbath Commandment and the laws taken up with issues of social justice presently in view.[53]

Sojourner, Orphan, and Widow (24:17f): Obligation

In a similar manner, the strategies employed by these two laws to persuade their audience to comply with their demands bring them into

[52] In addition to the three already named (14:21, 24:14, and 26:11), the sojourner also appears in a historical note contrasting Edom and Egypt (23:6f. [Eng 23:7f.]). Incidentally, this text lends support to the thesis that the sojourner may eventually be assimilated, as the Egyptian sojourner is allowed to enter the "assembly of YHWH" after three generations. Further on this, see generally Spina, "Israel as *gērim*," and Na'aman, "*HABIRU* and Hebrews."

[53] Notice that almost all these appearances occur within the Sabbath block of laws, within the material related to it (i.e., ch. 26), or within the laws we are presently discussing. The only exceptions are certain appearances of the sojourner, which appears as well at 14:21 and 23:8.

connection with the release-laws. Both employ the familiar sequence "law-consequence" and do so in a way which connects them first to the release-laws and second to the Sabbath block of laws.

Both the law which prohibits the judicial and economic mistreatment of the triad of dependents (24:17f.) and the one which provides for their physical welfare through the instruction to the landowner to leave the gleanings of the harvest (24:19-22) ground the motivation for their observance in the internal history of the nation, a strategy with which we are by now quite familiar.

The phrase is the same in both 24:18 and 24:22: "You shall remember that you were a slave in Egypt." In the manumission law, the phrase differs only by the inclusion of "the land."[54] Even more, this phrase occurs within the laws only at these three points and at 16:12 (in the feast of weeks), which, like the manumission law at Dt 15, occurs within the Sabbath block of laws.[55]

There are of course many other such phrases which make allusion to deliverance from Egypt. Only this phrase, however, directly highlights the slavery dimension of that experience. We noted this above in discussing the parallel slave law at 23:16f. (Eng 15f.). The closest parallel is "to redeem from the house of bondage," which appears at 13:6 and 11 (Eng. 5 and 10), as we have also noted.

Yet this parallel is actually more distant than is apparent at first glance, as the phrase "remember that you were a slave in Egypt" concentrates its attention not on redemption (though that is implied) but on the experience which the Israelite shares through that one's internal history with the slave, the sojourner, the dependent of any sort. To call upon this piece of Israel's internal history is thus completely appropriate in this context and serves to hook the audience into sympathy with the dependent and so to act in a way which sees to the dependent's protection and welfare.

Stated in terms of the ideology of social justice found in the Deuteronomic Code, we find confirmation here that those laws in Deuteronomy which deal with issues of social justice do so in a way that calls upon the deepest wells of Israel's experience and self-understanding. Israel takes care of its dependents not only because such is decreed by YHWH in the law but also because it shares with the dependent the memory of oppression.

---

54 That is, "you shall remember that you were a slave in *the land* of Egypt."

55 These citations are drawn from *Deuteronomy and the Deuteronomic School*, 327.

The laws dealing with the dependents in Israel hold out the promise of blessing in return for obedience.[56] As we noted above, the phrase which the law on gleanings uses to make this promise is yet another tie to the release-laws and the Sabbath block of laws. That phrase is "YHWH will bless you in all your work" (with slight variations as previously noted). To the hook of internal history is added the bait of blessing as a reward for compliance. The significance of this in terms of an ideology of the social justice laws in Deuteronomy is that it places the weal of the society as a whole upon its compliance to these laws.[57]

Conclusion

There are of course other laws which could be said to have some connection to the central concerns of an ideology of social justice—say, the law prohibiting bribing a judge. To admit that this is true is not to gainsay the pertinence of the laws discussed above or to undermine the analysis which has preceded. Rather, this analysis has chosen to center itself on those laws dealing with issues central to a system of social justice which have some connection to the release-laws of Dt 15, and so laws of an economic nature have been highlighted.

In the course of this analysis, however, we have discovered time and again the closeness of these connections, discoveries which give added weight to our analysis and to our thesis that in these laws enough is revealed to make some suggestions as to the attitudes and ideology which the Deuteronomic Code as a whole has toward those persons in special need of care in its community.

To continue with our two rubrics of "obligation" and "inclusion," we can summarize our findings in two parts.

I. Under the rubric of "obligation," the preceding analysis has given some nuance to a depiction of the ideology of social justice present in the laws of Deuteronomy in two ways.

First, it has highlighted the willingness of these laws to invoke phrases of deep evocative power, sprung from the central experiences of Israel. The phrases present in the laws just discussed have to do with the

---

56 On the relative rarity of this type of motive clause in the laws, see the discussion above, pp. 125-126.

57 The only other such enticement occurs in the law concerning just weights and measures, but this is a phrase which does not occur within the two blocks of laws associated with the "Chief Stipulation" and the Sabbath Commandment in which the others are clustered. On these exceptions to the general pattern, see the discussion under the law concerning loans on interest, pp. 125-126.

internal history of the community (which connects them to the release-laws and others in the Sabbath block of laws) and the right to choose a dwelling-place, a right normally reserved for YHWH (which connects them to the exclusiveness of relationship which is the "Chief Stipulation" of the First Commandment). Indeed, these evocative phrases and the experiences which they invoke create some problems for Deuteronomy, which tries to maintain a limited principle of inclusion while employing phrases admitting of no such limitation.

Second, tracing out the rhetoric these laws use to ensure assent and compliance reveals a general pattern which connects them to the blocks of laws associated with the First and Sabbath Commandments. One of these rhetorical patterns we have already mentioned, the evocative phrases used by several of these laws. The other is the consequence-phrase "YHWH will bless your work" and its variants, which, along with other such phrases promising blessing in return for obedience, also follow the same pattern of connection—that is, to the First Commandment and to the Sabbath Commandment. Under the rubric of "obligation," the significance of this observation is that the sequence "law-consequence," so fundamental to the promulgation of the laws, is here given a specific content: divine blessing and social weal.

II. The observation of the triangle of connections among the First Commandment block of laws, the Sabbath Commandment block of laws, and these laws has significance when viewed under the rubric "inclusion" as well. It shows that Deuteronomy has a well-focused understanding of what is at stake when the issue of social justice is broached. That these laws in chs. 23 and 24 which address various issues of social justice are so intimately connected to the two commandments of the Decalogue made central in Deuteronomy's version of that Decalogue shows us that there is an understanding here that these are issues of central importance to the health of the community. These laws, which are of a minor sort in comparison to the release-laws or to the stating of the great principles of exclusive worship, nevertheless enjoy a reflected glory and a heightened importance by their being connected to them. Stated in terms of the rubric "inclusion," the dependents who are the subject of these laws are therefore placed at the center of society, not at its margin.

This placing of the dependent at the center is evident in their being given the power within these laws to find redress with God. As with the release-laws, so too here choice and ultimate power are given to the dependent, not to the powerful. Those who have the power to see to it that justice prevails in economic relationships are given pointed reminders that they risk condemnation and divine retribution should they not exercise that power justly, that is, to the benefit of the dependent.

Lastly, the limitations apparent in the principle of inclusion have been shown to find contradiction and a certain amount of undermining within these laws. Were it not for those laws elsewhere which mete out harsh treatment to the natives of the land, one would be tempted to say that the key to this contradiction lies in the place of residence of the non-Israelite. The slave who escapes from another country to Israel and the sojourner who flees economic or political hardship are given a measure of protection and a degree of inclusion by these laws. Those who reside outside of Israel but with whom the Israelite has commerce are afforded no such protection or inclusion. This is not satisfactory, however, given those other contrary laws about treatment of the outsider who resides within Israel.

Perhaps instead the key lies in the identity of the exceptions to the limited principle of inclusion, both of whom (the slave and the sojourner) can claim to share with the people of Israel a basic common experience, that of living as oppressed dependents. The common experience of oppression binds together these two exceptional groups in every respect. Both can remember a time of slavery. Both have known the experience of crying to God for redress in a time of exploitation. Both have been placed at the center of God's attention. And, in the end, both have a claim to the blessing which that attention affords.

Having made these suggestive remarks concerning the shape of Deuteronomy's system of social justice, we turn finally to the place which the release-laws of Deuteronomy 15 occupy in that system and the underlying assumptions shared by the release-laws and Deuteronomy's system of social justice as a whole.

The Centrality of Deuteronomy 15

To bring together the two halves of this analysis of the place and influence of the release-laws within the other laws in the Deuteronomic Code, the preceding discussion can be spoken of in terms of four theses which together can serve as a summary of the system of social justice and the attitudes/ideology which underlie that system.

First, the laws in Deuteronomy insist that doing social justice is not an abstraction but is something which can be detailed. We saw this at work when we discussed the place of the release-laws in the Decalogic structure of the legal corpus where it became apparent that the laws which serve to give specificity to the Sabbath Commandment principle together paint a beatific portrait in which the dependents occupy the center in each case: they are the recipients of the tithe of the land, the ones for whom release is given from debt and the slavery which proceeds from it, the ones whom the law takes great pains to include as receiving the blessing of God and of participating in the great public festivals of worship.

But the laws in Deuteronomy are not content to leave the matter at the stage of beatific portrait. Rather, the laws get down to cases and safeguard the triad of dependents (sojourner, orphan, widow) from economic abuse, from physical deprivation, and from exclusion from participation in the community's reception of YHWH's blessing, both in these laws associated with the Sabbath Commandment and in the other laws we examined.

Second, the laws in Deuteronomy insist that the justness of society with respect to those within its midst in special need of care stands at the center of its program for the ideal society and, conversely, that their care serves as a barometer of the justness of society.

That the justness of society with respect to these stands at the center of the ideal society is made manifest by the fact that their treatment through the special tithe, the two forms of release, and the festivals draws from the Sabbath Commandment the quality of the cycle, as opposed to a treatment which is punctiliar and which therefore need not recur. The "holy rhythm" of Israel is given its beat by the treatment of the dependent, and those cyclical features of the life of the community whereby its relationship with YHWH is given reality in time features the dependents, whether slave, sojourner, orphan, or widow.

This is the Sabbatical principle: that rest comes, sustenance comes, release comes, celebration comes regularly, periodically, and for the sake of the dependent.

The language these laws employ to talk about the relationships obtaining between the powerful and the dependent makes this dimension clear and shows us what is at stake. The motive clauses which promise blessing, the deep evocative phrases by which law evokes assent and compliance, the use of words (in particular *néšek* and *nāgaś*) which connote a choice in whether this relationship will be just or unjust, tyrannical or not—all of these elements make it clear that what is at stake is the very health of this society.

That these very features of the social justice laws provide to a remarkable degree unique links to the two commandments given special prominence by the Deuteronomic version of the Decalogue only underscores that what is at stake here is considered crucial and fundamental.

Third, the laws of Deuteronomy aim their rhetorical weaponry at those who have the power to effect change. That rhetoric also pushes the breadth of obligation and the identity of the one to whom obligation is due to the widest possible compass.

The kinds of language just mentioned which give special prominence to these laws serve this function. For instance, the emotional hook of the remembrance of slavery in Egypt is set directly ("Remember that slaves you were . . .") and thereby catches the ones who have power to effect change on the line of their internal history. This emotional hook is also set indirectly through that cyclical cessation of labor given for the sake of the enslaved and dependent in Israel, a cessation which is akin in language and effect to the cessation of oppression by YHWH at the creation of the community.

So too the arguments given in favor of responding to the command to obey on behalf of the dependent are set forth both directly (e.g., "for he is poor, and sets his heart upon [his wages]") and indirectly, through dramatic explication of the divine court of retribution to which the wronged dependent one can appeal (e.g., "lest he cry against you to YHWH, and it be sin against you"). It is the powerful who are caught by these arguments.

It is at this point that we must note again the limited character of the principle of inclusion. This is a principle which in general gives breadth to the obligation inherent in these laws, yet it is a principle which is limited when the ones to whom the law applies are defined.

As we have seen, however, even this limitation is undermined from within by the very phrases which set the emotional hooks into the powerful. It is also undermined by the insistence that the outsider who seeks a home within the community due to flight from slavery (the fugitive slave) or from political and economic hardship (the sojourner) be given protection and a place to dwell.

Fourth and finally, the laws of Deuteronomy tell us that God serves as the advocate of the dependent and powerless. This is seen in the dramatic cry to God with which the dependent is said always to have recourse should that one receive unjust treatment rather than the justice which is due. More completely, it is by YHWH that the law is given, from YHWH that the reward of blessing should the dependent receive just treatment comes, for the renown of YHWH that thanks is given and public celebration is offered, to YHWH that the oppressed directs a cry for help and redress, and in YHWH that retribution is found. Were this a play, the characters would be three: the powerful, the dependent, and God. The system of social justice found in the laws would have its audience see this play as one in which the obligation which the powerful owes the powerless is adjudicated ultimately by God alone.

V

Toward the Present

Hermeneutical Considerations

The previous chapter concluded that the system of ideology of social justice in Deuteronomy displays four main features: that doing social justice is not an abstraction but is something which can be detailed; that both the identity of the one to whom obligation is owed and the breadth of that obligation are given the widest possible compass; that the justness of society can be measured by its treatment of the dependent; and that YHWH serves as an advocate for those in special need of care.

These conclusions, of course, are supported by a great deal of observation and discussion. To return to the language of the introduction, however, what remains is to see how these observations, discussions, and conclusions can inform the way in which the contemporary believer, a believer who takes this text as normative in some way, responds to analogous social problems in the present. It is the purpose of the present chapter to suggest several ways in which this can be done.

Several issues must be addressed before these suggestions can be made, however. These issues all have to do with responding to problems arising from the central task which is generally labeled "hermeneutics," which I take to mean the mechanics of how a text is not only read and understood but also made relevant to the reader's present.

This definition reflects an awareness that hermeneutics is a task which within the Christian tradition has historical roots in the interpretation and application of sacred texts, specifically the Bible. Only relatively recently has this subject once again been broadened to include non-sacred texts as well, perhaps because it is only relatively recently that such texts were considered worthy of such interpretation and application.

In any case, to invoke the issue of hermeneutics is to cause us to have to address, if only briefly, at least three areas of concern with relation to the text at hand and the subjects it addresses: 1) the differences between the socio-political relationships which obtained at the time in which Dt 15 was set down in its final form and those which obtain today, 2) the differences between economic and familial networks which were in practice then and those which are in practice today, differences which do not allow one to transfer directly the definition Dt 15 (and the rest of Deuteronomy) offers of those in special need of care, and 3) the differences between the understanding which the text has about its relationship with the realities of the time in which it was written (as best we can determine) and the relationships to reality it which can conceivably hold today.

As one can see by the way these areas of concern are worded, they can in fact be subsumed for the sake of discussion under a single topic, namely "difference," or more specifically "difference and transference." By this is meant the whole spectrum of difficulties, the most pertinent of which have been listed above, created by the span of years and custom which lie between the present of the text and the present of the reader. It is "difference" in this sense which does not allow the reader to transfer directly the injunctions and suggestions offered by Deuteronomy concerning issues of social justice, no matter how similar present issues may appear to those whom the book addresses today.

To take up the specific issues enumerated above in order under the control of the topic "difference and transference," we must first address the problems created by the differences between the socio-political system assumed by Deuteronomy and the socio-political system which holds today.

It is precisely at this issue that the book of Deuteronomy holds the greatest promise to the modern reader for satisfactory transference of its injunctions and suggestions.

This is so if one assumes an exilic date for the final form of the book, as seems reasonable given the current state of the discussion of this issue.[1] While the laws found in Deuteronomy, the framework which surrounds them, and the particular wording which they receive are the product no doubt of a long history of editing and redaction, it is the final form, the exilic form, of the text on which we have focused in this study. The reader of this study has no doubt noticed that little attempt has been made to trace out levels of redaction or editing in order to place them in time and space, nor has much distinction been made among the various sections of the book, except to concentrate on the laws themselves in order to observe the logic behind their sequence. This reflects a deliberate decision on the part of the writer, a decision which was made precisely with the hermeneutical, the "difference," issues presently under discussion in mind.

Because we have always kept this form of the text in view, certain features of the book of Deuteronomy can now be called upon which lend aid to an attempt to transfer the socio-political milieu of the release-laws from an ancient Near Eastern, specifically Israelite, society into a modern secular, pluralistic one (I should say specifically a contemporary North American one). This is so when one concentrates on an exilic formulation of the book because the "ideal society" outlined in the book holds an analogous position to the dominant culture in which Israel (the community which is envisioning its ideal self) found itself at that point in time as that which the church (taken as the "new Israel") finds itself in this secular, pluralistic North American society. That is, neither Israel in exile or in remnant nor the present-day church or synagogue has the capacity to dictate to the society at large the socio-political features which will hold sway. Despite those who assert that the United States is a "Judeo-Christian" nation, in the end neither the Christian church in its many denominations nor the Jewish synagogue in its divisions can dictate social policy to a secular government.

The task in both cases, then, is to find—for those who would still hold that the values, the ideology, and the loyalties embodied in life under the care and tutelage of YHWH are normative—a way in which those values, etc., can be spoken of in a society which does not necessar-

---

[1] This has been the case in some form or another since Martin Noth's seminal monograph, *Überlieferungsgeschichtliche Studien: Die sammelnden und bearbeitenden Geschichtswerke im Alten Testament*, specifically that portion more commonly known to English-speaking readers as *The Deuteronomistic History*. In terms of the book of Deuteronomy itself, important work has been done on the date of the final stage of editing of the book by N. Lohfink (especially *Das Hauptgebot*, and "The Deuteronomist and the Idea of Separation of Power") and J. Levenson ("Who Inserted the Book of Torah?").

ily hold them in the same high regard. It is in the light of this dilemma that the method of presentation, the rhetorical strategies, the structural sequence of laws, and the nuanced yet consistent perspective on issues of social justice which has been revealed by observation in the previous chapters must be seen.

Again, this is not to say that there were not earlier versions of the release-laws and earlier points in the history of the text when this material was not thought of as directly normative. It is rather to say that in trying to see how this material might find application, might be "transferred" or made relevant to the contemporary reader, it is the level of the text's history when they *could* not be thought of as directly normative (that is, the exile) which is most helpful.

As we move through the suggestions which this concluding chapter will try to outline, this feature of Deuteronomy will be ever before us—that we have in these laws, in this formulation of Israel's history and in this sense of absolute loyalty to YHWH a vision of an ideal which those who set them down surely realized could not have been put into effect in their immediate situation. How this reality can affect the way the church or synagogue acts in a contemporary society in which, like Israel in exile, the values and virtues which they hold in common or apart cannot be dictated to a secular society is something which will be explored as we proceed.

Of greater difficulty is the difference which lies between the identity of those whom Deuteronomy defines as the dependents of society and the criteria Deuteronomy used to make that definition, and those who can conceivably be defined as dependent in contemporary society.

To some extent, these definitions will overlap. The triad of sojourner, orphan, and widow are those whose position in our society is precarious as it was in Israel's.

It cannot be said, however, that they are in this precarious position in exactly the same way or for the same reasons. The family as a source of social welfare, most importantly, does not hold the same position in modern society as it did in theirs. Nor can the problem of the dependent be solved in exactly the same agrarian terms (e.g., through a putting into practice in our society of the law of gleanings), though perhaps the problem of the dependent in our society might move us in that direction.

Rather, some attention must be paid to the mechanics of dependence in our society and the way in which there is created a class of people who stand in special need of care.

Likewise, as has been noted above, some attention must be paid to the way in which those in special need of care find that care. Obviously, in a concluding chapter only a few suggestions can be made. Even so, it should be apparent in the suggestions which follow that this area of "difference" has been kept in mind.

Similarly, the area of "difference" spoken of at the outset having to do with the difference between the way this text sees its relationship to a real society and the way this text can be taken to relate to our own real society, has been kept to the fore.

To some extent, this area of difference can be seen as a variation on the first area discussed, that between the socio-political realities obtaining at the time of the exile and those which obtain today. Still, there remains some distinction between the two, because in this case we are speaking of Deuteronomy's system of social justice as a *text* which had an identifiable relation to cultural reality (as opposed to the relation its editors, as a socio-political force, had to that reality) which it does not have today.[2] This is the issue of textual authority as opposed to the political authority held by the community which holds that text to be normative. As with the other two areas of difference, this difference in the realm of the authority of the text will surface at key points in the suggestions which follow.

At this point, however, we can anticipate that discussion somewhat by echoing the comments we made concerning the first area of "difference." The book of Deuteronomy offers greater help for bridging this gap of difference than perhaps any other in the Old Testament. This is so because Deuteronomy is the most self-consciously a literary construct. It purports to set down the words of Moses to the people on the plains of Moab, just about to enter the land, outlining the responsibilities of the ideal society and its absolute loyalty to YHWH. In fact it received its final form in the exile. Of course there was a strong tradition placing the giving of the law in the mouth of Moses the lawgiver, but to put that law-giving at Moab rather than at Sinai represents a deliberate choice, a placing of this ideal at a time of potential which could resonate somehow with later times of potential (the writer's present).

All of this shows the degree to which Deuteronomy is conscious of itself as a text, a literary document, which is nevertheless intended to attain some very profound ends. It is this sense of itself as a text which makes Deuteronomy especially helpful in attempting to transfer its

---

[2] Again, the opinion of the "fundamentalist" substratum of Christianity and, I suppose, of Judaism to the contrary.

system of social justice into the present, since it is itself trying to effect a similar sort of transfer from a purported earlier ideal moment to a grim present. The careful attention we have paid to the rhetorical strings which the release-laws pull with such determination show how hard the text works at this task. Everything we have noted up to now, not just the conclusions reached at the end of the last chapter but those observations which carried us to that point, must be seen as the attempt of this text to cast itself off of the page or out of the mouth of its disseminator and into the lives of its audience.

This is the same task faced by the church or synagogue in the present-day United States which wonders how this text can become relevant to its own life and that of its members. Perhaps the text itself is the best instructor as to how this may be done.

Certainly there is much to learn from the masterful readers who have attempted this same task before us. Specifically, the suggestions which follow use the Gospel of Luke as a second point of reference. Luke has been chosen because, like Deuteronomy, it shows a particular concern for issues of social justice and, also like Deuteronomy, it presents itself as a retelling of events and content already known from other places (see Luke's "prologue," Luke 1:1-4).

Luke also provides an especially good discussion partner because it is the product of a community which has tried to grapple with issues of social justice while remaining faithful to the authoritative voices of the past (Deuteronomy among them).

Luke is a good selection, then, because it both employs the self-conscious literary strategy found in Deuteronomy (casting the ideal for the present back into the retelling of the past) and tries to remain faithful to the tradition of which Deuteronomy is a prime witness while making that tradition relevant to its present.

The Release-Laws for Today

Introduction

This is a study which has tried to uncover as much as possible the underlying structure of the text and the larger sequence of laws in which it is found, the rhetorical devices used by that text and laws related to it, and the system or ideology of social justice which these features reveal. It is also a study which has said that in terms of hermeneutics, the main issues involved are those of "difference" and "transference." It is thus a study which, while it has tried to maintain that distance and objectivity so prized of historical critics, has also tried to get inside the text as much as possible to the end that now, when the question of relevance is raised, some suggestions about the text's relevance can be made which echo the text's own attitudes about its subject and about itself.

The suggestions we will take up in the remainder of this concluding chapter will therefore closely follow the conclusions drawn in the previous study of the text itself. These suggestions will take account of both the areas of hermeneutical concern just spoken of and, in a small way, one of the other possible ways of treating these issues which have emerged in the interim between Deuteronomy and ourselves.

Social Justice/Human Rights as Obligation

We are encouraged by our living with this text for a while to see human rights as obligation, more particularly as a set of obligations which the powerful owe to the powerless.

This is in some contrast to the way we are accustomed to thinking of rights. Think of the difference, for instance, between the laws we have discussed and our Bill of Rights which, like the laws we have been dealing with, was intended to safeguard the rights of the individual from the encroachments of the powerful. The Bill of Rights tends to safeguard the liberty of the individual by spelling out what government or the powerful in society should *refrain* from doing—limiting peaceful assembly, censoring the press, etc. This view of human rights defines those things which individuals do which should not be placed in jeopardy.

The view of Deuteronomy, as we have seen, is more active. It defines that treatment which the dependent has a right to *expect* of society and that treatment which society *owes* to the dependent.

More specifically, we are encouraged to see the neighbor or kin to whom obligation is due in the widest possible terms. Our definition of those in a position of dependency should not be limited to the one next door or down the street. Rather, our definition of the one to whom obligation is due should proceed from these laws in the direction which Jesus took it in response to the question "Who is my neighbor?" We should, as Jesus did, resist the temptation to define once and for all who is neighbor and who is not. These laws have a built-in tendency to widen the compass of those who are to be included in their system of care.

So much has been made of the sense of obligation in the release-laws and the other laws in Deuteronomy having to do with problems of social justice that little more needs to be said on this score from that quarter.

There is another voice, however, which takes up this issue with great vigor. This voice is the community whose faith and convictions resulted in the formulation of the Gospel of Luke and its accompanying history of the infant church, the Acts of the Apostles.

The historiographic and intertextual ties between the Lukan corpus and Deuteronomy have been the subject of scholarly exploration for some time and have produced a bibliography too lengthy to summarize here.[3] For the sake of our discussion, only those ties pertinent to the subject at hand will be brought out.

In terms of the rubric of obligation, several themes which emerged in our investigation of the release-laws and legislation of similar intent find their parallels in Luke-Acts.

1. The most obvious of these themes is the breadth of that obligation. As was intimated in our preliminary comments on this suggestion, a key text here is the parable of the Good Samaritan which comes out of the narrative leading to the giving of the Great Commandment (Luke 10:25-37). The Good Samaritan is a tradition which appears in Luke and nowhere else in the gospels, and it comes as an elaboration of Jesus' answer to the lawyer's question, "What shall I do to inherit eternal life?"

When one compares this text with the other occurrences of the "Great Commandment" pericopes in Mark and Matt, several things become plain. First, as is indicated by the question which the lawyer puts to Jesus, the subject at hand is not law directly, but rather eternal life. This itself is in keeping with the attitude toward the law found in Deuteronomy. It is especially in keeping with those particular laws that attach to the law the consequences for the life of the community which fall from compliance or noncompliance.

Here the issue is put in more individual terms, but it is an issue which has community-wide implications when one notices, second, that the wider context in which this pericope is placed is that series of pericopes in Luke dealing with discipleship: the strenuousness of following Jesus (9:57-62), the mission of the seventy(-two) (10:1-20, with the interruption of the woe against Chorazin and Bethsaida in vv 13-15), and the

---

[3] Some important pieces of this bibliography, in no particular order, are J. Bligh, *Christian Deuteronomy (Luke 9-18)* (Scripture for Meditation 5; New York: Alba House, 1970); J. Dawsey, "Jesus' Pilgrimage to Jerusalem," *Pers. Rel. St.* 14 (1987), 217-232; D. Moessner, "Luke 9:1-50: Luke's Preview of the Journey of the Prophet Like Moses of Deuteronomy," *JBL* 102, (1983) 575-605, and *The Lord of the Banquet* (Minneapolis: Fortress, 1989); and C. Cave, "Lazarus and the Lukan Deuteronomy," *NTS* 15 (1968-69), 319-325.

conferral of authority (10:17-20) and insight (21-25) on the disciples. The pericope is followed in ch. 11 by further instructions to the disciples on the subject of prayer (11:1-13).

It is clear that in this context, the interaction between Jesus and the lawyer has to do with the discipleship, or in deuteronomic terms, of life in the community of those whose allegiance is to YHWH.

Third, when one compares this pericope with others which share with it certain narrative features (a setting of conflict in which one or each participant cites a portion of Old Testament legal material in resolving the dispute),[4] it becomes apparent that exhortation and example are key elements of the narrative. The resolution of the conflict in the narrative centers on the citation of a legal text. Both the opponent within the story and the reader who is allowed to overhear the exchange are the recipients of the instruction and exhortation which together are the point of the passage.

In the case of the inheritance of eternal life and the parable of the Good Samaritan, this narrative opens out into the issue at hand, namely the kind of obligation owed to those in special need of care and the identity of the one to whom that obligation is owed.

As we observed in the previous chapter, Deuteronomy itself is of two minds about these issues. At what point is one so far outside the realm of the community that obligation is no longer owed? Deuteronomy never resolves this issue completely, though as we have indicated, there is a tendency inherent in the language used to speak of the commonality of the experience of slavery which leans one toward a more radical resolution than the text is willing to state outright.

The community which produced the Gospel of Luke and which also considered this matter is willing to go further. Luke's Jesus refuses to answer the lawyer's question about the identity of the neighbor (10:29) in the speculative terms in which it was put. Jesus transforms the lawyer's question instead into an example which radicalizes the definition of the one in need of care.[5] The obligation to care is thus given even wider scope than the release-laws and their attendant social justice legislation are willing to say directly.

2. A second aspect of the rubric of obligation which is found in the Gospel of Luke is the centrality of the obligation to care for the depen-

---

4 Three close but, in the end, incomplete analogues are 4:4-13 (the contest with the devil in the wilderness), 18:18-30 (the rich ruler and eternal life), and 20:27-40 (the dispute about the nature of the resurrection).

5 E. Schweizer, *The Good News According to Luke* (Atlanta: John Knox, 1973) 137.

dent. As with the theme of the breadth of obligation, the texts which take up this matter give it a radical force. Indeed, when they consider the mission of Jesus, the gospel and the community from which it sprang list this very concern for the care of those in special need as primary. Jesus' inaugural sermon (4:16-21) strikes this theme at the outset of Jesus' public ministry. When the disciples of John the Baptist come to Jesus armed with the question of his identity, he responds by pointing to the care he has shown those in need as signs of his identity and of the veracity of his bringing in the "acceptable year of the Lord" (7:18-23).

The concern of Luke's gospel for the poor and the dependent is almost a truism and need not be elaborated further except to say that in so concentrating on the quality of relationship granted to the dependent upon the appearance of the acceptable year of the Lord, Luke's gospel is echoing and elaborating on a theme which it has taken up from Deuteronomy.

The obligatory nature of those relationships is clear in such texts as the discussion of eternal life, which is concluded by the parable of the Good Samaritan. It is also present in a more veiled form in the texts just mentioned concerning the identity and mission of Jesus who is to be taken as exemplar as well as redeemer.

Likewise, while the release-laws themselves are not alluded to in Luke-Acts, "release" is,[6] and the character of God who hears the cry of the oppressed and responds with speed and vigor is a favorite theme of this gospel.[7] In both of these, the centrality of this theme to the gospel is plain.

Luke's taking up of this theme found in Deuteronomy's system of social justice thus may not be direct in the sense that the gospel deliberately plays on Deuteronomy's particular outworking of the centrality of care for the dependent (though the thematic, historiographic, and intertextual ties between the two mentioned above at least make such a direct connection worth considering), but it is certainly of a piece with that deuteronomic outworking.

---

6 Cf. the inaugural sermon just mentioned, which quotes Isa 61:1-2, which in turn employs *dĕrôr*, the Hebrew cognate of the Akkadian *andurārum*. On the scope of influence of "release" on the gospel of Luke, see R. Sloan, Jr., *The Favorable Year of the Lord* (Austin, Tx: Schola, 1977).

7 Two prominent texts are the Magnificat (1:46-55) and the Lukan version of the Beatitudes, which are followed by their Woes to those who benefit from the present arrangement of society (6:20-26).

Further, Luke's dwelling on the various components of the theme of the centrality of care to the dependent places that theme in the center of the life of the community as it tries now to follow one whose authority exceeds even that of Moses in their minds.

We see in the way in which Luke's gospel deals with the breadth of obligation owed to the dependent and the centrality which that obligation holds in Luke's vision of society that Luke has radicalized the issue of human rights as obligation in both of its subdivisions—human rights/social justice as an obligation and an obligation which is owed to all in need of care, without definition.

In terms of the situation in which the church finds itself in the present, both the Lukan and the Deuteronomic formulations of this issue have weight and provide guidance. Despite the very good reasons[8] advanced by a secular society (which takes its cues on this issue from the Enlightenment rather than from scripture) to see rights as things to be safeguarded from encroachment rather than as a set of obligations owed, the church must insist that it demurs. Like the Lukan community, the contemporary community must retain as central the concern for social justice and insist that the right to be human is an obligation which society owes to each of its members.

There are other voices to be heard in the public square, certainly, and a good purpose served by allowing the debate to take place. Still, the community which takes as normative the laws of Deuteronomy, the Gospel of Luke, and the view of social justice contained in them is pushed to speak on one side of that debate, the side which says that the right to be human is an obligation which each of us owes the other, and that this is a right which can be detailed in positive acts of empowerment to anyone who stands in need of such care.

The Obligation of the Powerful

In following out the line of reasoning exhibited by the release-laws, we are encouraged to see our obligation to attend to those in need of care in such a way that palliatives or mere amelioration will not do. In the manumission law, the slave not only goes free, not only receives a stake with which to make a fresh start, but is garlanded with a wreath of good things and well-wishes. We should wish well for the powerless among us and give them the means to live well.

---

[8] Chiefly the danger of tyranny which arises when one portion of society, no matter how large, is allowed to define its view of what is right for society as an obligation owed by everyone.

This means that the obligation falls, as it does in Deuteronomy, on those who have the capacity, the resources, to see that such a change from dependent living to good living is carried out. Rather than advancing an "up-by-your-bootstraps" mentality, our exposure to the Deuteronomic way of thinking about social justice encourages us to confront those who *can* shape society for the better to do so.

We have noted throughout this study and especially in the conclusion at the end of the previous chapter that the rhetoric and thrust of the legislation in Deuteronomy dealing with issues of social justice are aimed at the powerful, at those who have the capacity to shape society in this regard. As we said, the powerful are reminded that the decision is, in the end, up to the dependent one who may always cry to God in whom that one will find a quick ear. And the powerful are reminded that the health of society is defined both by the absoluteness of its allegiance to YHWH and by its treatment of the dependent in its midst. The responsibility, the moral imperative, is thus not on the dependent but on the powerful who can make that cry unnecessary and that society a just one.

Again, Luke's gospel takes up this theme quite pointedly. One place where the obligation of the powerful is seen most strongly is in the parable of the Rich Ruler (18:18-30).

As with the parable of the Good Samaritan, the subject here is eternal life, and in fact these two texts have a great deal in common. Both involve a discussion between Jesus and another in which a piece of legal material is quoted as part of the resolution of the discussion. Both deal with the nature of discipleship (i.e., following Jesus) and carry an element of social teaching in so doing.

In the case of the parable of the Rich Ruler, the social teaching is quite pointed. Luke puts it the most vigorously of the three synoptics with the inclusion of the emphatic "sell *all* that you have," where Matt and Mark say simply "sell what you have" with only slight variation between them.[9] What is clear in all three cases is that the wealthy one who approaches Jesus has an obligation to the poor which goes beyond that one's observance of the law—beyond even the Decalogue which he quotes.

The perspective seen here, however, is not quite the same as that present in Deuteronomy. Clement of Alexandria, in discussing the Marcan version of this pericope in his treatise "Who is the Rich Man that Shall be Saved?", makes the point that should the wealthy give all of

9 Luke 18:23; cf. Mark 10:24 and Matt 19:21.

their wealth away, the poor are little served, since the end result is that the one who was formerly rich is now simply another of the poor. This comes closer to the attitude struck by Deuteronomy. Deuteronomy, at least by implication, does not ask the wealthy to give up their wealth[10] but rather to use it for the benefit of the poor.

Clement, in his short treatise on Mark 10:17-31, "Who is the Rich Man That Shall be Saved?," focuses a great deal of attention on the spiritual dimensions of the Marcan text. Putting the focus here is not meant to be taken as an apology for wealth, along the lines of there being a spiritual dimension of reality which makes one's immediate, corporeal situation unimportant, and indeed Clement opens his treatise with a condemnation of those who flatter the rich.[11] His concern can rather be called pastoral in the sense that he wants to show the wealthy that the Lord's love extends to them as well, despite the seemingly absolute handicap placed upon them by Jesus' having said that it is easier for a camel to pass through the eye of a needle than a rich man to enter the kingdom of God (pp. 591-592, ch. 3).

Clement, then, is wrestling with a particular aspect of the subject at hand, namely the presence and purpose of the wealthy in a community which does not see wealth as necessarily a virtue, indeed which can suggest in the strongest terms that God sides with the poor and that salvation comes to the rich only by the grace of God.[12]

In doing so, however, Clement does not go so far as to say that what one does with wealth is not important. Rather he says that while it is certainly true that the difficulty of the rich in entering the kingdom is to be taken spiritually, that sin and virtue are found in poor and rich alike, and that therefore the state of one's soul before God is to be of the first concern (596, ch. 28), still the one who is truly rich is rich in virtue and therefore able to make faithful use of wealth (596, ch. 19).[13]

The opposite is also true, in Clement's mind—that one can give away one's wealth to the poor for all the wrong reasons (arrogance, pretension,

---

[10] In fact, at one point in the parallel law on gleanings, the property of the landholder is safeguarded from exhaustive gleaning by the poor—cf. Dt 23:25f (Eng 24f).

[11] "Who is the Rich Man that Shall be Saved?," in *The Ante-Nicene Fathers, Vol. 2: Fathers of the Second Century* (Trans. W. Wilson; Grand Rapids: Eerdmans, 1951) p. 591, ch. 1. All further references to the treatise will be given in the body of the discussion and will be paginated according to this edition.

[12] Or as Clement puts this last more eloquently, "God conspires with willing souls (597, ch. 21)," whether those souls be rich or poor in their physical state.

[13] Though here again, Clement quickly moves back to the point that it is inner wealth or poverty which is the important thing.

vainglory, and self-righteousness) and come no closer to salvation than if one had kept it (594, ch. 12). One should not desire to be destitute unless one also has a special object for that desire, namely the banishment of the morbid feelings and anxieties which can accompany wealth (594, ch. 11). Instead, the greater good is done when the one rich in virtue and in wealth uses that wealth to assist those without (594, ch. 13). Wealth in this sense is to be seen as another of God's blessings, useful for the benefiting of one's neighbors, an instrument which can be played skillfully or not, depending on how it affects one's soul (595, ch. 14). Always, always, the effect on the inward disposition of the believer is that which determines the good or ill of any outward circumstance.

Thus Clement is at least in sympathy with Deuteronomy's perspective on the responsibility which the wealthy, the powerful, have toward the poor, the dependent, as over against the absoluteness of the parable of the Rich Ruler in the synoptics. One should note along these lines that Clement avoids the alternatives which lie to either side of their position, either toward the fawning appreciation of the power of the wealthy on the one hand[14] or toward asceticism which simply denounces material property on the other hand.[15]

This balancing act is in keeping with the attitude expressed in Deuteronomy which does not denounce wealth *per se* nor offer up denial and asceticism as the ideal, and which does not congratulate the wealthy for their power and riches. Instead, in opposition to both possibilities, Deuteronomy challenges them to use their wealth and power to good effect, to the increased justness of society.

The goal is not for the wealthy to renounce their wealth, but rather for the wealthy to empower the dependent so that they too may enjoy the blessed life. Luke's gospel tells a story along these lines which the other synoptics do not preserve, the story of Jesus' encounter with Zacchaeus the tax collector upon whom salvation is pronounced when Zacchaeus vows to give half to the poor (Luke 19:1-10). Again, something less than full denial is held up as an example to the wealthy.

One might infer that having put this plan into action, the contrast between rich and poor in the ideal society would inevitably shrink,

14 Note Clement's opening opprobrium against those who cater to the wealthy among the community spoken of above.

15 Clement warns that it is possible to give away wealth for self-righteousness' sake or that, having relinquished one's property, one might all the more desire what one had once and has no longer ("Who is the Rich Man that Shall be Saved?" 594, ch. 12).

though Deuteronomy does not hold this out specifically as a goal. The beatific portrait painted in the laws concerning the festivals is that of the *whole* community, rich and poor alike, participating in the public worship of the community and enjoying the blessings of YHWH.

The special role and responsibility of the powerful in seeing that this portrait becomes reality is inescapable, and Deuteronomy does not draw back from putting this in the most pointed terms. While Deuteronomy does not have the same emphasis on the life of the soul found in Clement nor the call for giving up one's wealth found in the synoptics, it does pay particular attention to the attitude of the lender or the slaveholder. It is careful to admonish them to let go of their overabundance for the benefit of the poor without doing so grudgingly, and so it addresses the concern which both of these other positions (Luke and Clement) speak to, the attitudinal handicap which having wealth can place in the way of meeting one's obligation to the poor.

Social Justice as Barometer of the Health of a Society

Our sitting for a while with this text also encourages us to see the extent to which society meets its obligation to the dependent in need of care as one of the two most important barometers of social well-being (the other of course is a proper and worshipful relationship with YHWH).

In ancient Israel, or at least in ancient Israel as Deuteronomy would have us see it, this is the function which the Levites filled. They were dependent on the community for their well-being on the one hand, but on the other hand, as those without an inheritance save YHWH, they constantly held before the community a portrait of itself. This portrait was of a people without a portion except that which God's good mercy provided, without sustenance except that which God's gracious law allotted to them. The Levites were without function except to be dependent and so to remind Israel that it too was as dependent as they, had Israel only the courage to see it.

Such can be said on a less programmatic level of all the dependents of Israelite society. How Israel treated the Levite, how Israel treated the sojourner, the orphan, the widow, the indebted one, the slave, all of them completely dependent in the end on a God who sees to their care, was in this sense a reflection of the extent to which they respected themselves in their position of dependence on a God who answers the cry of the oppressed with compassion.

Would they cast these dependents in the role of "other" whose presence could then be thought of as a cancer to be rooted out or consigned to places where no one cared to go? Would they see the Levite, the sojourner, the widow, the orphan as weak morally or physically and hence absolve themselves of responsibility? Or would their powers of inclusion and compassion extend even to these who had no portion, no family claim, no redeemer should they fall into slavery? These are the kinds of questions which we should ask ourselves of the dependents in our society when we try to transfer into the present the conviction expressed in Deuteronomy that the treatment of these groups of people is the most important indicator of the justness of society.

Such an attitude toward the treatment of the dependent is mirrored in the Lukan texts already mentioned, Luke 4:16-21 and 7:18-23, in which Jesus speaks about his identity and his mission.

In both of these instances in Luke's portrait of Jesus, when Jesus speaks directly about these matters, it is always in terms of what Jesus has done for these, the handicapped, the outcast, the poor. This portrait is reinforced at those points where Luke offers a summary of Jesus' ministry, for instance at 6:17-19, where Jesus' ministry is summarized as one of teaching, healing, and comfort.

Here, by implication, an attitude is revealed in which society and its members are judged according to what they do for the dependent, since the figure of Jesus in Luke serves as an example of the right way to live as a follower of Jesus as well as news of their having been given salvation by this one. The question of how society treats the dependent is thus never far from this community's mind as it constantly measures its behavior against the behavior of Jesus who came for the sake of the release of the dependent.

For the community which takes both of these books as normative, this question and the ones related to it enumerated above must be ever to the fore. As with the first two suggestions, however, the questions of difference and transference must be taken account of.

In the case of those other two suggestions ("social justice/human rights as obligation" and "the obligation of the powerful"), this was not as tricky a matter as might be feared, at least on the fairly abstract level with which we are dealing with these issues at present. Such a level of abstraction is appropriate for a study of this sort, since what we are after is not so much a blueprint for public policy as the broad outlines of how transference may take place.

In the case of the suggestion presently in view, "social justice as social barometer," this level of abstraction is also appropriate. In addressing a society which no longer has this attitude, establishing the centrality of care for the dependent as an indicator of the health of that society must come before any specific proposal. Such is not the case with the last suggestion, which must define the actual social role which the contemporary community can play on behalf of those in special need of care in this secular society.

The Church as Advocate for the Dependent

Finally, we, as the community which takes these texts and these opinions as normative, are encouraged to seek an active role in bringing about this vision of human rights as a good life even for those lacking in the immediate means to achieve that end. The church and the synagogue need to find a proper role in our society, a society which is deliberately secular and whose values are not our own. We have lost the power to dictate policy (if we ever really had it) and find ourselves increasingly on the margins in a community which listens to other, more pragmatic, or at least more comforting, prophets.

The role suggested here is in keeping with the conclusions we have drawn from this study of the release-laws. That role is one of an *advocate.* The church and the synagogue can function as advocates on behalf of the dependent. They can identify as their constituency those who are without the normal system of support in our community, those without a voice to catch the ear of the powerful, those who command the support of no center of economic or political power. They can as advocates serve as the mouthpiece of YHWH in a society which no longer accepts the divine as a source for legislation.

Part of this role involves the task of identification, a task which brings us back around to our first suggestion, that rights are an obligation owed to the powerless. Who in our society are the powerless, the dependent? No final answer can be given here, but questions can be raised which point the way toward the identification of the church's constituency. These questions are in fact derived from the language of the release-laws, which remind their audience that the dependent do have an advocate upon whom they can call for redress.

Who in our community has no recourse but to cry to God? Who has been barred either by constricting legislation or the constraints of a withered imagination from any court of appeal other than the divine?

However we may answer these question, *these* are our constituents, these are the ones for whom we can act as an advocate before the powerful who owe them care and attention, would they only recognize that responsibility.

That the community of Luke's gospel saw the matter this same way is evident in the summary passages mentioned above where the people who come to Jesus are identified as infirm and as those eager to hear the good news of release and forgiveness (e.g., 4:14-15; 4:40-44; 6:17-19; 8:1-3). The inaugural sermon (4:16-20) also shows this mission to the dependent.

We cited these passages above to show how Luke's portrayal of Jesus reveals one in basic agreement with Deuteronomy's attitudes toward social justice. Here they may be cited to show how the Lukan community, in telling itself what Jesus was like, placed upon itself Jesus' mission to the dependent as well.

Put in terms of the hermeneutical concerns with which this chapter began, such a noting of the polyvalent quality of the Gospel of Luke is in this sense similar to Deuteronomy as well in that it serves two purposes: it purports to hand on an "orderly" account of what happened in the life of Jesus of Nazareth and what happened after his crucifixion to those who followed him, and it sets forth an ideal for the benefit of a community in which eyewitnesses are becoming increasingly rare but which needs to redefine, to remember, and to recharge its past for a new day and time.

It is this same sort of redefining which needs to be done by the contemporary community. The suggestion that the church serve as advocate for the dependent is an attempt to do this. Such a role transfers to the people of YHWH in a secular society the role which YHWH played in a theocentric society. As such, the church makes what could otherwise be a secular undertaking, providing for the welfare and empowerment of the poor, into a sacred undertaking in much the same way in which Deuteronomy made sacred this same undertaking in its portrait of the ideal society, or in the same way in which the Lukan community did so to this same undertaking in its day by making this aspect of the community's behavior a mimicking of the example of Jesus.

This is hermeneutics by analogy. In each case a similar task is treated in an analogous manner by three communities of widely varying times, cultures, and situations. In this way, fidelity and transformation coexist.

The important thing to note, however, is that the text itself has shown us the way this can be done. In placing release in Israel on the "holy rhythm" of the cycle, in investing these release-laws with the language and drama of the most basic and deeply felt of Israel's experience of its history and its relationship with God, in presenting these laws and related social justice legislation in the most persuasive and coercive manner at its disposal—in all of these ways, Deuteronomy has insisted that this task is to be regarded as sacred.

The contemporary church must then also see it thus and must therefore seek a role for itself which partakes of this way of viewing the task of granting to all of society's members the right to be human, of calling upon the powerful to use that power to good effect, and of providing for the justness of society as a task of the most sacred sort.

Just as Deuteronomy allows the fugitive slave to take on the characteristics of YHWH, at least insofar as that one is allowed the divine right to choose a place, so too the church must allow itself to consider itself the very mouthpiece and image of the God who is the advocate of the dependent in a society which no longer looks for God in the ordinary course of events.

Conclusion

This last suggestion then represents the end point of our study, as it identifies the role and the attitudes which the contemporary community is to have toward issues of social justice. It is not the intention of this study to specify policy but rather to point the way toward how policy can be invested with the authority of scripture without assuming that one can simply read from the release-laws prescriptions for that policy. What we have uncovered in this study are the touchstones of an attitude, an ideology, a system of dealing with issues of social justice which can have great relevance for the way the present community addresses those issues in a society in which its influence is only indirect.

In such a society, the primary task of the exegete is not the naming of policy but the identification of attitude. By this is meant that what the church needs more than the specific is the general. How are we to feel about the poor, the powerless, the dependent, all those who ask for and need our care? Is there a point at which our neighborly obligation ends? What sort of attitude does the community represent to the world at large when it comes to these issues? *These* are the difficult questions, even more than the specifics of cost-effectiveness and effective empowerment.

While in terms of the specifics perhaps more questions have been raised than answered, in terms of the broader questions, old imperatives have been sounded again: The right to be human, to be a full participant in the blessings of one's society, is not only a privilege but a right. Of those to whom much is given, much is expected on behalf of the powerless. The treatment and condition of the least in society is indicative of the health of the whole of society. The drama of human existence dictates that those who ordinarily have no voice should find a voice in the church, just as they find an advocate in God.

Each of these resonates with the attitude found in the release-laws of Deuteronomy 15, and each rings forth from that text as it finds distinction from comparable systems. To the contemporary audience of this chapter faced with comparable situations of dependence and poverty, these imperatives gain new authority and greater weight for their having this resonance. It is then up to that audience to give melody to what is at this point only an echo.

Bibliography

Alexander, J. B. "A Babylonian Year of Jubilee?" *JBL* 57 (1968) 75-79.

Alt, A. "Die Ursprünge des israelitischen Rechts," in *Kleine Schriften* I, 278-332. München: C. H. Bech'sche, 1953. Eng. Trans. "The Origins of Israelite Law," in *Essays on Old Testament History and Religion*. Trans. R. Wilson; Oxford: Basil Blackwell, 1966.

Anderson, H. "Broadening Horizons: The Rejection of Nazareth Pericope of Luke 4:16-30 in Light of Recent Critical Trends," *Int* 18 (1964) 259-275.

Andreasen, N.-E. "Recent Studies of the Old Testament Sabbath: Some Observations," *ZAW* 86 (1974), 453-469.

Bal, M. *Narratology: Introduction to the Theory of Narrative*. Toronto: University Press, 1985.

Bietenhard, H. *Der tannaitische Midrasch: Sifre Deuteronomium*. Bern: Peter Lang, 1984.

Bligh, J. *Christian Deuteronomy (Luke 9-18)*. Scripture for Meditation 5; New York: Alba House, 1970.

Borger, R. *Die Inschriften Asarhaddons Königs von Assyrien*. AfO Beiheft 9; Graz: Weidner, 1956.

Bottero, J. "Le ʿCode' de Hammurabi," *Annali della Scuola Normale Superiore di Pisa* 12 (1982) 407-444.

Boyce, R. *The Cry to God in the Old Testament*. SBLDS 103; Atlanta: Scholars, 1988.

Braulik, G. "Die Abfolge der Gesetz im Dt. 12-26 und der Dekalog" in *Das Deuteronomium: Enstehung, Gestalt und Botschaft*, N. Lohfink, ed. Leuven: University Press, 1985.

———. "Die Ausdrücke fur ʿGesetz' im Buch Deuteronomium," *Bib* 51 (1970), 39-66.

———. "Law as Gospel: Justification and Pardon According to the Deuteronomic School," *Int* 38 (1984), 5-14.

———. *Die Mittel Deuteronomischer Rhetorik: Erhoben aus Deuteronomium 4,1-40*, AnBib 68. Rome: PBI, 1978.

———. *Testament des Mose*. Stuttgart: Katholische Bibelwerk, 1976.

———. "Zur Abfolge der Gesetze in Deuteronomium 16,18-21,23. Weitere Beobachtungen," *Bib* 69 (1988) 63-92.

Bright, J. "The Apodictic Prohibition: Some Observations," *JBL* 92 (1973) 185-204.

Buis, P. *Le Deutéronome*. VS 4; Paris: Beauchesne, 1969.

Calvin, J. *Commentaries on the Four Last Books of Moses Arranged in the Form of a Harmony*, Vol I & II. Trans. C. Bingham; Grand Rapids: Eerdmans, 1950.

———. *Sermons on the Ten Commandments*. Ed. and Trans. B. Farley; Grand Rapids: Baker Book House, 1980.

Cardascia, G. "La transmission des sources juridiques cuneiformes," *RIDA* 7 (1960) 31-50.

Cardellini, I. *Die biblischen "Sklaven"-Gesetze im Lichte des keilschriftenlichen Sklavenrechts*. BBB 55; Bonn: Peter Hanstein, 1981.

Carmichael, C. *Law and Narrative in the Bible: The Evidence of the Deuteronomic Laws and the Decalogue*. Ithaca: Cornell, 1985.

———. *The Laws of Deuteronomy*. Ithaca: Cornell, 1974.

Cave, C. "Lazarus and the Lukan Deuteronomy," *NTS* 15 (1968-69) 319-325.

Castellino, G. "Urnammu: Three Religious Texts," *ZA* 52 (1957), 1-57; 53 (1958), 106-132.

Cazelles, H. "De l'ideologie royale," *JANESCU* 5 (1973) 59-73.

———. *Études sur le Code de l'Alliance*. Paris: Letouzney et Ane, 1946.

———. "The Hebrews," in *Peoples of Old Testament Times*, 1-28. Ed. D. J. Wiseman; Oxford: Clarendon, 1973.

Childs, B. *The Book of Exodus*. Philadelphia: Westminster, 1974.

Cholewski, A. *Heiligkeitsgesetz und Deuteronomium: Eine vergleichende Studie*. AnBib 66; Rome: PBI, 1976.

Chumash with Targum Onkelos, Haphtaroth and Rashi's Commentary. Trans. Rabbi A. Silbermann and Rev. M. Rosenbaum; Jerusalem: Silbermann, 1973.

Civil, M. "New Sumerian Law Fragments," *AS* 16 (65), 1-12.

Clement of Alexandria. "Who is the Rich Man that Shall be Saved?" in *The Ante-Nicene Fathers, vol. 2: Fathers of the Second Century*. Trans. W. Wilson; Grand Rapids: Eerdmans, 1951.

Clements, R. E. *God's Chosen People: A Theological Interpretation of the Book of Deuteronomy*. Valley Forge: Judson, 1969.

Craigie, P. C. *Deuteronomy*. NICC; Grand Rapids: Eerdmans, 1976.

David, M. "Eine Bestimmung über das Verfallspfand in den Mittelassyrischen Gesetzen," *Bibliotheca Orientalis* 9 (1952) 170-172.

———. "The Manumission of Slaves Under Zedekiah," *OTS* V (1948) 63-79.

Dawsey, J. "Jesus' Pilgrimage to Jerusalem," *PersRelSt* 14 (1987) 217-232.

Diakonoff, I. M. "Some Remarks on the ‹Reforms' of Urukagina," *RA* 52 (1958), 1-15.

Dossin, G. "L'inscription de fondation de Iaḫdun-Lim, roi de Mari," *Syria* 32, 1-28.

Driver, G. R. and C. J. Miles. *The Assyrian Laws*. Oxford: Clarendon, 1935.

———. *The Babylonian Laws, Vols I and II*. Oxford: Clarendon, 1955, 1956.

Driver, S. R. *A Critical and Exegetical Commentary of Deuteronomy*. ICC; New York: Scribners, 1895.

Eagleton, T. *Literary Theory: An Introduction*. Minneapolis: University of Minnesota, 1983.

Ellis, M. d. J. "*Ṣimdatu* in the Old Babylonian Sources", *JCS* 24 (1972), 74-82.

Ellison, H. L. "The Hebrew Slave: A Study in Early Israelite Society," *EvQ* 45 (1973) 30-35.

Epsztein, L. *La Justice dans le Proche-Orient Ancien et le Peuple de la Bible*. Paris: Les Editions du Cerf, 1983. Eng. Trans. *Social Justice in the Ancient Near East and the People of the Bible*. Trans. J. Bower; London: SCM, 1986.

Etheridge, J. W. *The Targums of Onkelos and Jonathan ben Uzziel On the Pentateuch*. London: Longman, Green, Longman, Roberts and Green, 1865.

Fensham, F. C. "Widow, Orphan, and the Poor in Ancient Near Eastern Legal and Wisdom Literature," *JNES* 21 (1961), 129-139.

Finkelstein, J. J. "Ammiṣaduqa's Edict and the Babylonian ‹Law Codes,'" *JCS* 15 (1961), 91-104.

———. "The Edict of Ammiṣaduqa: A New Text," *RA* 63 (1969), 45-64.

———. "On Some Recent Studies in Cuneiform Law," *JAOS* 90/2 (1970), 243-256.

———. *The Ox That Gored*. Philadelphia: American Philosophical Society, 1981.

———. "Some New *Misharum* Material and Its Implications," *AS* 16 (1965), 233-246.

Gadd, C. J. "Forms and Colors," *RA* 19 (1922), 149-159.

Gamoran, H. "The Biblical Law Against Loans on Interest," *JNES* 30 (1971) 127-135.

Gemser, B. "The Importance of the Motive Clause in Old Testament Law," *VTSup* 1 (Congress Volume); Leiden: E. J. Brill, 1953, 50-66.

Gerstenberger, E. *Wesen und Herkunft der ‹apodiktischen Rechts'*. Neukirchen-Vluyn: Neukirchener, 1965.

Gilmer, H. W. *The If-You Form in Israelite Law*. SBLDS 15; Missoula: Scholars, 1975.

Goetze, A. *The Laws of Eshnunna*. New Haven: ASOR, 1956.

Gowan, D. "Wealth and Poverty in the Old Testament: The Case of the Widow, the Orphan, and the Sojourner," *Int* 41 (1987) 341-353.

Grasser, E., A. Strobel, R. C. Tannehill, and W. Eltester. *Jesus in Nazareth*. Berlin: Walter de Gruyter, 1972.

Greenberg, M. *The Hab/piru*. AOS 39; New Haven: American Oriental Society, 1955.

———. "More Reflections on Biblical Criminal Law." in *Scripta Hierosolymitana* 31, 1-17. Ed. S. Japhet; Jerusalem: Magnes, 1986.

———. "Some Postulates of Biblical Criminal Law," in *Y. Kaufmann Jubilee Volume*. Jerusalem: Magnes, 1960, 5-28

Grelot, P. "Hofšî (PS.LXXXVIII 6)," *VT* 14 (1964) 256-263.

Gurney, O. R. and S. N. Kramer. "Two Fragments of Sumerian Law," *AS* 16 (1965), 13-19.

Halivni, D. *Midrash, Mishah, and Gemara*. Cambridge: Harvard, 1986.

Hammer, R. *Sifre: A Tannaitic Commentary on the Book of Deuteronomy*. New Haven: Yale, 1986.

Hincke, W. J. *A New Boundary Stone of Nebuchadnezzar I*. BERes 4; Philadelphia: University of Pennsylvania, 1907.

Hirsch, S. R. *The Pentateuch. Vol 5: Deuteronomy*. Trans I. Levy; London: L. Honig and Sons, 1966.

Hoffner, H. "The Old Hittite Version of Laws 164-166," *JCS* 33 (1981) 206-209.

Horst, F. *Das Privilegrecht Jahwes*. FRLANT 45; Göttingen: Vandenhoeck & Ruprecht, 1930.

Jacobsen, T. *Toward the Image of Tammuz*. Cambridge: Harvard, 1970.

Janzen, J. G. "On the Most Important Word in the Shema," *VT* 37 (1987), 280-300.

———. "The Yoke That Gives Rest," *Int* 41 (1987), 256-268.

Japhet, S. "The Relationship Between the Legal Corpora in the Pentateuch in Light of Manumission Laws," in *Scripta Hierosolymitana* 31, 63-89. Ed. S. Japhet; Jerusalem: Magnes, 1986.

Jirku, A. *Das weltliche Recht im Alten Testament*. Gütersloh: Bertelsmann, 1927.

Johns, C. H. W. *Assyrian Deeds and Documents, vol. I*. Cambridge: Deighton Bell and Co., 1898.

———. *Babylonian and Assyrian Laws, Contracts and Letters*. New York: Scribners', 1904.

Kaufmann, S. "Deuteronomy 15 and Recent Research on the Dating of P," in *Das Deuteronomium: Entstehung, Gestalt und Botschaft*, 273-276. Ed. N. Lohfink; Leuven: University Press, 1985.

———. "A Reconstruction of the Social Welfare Systems of Ancient Israel," in *In the Shelter of Elyon: Essays on Ancient Palestinian Life and Literature in Honor of G. W. Ahlstrom*, 277-286. Ed. W. B. Barrick and J. R. Spencer; JSOTSup 31; Sheffield: JSOT Press, 1984.

———. "The Structure of the Deuteronomic Law," *Maarav* 1 (1978-79), 105-158.

———. "The Temple Scroll and Higher Criticism," *HUCA* 53 (1982) 29-43.

Kessler, M. "The Law of Manumission in Jer. 34," *BZ* 15 (1971) 105-108.

Klein, M. L. *The Fragment-Targums of the Pentateuch*. AnBib 76 (in two volumes); Rome: PBI, 1980.

Kline, M. G. *Treaty of the Great King: The Covenant Structure of Deuteronomy*. Grand Rapids: Eerdmans, 1963.

Kohler, J. and A. Ungnad. *Assyrische Rechtsurkunden*. Leipzig: Eduard Pfeiffer, 1913.

Kohler, J., A. Ungnad, and P. Koschaker. *Hammurabi's Gesetz*, vol. 4-6. Leipzig: Eduard Pfeiffer, 1910.

Kramer, S. N. and A. Falkenstein. "Ur-Nammu Law Code," *Or* n.s. 23 (1954) 40-51.

Kraus, F. R. *Ein Edikt des Königs Ammiṣaduqa von Babylon*. Leiden: E. J. Brill, 1958.

———. "Ein Edikt des Königs Samsu-iluna von Babylon," *AS* 16 (1965), 225-231.

———. "Ein mittelbabylonischer Rechtsterminus," in *Symbolae David* II, 9-40. Leiden: Brill, 1968.

———. "Ein Zentrales Problem des Altmesopotamischen Rechts: Was ist der Codex Hammurabi?" *Genava* 8 (1960) 283-296.

Kupper, J. R. "Northern Mesopotamia and Syria," in *The Cambridge Ancient History, Vol II:1*, Edwards, et.al., eds. Cambridge: Univ., 1973.

Lambert, M. "Les 'Reformes' d'Urukagina," *RA* 50 (1956) 169-184.

Landsberger, B. "The Date List of the Babylonian King Samsu-Ditana," *JNES* 14 (1955) 137-160.

———. "Die Babylonischen Termini fur Gesetz und Recht," in *SDIOP* II (Fs. Koschaker), 219-234. Leiden, Brill 1939.

Langdon, S. "Assyrian Grammatical Texts," *RA* 13 (1916), 181-192.

———. *Die neubabylonischen Königsinschriften*. Leipzig: J. C. Hinrich's, 1912.

Larsen, M. T. *The Old Assyrian City-State and Its Colonies*. Copenhagen: Akademisk Verlag, 1976.

Leemans, W. F. *Foreign Trade in the Old Babylonian Period*. Leiden: E. J. Brill, 1960.

———. "King Hammurabi as Judge," *Symbolae David* II. Leiden: E. J. Brill, 1968.

———. *The Old Babylonian Merchant: His Business and Social Position*. Leiden: E. J. Brill, 1950.

Lemche, N. P. "*Andurārum* and *Mīšarum*: Comments on the Problem of Social Edicts and Their Application in the Ancient Near East," *JNES* 38 (1979), 11-22.

———. "The 'Hebrew Slave'. Comments on the Slave Law Ex. XXI, 2-11," *VT* 25 (1975), 129-144.

———. "*ḤPŠY* in 1 Sam xvii 25," *VT* 24 (1974), 373-374.

———. "The Manumission of Slaves—the Fallow Year—the Sabbatical Year—the Jobel Year," *VT* 26 (1976), 38-59.

Levenson, J. "Poverty and the State in Biblical Thought," *Judaism* 25 (1976) 230-241.

———. "The Theologies of Commandment in Biblical Israel," *HTR* 73 (1980) 17-33.

———. "Who Inserted the Book of the Torah?" *HTR* 68 (1975) 203-233.

Lewy, J. "The Biblical Institution of *Dᵉror* in the Light of Akkadian Documents," *Eretz-Israel* 5 (1958) 21*-31*.

Lipiński, E. "L''Esclave Hebreu,'" *VT* 26 (1976), 120-123.

Lohfink, N. "Der Bundesschluss im Land Moab: Redaktionsgeschichtliches zu Dt. 28,69-32,47," *BZ* 6 (1962) 32-56.

———. "The Cult Reform of Josiah of Judah: 2 Kgs. 22-23 as a Source for the History of Israelite Religion," in *Ancient Israelite Religion: Essays in Honor of Frank Moore Cross*, 459-475. Trans. C. Seitz; Ed. P. Miller, Jr., P. Hanson, and S. D. McBride; Philadelphia: Fortress, 1987.

———. "The Deuteronomists and the Idea of Separation of Powers," Unpublished paper read at the Los Angeles International Congress of Learned Societies in the Field of Religion, 1972.

———. "Deuteronomy," *IDBSup*, 229-232.

———. *Great Themes from the Old Testament*. Edinburgh: T & T Clark, 1982.

———. *Das Hauptgebot: Ein Untersuchung literarischer Einleitungsfragen zu Dtn. 5-11*. AnBib 20; Rome: PBI, 1963.

———. "Hos. 9:5 als Bezugstext von Dt. 17:16," *VT* 31 (1981), 226-228.

———. "Zur Dekalogfassung von Dt. 5," *BZ* ns 9 (1965), 17-32.

Loretz, O. *Habiru-Hebraeer: Eine sozio-linguistische Studie über die Herkunft des Gentiliziums ʿibrî vom Appelativum habiru*. Berlin: Walter de Gruyter, 1984.

McBride, S. D., Jr. "Polity of the Covenant People," *Int* 41 (1987), 229-244.

———. "The Yoke of the Kingdom: An Exposition of Dt. 6:4-5," *Int* 27 (1973), 273-306.

McCarthy, D. "Notes on the Love of God and the Father-Son Relationship between Yahweh and Israel," *CBQ* 27 (1965), 144-147.

———. *Treaty and Covenant*. AnBib 21A; Rome: PBI, 1978.

McGonville, J. G. *Law and Theology in Deuteronomy*. JSOTS 33; Sheffield: JSOT, 1984.

McKay, J. "Man's Love for God in Dt. and the Father/Teacher—Son/Pupil Relationship," *VT* 22 (1972), 428-435.

Maloney, R. P. "Usury and Restrictions on Interest-Taking in the Ancient Near East," *CBQ* 36 (1974), 1-20.

Mayes, A. D. H. *Deuteronomy*. NCB; Grand Rapids: Eerdmans, 1981.

Mays, J. L. "Justice: Perspectives from the Prophetic Tradition," *Int* 37 (1983) 5-17.

Meinhold, A. "Zur Beziehung Gott, Volk, Land im Jobel-Zusammenhang," *BZ* 29 (1985) 245-261.

Mendelsohn, I. "New Light on the *Ḫupšu*," *BASOR* 139 (1955), 9-11.

———. "Slavery in the Ancient Near East," *BA* 9/4 (1946), 74-88.

———. *Slavery in the Ancient Near East*. New York: Columbia, 1949.

Mendenhall, G. *Law and Covenant in Israel and the Ancient Near East*. Pittsburgh: The Biblical Colloquium, 1955.

Miller, P. D., Jr. "The Gift of God: A Deuteronomic Theology of the Land," *Int* 23 (1969), 451-465.

———. "The Human Sabbath: A Study in Deuteronomic Theology," *Princeton Seminary Bulletin* 6 (1985), 81-97.

———. "Israel as Host to Strangers," in *Today's Immigrants and Refugees: A Christian Understanding*, 1-19. Washington: United States Catholic Conference, Inc., 1988.

———. "Luke 4:16-21," *Int* 29 (1975), 417-421.

———. "The Most Important Word: The Yoke of the Kingdom," *Iliff Review* (1984), 17-29.

———. "Sin and Judgment in Jeremiah 34:17-19," *JBL* 103 (1984) 611-613.

———. "The Way of Torah," *Princeton Seminary Bulletin* 8 (1987) 17-27.

Mitchell, C. W. *The Meaning of BRK "To Bless" in the Old Testament*. SBLDS 95; Atlanta: Scholars, 1987.

Mittmann, Siegfried. *Deuteronomium 1:1-6:3 literarkritisch und traditionsgeschichtlich untersucht*. Berlin: Walter de Gruyter, 1975.

Moessner, D. *Lord of the Banquet: The Literary and Theological Significance of the Lukan Travel Narrative*. Minneapolis: Fortress, 1989.

———. "Luke 9:1-50: Luke's Preview of the Journey of the Prophet Like Moses of Deuteronomy," *JBL* 102 (1983) 575-605.

Moran, W. "The Ancient Near Eastern Background of the Love of God in Deuteronomy," *CBQ* 24 (1963), 77-87.

Moses ben Nahman (Ramban). *Commentary on the Torah*. Trans. Rabbi C. Chauel; New York: Shilo, 1976.

Muilenberg, J. "Form Criticism and Beyond," *JBL* 88 (1969) 1-18.

Na'aman. N. "*ḪABIRU* and Hebrews: The Transfer of a Social Term to the Literary Sphere," *JNES* 45 (1986), 282-287.

Niebuhr, H. R. *The Meaning of Revelation*. New York: MacMillan, 1941.

Neufeld, E. *The Hittite Law*. London: Luzac and Co., 1951.

———. "The Prohibitions Against Loans at Interest in Ancient Hebrew Laws," *HUCA* 26 (1955), 355-412.

Newman, L. E. *The Sanctity of the Seventh Year: A Study of Mishnah Tractate Shebiit*. BJS 44; Chico: Scholars, 1983.

Nicholson, E. W. *Deuteronomy and Tradition*. Philadelphia: Fortress, 1967.

———. *God and His People*. Oxford: Clarendon, 1986.

Nies, J. B. and C. E. Keiser. *Babylonian Inscriptions in the Collection of J. B. Nies, vol II: Historical, Religious and Economic Texts and Antiquities*. New Haven: Yale Univ., 1920.

North, R. *Sociology of the Biblical Jubilee*. AnBib 4; Rome: PBI, 1954.

———. "*Yâd* in the Shemitta-Law," *VT* 4 (1954), 196-199.

Noth, M. *The Deuteronomistic History*. Trans. J. Doull; JSOTSup 15; Sheffield: JSOT Press, 1981

———. *Exodus*. Trans. J. Bowden; OTL; Philadelphia: Westminster, 1962.

Olivier, H. "The Effectiveness of the Old Babylonian *Mêšarum* Decree," *JNSL* 12 (1984) 107-113.

———. "The Periodicity of the *Mêšarum* Again," in *Text and Context: Old Testament and Semitic Studies for F. C. Fensham*, 227-235. Ed. W. Claason; JSOTSup 48; Sheffield: JSOT Press, 1988.

Paul, S. *Studies in the Book of the Covenant in the Light of Cuneiform and Biblical Law*. Leiden: E. J. Brill, 1970.

The Pentateuch and Haftorahs. Trans. with Comm. J. H. Hertz; London: Humphrey Milford, 1936.

Phillips, A. "The Laws of Slavery: Exodus 21:2-11," *JSOT* 30 (1984) 51-66.

Porteous, N. W. "The Care of the Poor in the Old Testament," in *Living the Mystery: Collected Essays*, 143-155. Oxford: Basil Blackwell, 1967.

Postgate, J. N. *Taxation and Conscription in the Assyrian Empire*. Rome: PBI, 1974.

Preuss, H. D. *Deuteronomium*. Darmstadt: Wissenschaftliche Buchgesellschaft, 1982.

Rad, G. von. *Deuteronomy*. Trans. D. Barton; OTL; Philadelphia: Westminster, 1966.

———. *Old Testament Theology*, 2 Vols. Trans. D. Stalker; New York: Harper and Bros., 1962.

———. *The Problem of the Hexateuch and Other Essays*. Trans E. Dicken; London: SCM, 1984.

———. *Studies in Deuteronomy*. London: SCM, 1953.

Reider, J. *Deuteronomy*. Philadelphia: JPS, 1937.

Rendtorff, R. "The 'Yahwist' as Theologian?" *JSOT* 3 (1977) 2-10.

Rennes, J. *Le Deutéronome*. Geneve: Labor et Fides, 1967.

Ridderbos, J. *Deuteronomy*. Grand Rapids: Zondervan, 1984.

Ringe, S. *Jesus, Liberation, and the Biblical Jubilee*. OBT 19; Philadelphia: Fortress, 1985.

Scheil, V. "Notules," *RA* 14 (1917) 139-163.

Schneider, D. *Das fünfte Buch Mose*. Wuppertal: R. Brockhaus, 1982.

Schorr, M. *Urkunden des altbabylonischen zivil- und Prozessrechts*. VAB, vol 5; Leipzig, 1913.

Schrey, H.-H., H. Wolz and W. A. Whitehouse. *The Biblical Doctrine of Justice and Law*. EcuBibSt 3; London: SCM, 1955.

Schweizer, E. *The Good News According to Luke*. Atlanta: John Knox, 1973.

Seeligmann, I. L. "Lending, Pledge and Interest in Biblical Law Biblical Thought" (Eng. sum.), in *Studies in Bible and the Ancient Near East* (Fs. S. E. Loewenstamm), 209-210. Jerusalem: Magnes, 1978.

Seitz, G. *Redaktionsgeschichtliche Studien zum Deuteronomium*. Stuttgart: W. Kohlhammer, 1971.

Sloan, R., Jr. *The Favorable Year of the Lord: A Study of the Jubilary Theology in the Gospel of Luke*. Austin, Tx: Schola Press, 1977.

Snaith, N. H. "The Daughters of Zelophephad," *VT* 16 (1966) 125-127.

Soden, W. von and P. Ackroyd. "*Yâd*," *TDOT* V:393-426.

Sonsino, R. *Motive Clauses in Hebrew Law: Biblical Forms and Near Eastern Parallels.* SBLDS 45; Chico: Scholars, 1980.

Speiser, E. A. "Early Law and Civilization," in *Oriental and Biblical Studies: Collected Writings,* 534-555. Ed. J. J. Finkelstein and M. Greenberg; Phila: Univ. of Penn., 1967.

Spina, F. A. "Israelites as *gērim*, 'Sojourner', in Social and Historical Context", in *The Word of the Lord Shall Go Forth* (Fs. Freedman), 321-335. Winona Lake, IN: Eisenbrauns, 1983.

Stephens, F. J. "A Cuneiform Tablet from Dura-Europa," *RA* 34 (1937), 183-190.

Steuernagel, C. *Das Deuteronomium*. Göttingen: Vandenhoeck & Ruprecht, 1923.

Thompson, R. C. *The Reports of the Magicians and Astrologers of Ninevah and Babylon*. London: Luzac and Co., 1900.

Thureau-Dangin, F. "La Correspondence de Hammurapi avec Šamaš-Ḫâṣir," *RA* 21 (1924) 1-58.

———. *Lettres et Contrats de l'Epoque de la Premier Dynastie Babylonienne*. TCL I; Paris, 1910.

———. *Die Sumerischen und Akkadischen Königsinschriften*. VAB I; Leipzig: J. C. Hindrichs', 1907.

Toulmin, S. *The Uses of Argument*. London: Cambridge, 1958.

Vaux, R. d. *Ancient Israel: Its Life and Institutions*. London: Darton, Longman, and Todd, 1961.

Virolleaud, C. *L'astrologie chaldeene*, vol. 2. Paris: Paul Geuthner, 1909.

Waldow, H. E. von. "Social Responsibility and Social Structure in Early Israel," *CBQ* 32 (1970) 182-204.

Weidner, E. F. "Ilusumas Zug nach Babylon," *ZA* 43 (1936) 1935.

Weinfeld, M. *Deuteronomy and the Deuteronomic School*. Oxford: Clarendon, 1972.

———. "The Emergence of the Deuteronomic Movement: The Historical Antecendents," in *Das Deuteronomium: Enstehung, Gestalt und Botschaft*, N. Lohfink, ed. Leuven: University Press, 1985.

———. "Judge and Officer in Ancient Israel and the Ancient Near East," *Israel Oriental Studies* 7 (1977) 65-76.

———. "'Justice and Righteousness' in Ancient Israel Against the Background of 'Social Reforms' in the Ancient Near East," in *Mesopotamien und Seine Nachbaren*, 491-519. Ed. H. Jorg and J. Renger; Berlin: Dietrich Reimer, 1987.

Weingreen, J. "The Case of the Daughters of Zelophephad," *VT* 16 (1966) 518-522.

Weippert, M. "Semitische Nomaden des Zweiten Jahrtausends: Über die S;sw der Aegypten Quellen," *Bib* 55 (74), 265-80.

———. *The Settlement of the Israelite Tribes in Palestine*. SBT 21; London: SCM, 1971.

Welch, A. C. *The Code of Deuteronomy: A New Theory of Its Origin*. London: James Clarke, 1924.

Westbrook, R. "Biblical and Cuneiform Law Codes," *RB* 92 (1985), 247-264.

Whitelam, K. W. *The Just King: Monarchical Authority in Ancient Israel*. JSOTSup 12; Sheffield JSOT, 1979.

Williams, R. J. *Hebrew Syntax: An Outline* (2nd Ed.). Toronto: University of Toronto, 1976.

Wright, C. "What Happened Every Seven Years in Israel?" *EvQ* 56/3 (1984), 129-138; 56/4, 193-201.

Yaron, R. *The Laws of Eshnunna*. Jerusalem: Magnes, 1969.